The Great Awakening

The Great Awakening

DAVE HAYES

dhayesMEDIA

DEDICATION

To Lieutenant General Michael Flynn
and his family.
Thank you for your unwavering commitment
to America—and we, the people.
We are with you.

ACKNOWLEDGMENTS

We are grateful to our supporters and friends who persist with us in our efforts to uncover the truth. Special thanks to the digital army of researchers and citizen journalists for their enduring work. Together, our collective voices provide a clear alternative to the mainstream narrative that is called "the news."

TABLE OF CONTENTS

INTRODUCTION

This is the second book in my *Q Chronicles* series covering the messages posted by the anonymous entity known as Q. It is not necessary to have read the first book in the series, *Calm Before the Storm*, to understand the material in this second book. However, after you finish this book, you might want to go back and read *Calm Before the Storm* for insight on other important topics covered at the beginning of the Q operation. For those who have read *Calm Before the Storm*, this introduction provides new information that has come to light since its publishing. For new readers, a brief overview of subjects covered in the previous book is provided to explain key elements of Q's operation.

Jeffrey Epstein was convicted in 2008 of procuring an underage girl for prostitution and for soliciting a prostitute. Although investigators identified 36 girls he had abused, he pled guilty to the two charges related to one victim and served a 13-month sentence. Many questions were later raised about his very lenient treatment while incarcerated. Open source articles report that Epstein was held in a private wing of the Palm Beach County jail. In most cases, work-release programs in Florida are reserved for inmates with less than ten months left on their sentence, and are not available for people convicted of sex crimes. Despite that, Epstein was allowed to leave the jail to work in his office 12 hours a day, six days a week. He was accused of sexually abusing other women while serving his sentence.

In July of 2019, Epstein was arrested again for sex trafficking minors in Florida and New York. Epstein died in his jail cell about a month later. The medical examiner deemed his death a suicide, but there has been considerable public skepticism surrounding that determination. Multiple egregious errors in the jail system enabled this high-profile prisoner's life to be ended before he could stand trial.

Cases like Epstein's have caused many people to believe there are two systems of justice in the world—one for the rich and powerful, and one for everyone else.

On June 19th, 2020, U.S. Attorney General William Barr announced that he asked for the resignation of U.S. Attorney Geoffrey Berman of the Southern District of New York (SDNY). Berman refused to step down. After receiving a letter from Barr explaining that he was being replaced at the request of President Trump, Berman finally stepped aside. Q suggested that Berman's departure would pave the way for action on many high-profile cases in SDNY's jurisdiction, including those related to Jeffrey Epstein. Less than two weeks later, on July 1st, 2020, Epstein's alleged accomplice, Ghislaine Maxwell, was arrested on a 6-count indictment that included conspiracy, enticement, and transporting of minors with intent to engage in illegal sexual activities. She was also indicted on perjury charges.

The purpose of this series of books is to explain how, until recently, there existed a two-tiered system of justice that allowed rich and powerful people to commit crimes and avoid prosecution. It is my belief that this two-tiered system of justice is being dismantled, and a system of equal justice is being set in its place. The arrest of Ghislaine Maxwell is one example of how equal justice is being restored.

The information Q provides helps us connect events like U.S. Attorney Berman's departure and Ghislaine Maxwell's arrest. When such events are properly connected, we get a better understanding of the forces at work behind the scenes.

Q's operation involves the disclosure of information available in the public domain. Links to documents, articles, and videos are provided. Questions are presented, and hints are given that help researchers connect various people, organizations, and events. When the information is assembled correctly, it reveals the truth about corruption. Millions of people from all walks of life who follow Q's posts conduct their research and report what they've found. Anyone is free to take the information and disseminate it. In function, the operation is similar to that of a beehive, where researchers work together. Rather than being consumers of news, citizens become reporters.

Q claims to have access to classified information, but national security laws prevent it from being disclosed in plain terms. The essence of that information can be understood if one properly decodes the clues, and infers the correct meaning from Q's questions. The reader ends up with a set of assumptions that convey information that would normally require a classified briefing.

Q's operation involves the exposure of corruption; those whom he exposes are his opponents. Researchers are not the only ones interested in Q—his opponents also read his posts. The strategies and tactics of game theory are used to keep opponents off guard and lure them into traps. Varying degrees of deception, distraction, disinformation, and bluffing are incorporated into Q's messages.

For example, during the first week of November, 2017, Q frequently promised that former Secretary of State Hillary Clinton, her campaign manager John Podesta, and her personal assistant Huma Abedin would be arrested. During that week, these political figures were *not* arrested, but members of the Saudi royal family *were*. Q had also posted messages about Saudi Arabia that week but did not mention arrests. Is it possible that Q wanted attention to be focused on U.S. political figures that week while the arrests in Saudi Arabia were being planned?

Q uses the Socratic method of instruction, which is a form of cooperative dialogue. The alternating asking and answering of questions encourages critical thinking, the analysis of ideas, and the examination of underlying presuppositions. Stronger hypotheses emerge by identifying and eliminating weaker ones. Q asks if our beliefs are logical. He hints at facts we may not be aware of and suggests alternative hypotheses.

Q claims to be closely connected to President Trump. Rather than confirming this relationship directly, it is done indirectly. For example, Q will sometimes post a message 20 or 30 seconds before the President sends out a tweet on his Twitter account. Q posts, on average, five times a day. The President might tweet a dozen times a day. The odds are small that they would coincidentally post at the same time, given that Q posts first. If it happened only once, it could be attributed to coincidence, but Q has posted before the President, and within 60 seconds, on more than 25 occasions.

The President often retweets Twitter accounts that follow Q. The mainstream media have made much of this habit, claiming, on the one hand, that Trump is lending credibility to the Q movement, but on the other hand, insisting that he is in no way involved in the operation. Trump's retweets tacitly confirm Q, but they also provide a degree of plausible deniability.

Q intends to reveal as much information to the public as possible, but some subjects pose a risk if too much is said about them. National security laws are one obstacle to disclosure. If released, some information could do irreparable harm to allies of the United States, which could precipitate war and cause worldwide (WW) suffering.

> Feb 11, 2018
> Understand one simple fact - the US is connected to the rest of the world.
> Knowing that, understand, by default, if certain intel is released it would cause a WW/mass suffering. We share the idea of open source but value life and must make decisions base decisions on outcomes and containability.
> Q

In this book, when I refer to Q as "he" or "him," it is strictly for ease of writing. I do not know if Q is a male or female, an individual or a group.

Q originally posted on the 4chan board *politically incorrect* (sometimes called /pol/). 4chan users can remain anonymous, which is why government employees sometimes use it to post information about public corruption. By day, anonymous users (also called anons or autists) work as systems analysts, coders, and game designers. By night, they research the clues people drop.

The presence of thousands of researchers was one reason Q initially posted on 4chan. Anons are excellent internet researchers. They've examined posts from intelligence community insiders (both real and fake) for years. Dealing with phonies makes them highly skeptical. Q's messages needed to be vetted for legitimacy. He knew that anons would scrutinize his posts, looking for flaws. If they could be verified, he would gain the trust of a group of hardened skeptics. Once Q's information was verified, anons became a conduit of information about the real stories behind world events and the facts of history that have been hidden from society.

Conversations on 4chan, 8chan, and 8kun are hosted on various subdomains called *boards*. Each board hosts discussions on a particular topic. The boards are operated by volunteers (board volunteers or BVs) who create and moderate conversations (threads). Board volunteers are sometimes called *bakers*. The threads are called *breads*. When a baker creates a new thread, they're said to be "baking a bread." A single comment in a thread is called a *crumb*. Helpful information on a topic is called *sauce*. The term sauce is derived from the word "source." If a point is made that isn't common knowledge, others will ask for the source (sauce) of the information.

Currently, Q communicates on two different boards hosted on 8kun. Messages on the read-only board can be viewed, but readers cannot leave comments. Posts that are intended for discussion are posted on a research board where anyone can comment.

Some people are shocked to find nudity when visiting some of the message boards on 4chan, 8chan, and 8kun. Most people are accustomed to social media platforms where nudity isn't allowed. Although these platforms are family-friendly, these restrictions are a form of censorship. Q's posts about global corruption are controversial enough that they would eventually be removed from such platforms. In fact, even 8chan was ultimately deplatformed in an effort to silence Q. The site's owner and his team then worked to replace it with 8kun, and have kept it operating as a free speech platform despite massive attacks from those seeking to disrupt it.

Q has posted more than 4,800 messages to date. Instead of covering every post, each book in this series will examine a sample of posts over a span of time and explore the main subjects discussed during that period. This book covers topics discussed by Q from mid-December of 2017 through March of 2018. Whenever possible, details of those discussions will be examined from the time they were first mentioned until the present.

There are posts of every kind to be considered—including links to news articles, videos, and photographs. I'll provide information from news reports and videos when appropriate. I'll describe images and provide commentary on them, however copyright laws, privacy concerns, and space constraints make it impossible for the pictures themselves to be included in this book. Thankfully, the Q posts are still archived on several websites so you can check them out for yourself.

Many of Q's posts contain abbreviations, acronyms, diagrams, and the initials of people and government agencies with which you may not be familiar. I've included a glossary at the back of the book to help explain them.

Please note that the formatting of Q's posts when they appear in this book will adhere to the following guidelines:

- If there were typos in a post by Q or an anon, the typos will also appear in this book. Note: Some of Q's "typos" are intentional and convey a message.

- In some cases, an original post by Q or an anon may contain blank lines between sections of text. We have tried as much as possible to preserve the original use of paragraph returns, but occasionally, they may be removed due to space constraints.

• Dates will always be provided when I display a post by Q if they are relevant. I will occasionally break a long post into multiple sections and explain each part individually. In those cases, the date will appear at the top of the first section, but the sections that follow will not have a date because they're part of the same post.

• I will occasionally explain a conversation thread between two people that occurs on a single day. In those cases, the date of the first post will be displayed but the dates of the responses may be omitted.

• To limit distracting data, I've opted in most cases to omit the time-stamps and user IDs from Q's posts. That information usually isn't relevant to the discussion. In the few cases where it is, timestamps and user ID's will be included.

• I've chosen, at times, to cut out certain parts of Q's posts while including other parts because, from a teaching standpoint, it's best if we focus on the part of the post that's relevant to the subject we're discussing. Some Q posts cover many topics, and it's easy to become confused or distracted by off-topic information. When I need to display only a section of a post, you'll see three diamonds like this: ♦♦♦ to indicate where part of the original message has been omitted.

CHAPTER 1

Red Castle Green Castle

WE'LL BEGIN THE BOOK BY decoding a single, cryptic post. Some of Q's messages don't give us much information to go on. We see an odd string of letters and numbers and a few seemingly unrelated words. The first step to decoding these posts is looking for information we already understand. The second step is researching key terms. The third step is waiting for a news story to confirm our theory.

On March 23rd, 2018, Q posted the following message.

Mar 23 2018
Clock activated.
RED_CASTLE.
GREEN_CASTLE.
Stage_5:5[y]
Q

From previous posts by Q, I understood the term "clock activated" to indicate that the meaning of a message would be revealed to us at a later time.

The word "stage" usually speaks of something being prepared for public disclosure, i.e., "the stage is being set."

"Five by five" (5:5) is military jargon. Radio transmissions are rated for signal clarity and strength on a scale from one through five, with one being the lowest and five being the highest. Five by five indicates the signal is loud and clear.

The letter "y" in brackets [y] often means, "yes," conveying a "go" signal.

My internet search for the meaning of "RED_CASTLE" provided a couple of possibilities. I noted that the U.S. Army Corps of Engineers has a red-colored castle as part of their logo. My search for the meaning of GREEN_CASTLE returned an interesting finding; the Army Corps of Engineers has a location in Green Castle, Indiana.

When this message was posted, President Trump was battling Congress over funding for the wall on the southern border. He had asked repeatedly for money to fund the construction of a border wall, but Democratic leaders in Congress refused to approve it. I suspected that perhaps the President planned to fund the border wall with money from the military budget and that he would use the Army Corps of Engineers to complete the construction. The political wrangling over funding may have been merely theater—a distraction to keep someone's eyes off the real plan.

In the Twitter thread that I composed in March of 2018, I explained that this seemed to be the most likely decode, but we would have to wait for confirmation. There were no public discussions about using the military to build the wall until nine months later, when, in December of 2018, the President suggested he could use the military to build a wall on the border. On January 4th, 2019, he explained that he intended to declare a national emergency at the border. The following day, *The New York Times* wrote an article excoriating President Trump for his idiotic idea. A few days later, Q confirmed to anons on the board that the Army Corps of Engineers and the border wall project was the correct decode for RED_CASTLE, GREEN_CASTLE.

Jan 11 2019
At what point is it mathematically impossible?
The very next day.
Red Castle.
Green Castle.
Public access to intel?
Q

The President diverted money from the Defense Department budget, and the Corps of Engineers began construction on the wall. During the first year, approximately 100 miles of the wall was built, but a lawsuit slowed construction. In January of 2020, after winning a decision by the 5th Circuit Court, President Trump announced that he would divert an additional 7.2 billion dollars in Pentagon funding to the wall. The total number of miles to be built would increase from 509 miles to 885 miles.

Anons who decoded the "red castle, green castle" stringer had a scoop on the President's plans months before anyone else. This post confirmed Q's foreknowledge of the President's plans. But it also demonstrated the President's foreknowledge that Congress would not agree to fund the wall, making it necessary to plan for it to be built by the military. Q provides information before it is announced by the President or reported by the media.

One month before posting the "red castle, green castle" stringer, Q dropped another coded message. It isn't easy to grasp the full meaning of this message, because it is full of military terms, but parts of it can be understood. We know the meaning of RED_CASTLE. Another chapter in this book will reveal the meaning of RED_RED. Does "COMM_SAT" refer to satellite communications? Does "TELCON" refer to telephone conversations or communications? Is this message meant for military operators on a mission? I would encourage the curious among you to search the terms in the coded message below.

Feb 14 2018
dZ68J_729282D_B^02928xABVtZ
b7al8920289-sLBTCZA99_jXK
382018202810282018204843739201837474
B_1
B_2
KILL_CHAIN
SKY_TAR_[E_BZ_y]
[]
[]PAK[]
[]-13-[]
A-9zBT1-033
"Republic-D"
"Republic-E"
"Republic-F"

"Republic-MILMAR-E"
INFIL-[2]-OP_TAKE_O_
WATCH_TOWER_OK
RED_RED_OK
RED_CASTLE_OK
NIGHT_BOX_OK
SKY_BEAM_OK
NORTH_TRADE_OK
MOUNTAIN_DEEP_OK
COMM_SAT_6_OK
COMM_SAT_7_OK
COMM_SAT_8_FALSE
COMM_SAT_9_OK
COMM_SAT_SEC_R140_OK
TELCON_SIG_CONF_C-83028
ZEBRA_PACIFIC_SIG_COMM_[GOOD]
DESIGNATE CODE: [_D7_UND<93829]
ACTIVATE CODE: [0 0000 018739 7-ZjG]
Q, DELTA

CHAPTER 2

Conspiracies Great and Small

DURING MOST OF MY LIFE, I've trusted the official explanations for mass shootings and terrorist attacks. My friends have chided me for believing the lies of the government and the mainstream media, but there's a reason why I've been reluctant to accept alternative explanations. As alternative theories are developed to explain suspicious events, these theories are sometimes proven wrong by new evidence. While an official news account may not reveal the entire truth, the alternative explanations may also be equally murky.

Q's messages first attracted *truthers*. I would describe truthers as independent thinkers. Rather than accepting a news report on its face, they prefer to evaluate the presentation of facts—both those that are included and those that are excluded. They consider a reporter's bias and personal motivation. They may review other reports about the event, including those that are developed by non-mainstream sources. Sometimes mainstream statements accurately reflect the facts. Sometimes, they do not.

Truthers had long suspected that the official story that a lone gunman assassinated President John F. Kennedy was a lie. They developed an alternate theory that two shooters were involved. When President Trump declassified documents in 2017 related to the assassination, a report from the medical examiner vindicated them. Kennedy was killed by two gunshots fired from two different angles, indicating that two shooters were involved. Ironically, the term "conspiracy theorist" was popularized by the CIA (and the media) in the 1960s to shame those who refused to accept the Kennedy assassination's official story. This shaming continues today.

Q could have posted about any one of a thousand topics on any platform. Instead, he chose specific subjects, and he selected a forum that would draw the interest of those who question the mainstream media and government narratives. And it seems he did this by design.

Why?

Q's mission happens to involve important topics to the truther community—such as the mass shooting in Las Vegas, Nevada, and the September 11th terrorist attack in New York. Skeptics have hotly debated the truth behind these incidents; however, Q's discussion of these events has—thus far—been limited. I believe Q needed to develop a core group of dedicated researchers. He provided just enough information on these subjects to draw researchers' interest, but not enough to cause the public to dismiss the operation as just another conspiracy theory. As the mission progressed, Q turned to subjects currently in the headlines, and topics that are more mainstream in nature—like the media's opposition to President Trump, and the FBI's investigation of his former National Security Advisor, retired General Michael Flynn.

The FBI accused General Flynn of conspiring with Russia and of lying to FBI agents. Although FBI agents Strzok and Pientka, who interviewed him, said they did not think Flynn had lied to them, he became a target of Robert Mueller's Special Counsel investigation. In a handwritten note, an FBI official asked what the goal of Flynn's interview was—"to get him to lie, so we can prosecute him or get him fired?" Some believe the note was written by Strzok's supervisor Bill Priestap, the FBI's former head of counterintelligence. The author of the note suspected that agents had set a trap for Flynn. Agent Strzok was later fired.

When it was revealed that Mueller's prosecutors withheld exculpatory evidence (evidence that proves a defendant's innocence) from Flynn's legal team, the DOJ felt it could not prove its case against him, and dismissed the charges. Despite this, Judge Emmet Sullivan has refused to dismiss Flynn's case. As this book goes to print, Flynn's attorney, Sidney Powell, is seeking to have Sullivan recused from the case.

Mainstream commentators have concluded that Q is just another person propagating conspiracy theories. I have carefully examined Q's posts and stated objectives, and my research has led me to reach the exact opposite conclusion. Rather than spreading *more* conspiracy theories, Q intends to resolve them. Q aims to expose the facts regarding many historical events for which the truth was never publicly revealed. The problem for someone with an alternate theory of an event is that they don't always have access to conclusive evidence to confirm their hypothesis.

Q claims to be the ultimate intelligence insider—someone who has current access to the highest levels of classified information in the world. Not a retired CIA agent. Not a former government official. Q appears to be a person (or team) currently working closely with the President of the United States. And at times, it seems the President himself is the one sending the messages.

Think about what that means. Q would have access to secret files the government has never allowed the public to see. He would have information about secret government programs that even Congress hasn't seen. Q might read intelligence reports found in the President's daily briefing and have knowledge of Justice Department investigations. While mainstream reporters hunt for scoops—leaked by senators or Congress members under the agreement that they won't be named as the source—Q may have approval from the President to discuss what happened during the latest military operation.

What would happen if the President decided to make all the secret files, the secret programs, and truths about historical events publicly known through Q? What if Q provided evidence (or helped us find evidence) that conclusively proved the truth about all modern conspiracies? Once the truth is established with evidence, there is no need for alternate explanations. And that is what I believe Q intends to do.

Mainstream media outlets have increased their attacks against Q. In most articles, followers are falsely accused of being violent and delusional. Those claims are based on an article published by *Yahoo News* in 2019. The article claimed the FBI's Phoenix field office issued a bulletin warning that conspiracy theory extremists are prone to acts of violence. The so-called FBI bulletin linked in the article was hosted on a private Scribd account. I contacted the reporters who wrote the article and asked how they obtained the bulletin. I asked them to provide a link to the document on a government website. My inquires went unanswered. I contacted the FBI's Phoenix field office, the National Press Office and filed a FOIA request and received no confirmation that the bulletin is legitimate. I was directed by an agent to a website where the bureau outlines its four classifications of domestic violent extremism. None of the categories describe the conspiracy theory extremism mentioned in *Yahoo's* bulletin. Because of the unsubstantiated claim that Q followers are violent, social media platforms are ramping up censorship and banning the accounts of those who comment positively about Q. Even church pastors have become increasingly hostile toward the movement.

We are all entitled to our opinions about Q, but not all opinions are equal. I have opinions about nuclear energy, but I have no expertise from which to speak. My opinions are uninformed. Like nuclear energy, Q is a field of study unto itself. One cannot learn anything useful about Q by reading mainstream media articles. You can only understand Q's messages by reading them. It's taken researchers years to develop their understanding of Q's messages, and still, their grasp of the big picture is incomplete. Critics of Q don't base their views on knowledge of the posts. This is evidenced by that the fact that they don't mention them in their articles. The goal of critics is to shame and dismiss anyone who attempts to understand the messages. As you read this book, I encourage you to thoughtfully and objectively consider what Q has to say and come to your own conclusions.

CHAPTER 3

Decoding Q's Posts

ANYONE WHO READS Q'S MESSAGES will, over time, develop
their own approach to deciphering them. On November 9th, 2017, Q told
anons that keeping an accurate graphic was critical to the success of his
mission. The previous week, anons had been posting updated graphics
containing all of Q's posts.

After posting more than 100 messages, Q said a coordinated effort
was underway to misdirect his followers. A guide to reading his crumbs
was necessary. The guide would be the following post, which contains
instructions for deciphering his messages. The instructions come in the
form of hints and questions. In this chapter, we'll examine this post, and I'll
explain, line by line, how Q wants us to read and understand his messages.

Q !ITPb.qbhqo
Nov 9 2017
1510280445405.jpg
Trip added.
[C]oordinated effort to misdirect.
Guide to reading the crumbs necessary to cont[I]nue.
Attached gr[A]phic is correct.

Linked graphics are incorrect and false.

Graphic is necessary and vital.

Time stamp(s) and order [is] critical.

Re-review graphic (in full) each day post news release.

Learn to distinguish between relevant/non-relevant news.

Disinformation is real.

Disinformation is necessary.

Ex: US ML NG (1) False SA True

Why was this necessary?

What questions were asked re: SA prior to SA events?

Why is this relevant?

Think mirror.

Look there, or [here], or there, truth is behind you.

What is a map?

Why is a map useful?

What is a legend?

Why is a legend useful?

What is a sequence?

Why is this relevant?

When does a map become a guide?

What is a keystone?

Everything stated is relevant.

Everything.

Future provides past.

Map provides picture.

Picture provides 40,000ft. v.

40,000ft. v. is classified.

Why is a map useful?

Think direction.

Think full picture.

Who controls the narrative?

Why is this relevant?

What is a spell? Who is asleep?

Dissemination.

Attention on deck.

There is an active war on your mind.

Be [p]repared.

Ope[r]ations underway.

Operators [a]ctive.

Graphic is essential.
Find the ke[y]stone.
Moves and countermoves.
They never thought she would lose.
Snow white.
Godfather III.
Iron Eagle.
Q

In the above post, Q included a JPG image. It can still be found online with a search of the filename. The image is a graphic (created by an anon) showing all of Q's posts up to that point in time.

Q explained that he added a tripcode to his login credentials.

♦♦♦
Trip added.
♦♦♦

Most people post on imageboards anonymously. It is difficult to distinguish one user from another because all users are by default labeled "anonymous" and given a randomized set of characters as a user ID. Some people use a tripcode to identify themselves or for security purposes. A tripcode is a password that identifies a user by displaying a unique set of characters instead of the word "anonymous." In this post, Q's tripcode is Q !ITPb.qbhqo.

This is the next line in the post.

♦♦♦
[C]oordinated effort to misdirect.
♦♦♦

There have been—and after thousands of posts by Q, there still are—coordinated efforts underway to misdirect those who wish to learn from Q. People have created profiles on virtually every social media platform for the sole purpose of misleading those who are interested in learning about Q. Websites have been created for the same purpose. Some websites provide false information aimed at discrediting Q. Many of the users who respond to Q on the research board are there only to sow division, create confusion, and discredit Q's operation. Note the letter C is in brackets. The use of bracketed letters will be discussed at the end of the chapter.

♦♦♦
Guide to reading the crumbs necessary to cont[I]nue.
♦♦♦

A guide to reading Q's crumbs (messages) was needed and he would provide it. This post is the guide.

♦♦♦
Attached gr[A]phic is correct.
Linked graphics are incorrect and false.
Graphic is necessary and vital.
♦♦♦

Q had asked anons to regularly compile all of his posts in a single graphic for review. He confirmed the current graphic was correct, but linked graphics were incorrect.

♦♦♦
Time stamp(s) and order [is] critical.
♦♦♦

Anons did not yet know the value of timestamps, but Q emphasized here that keeping track of them would be essential. Q and President Trump would post at the same time or at pre-determined intervals. Only by careful analysis of timestamps would anons be able to make the necessary connections.

♦♦♦
Re-review graphic (in full) each day post news release.
♦♦♦

Anons were instructed to review past posts after big news events and search them for topics that were mentioned in the news. Many people have incorrectly assumed that Q's posts are to be used to predict the future. That is not Q's intent. Q provides clues about future events, but they are not to be used to predict the future. After news events are reported, Q wants us to go back over his past posts and find the clues that hinted about an event. This shows Q's foreknowledge of certain events.

◆◆◆

Learn to distinguish between relevant/non-relevant news.

◆◆◆

A story being in the news doesn't make it relevant. Curiosity about "interesting" but irrelevant information distracts us from seeing what is important. I'm a voracious consumer of news, but I've had to learn how to discard irrelevant, poorly sourced, sensational, or distracting news. On any given day, perhaps 20 percent of what I find is worthy of attention. Because many mainstream sources have become so biased, I look for citizen journalists who stay within their area of expertise, research deeply, and have a track record of accuracy. It takes time and discernment to find good reporting, but with practice it gets easier.

◆◆◆

Disinformation is real.
Disinformation is necessary.
Ex: US ML NG (1) False SA True
Why was this necessary?

◆◆◆

Disinformation and distractions are provided by Q to mislead his opponents. His warning the first week of November 2017 about the military (ML) and the National Guard (NG) being deployed was false for the United States (US), but true for Saudi Arabia (SA). This deception was necessary because Q says, prior to their arrest, Saudi royalty controlled many U.S. politicians. A threat was issued that American politicians were about to be arrested. That threat caused Saudis to make plans to secure the safety of U.S. political figures when they should have been securing their own. Thus, their own arrest came as a surprise.

◆◆◆

What questions were asked re: SA prior to SA events?
Why is this relevant?

◆◆◆

Q asks relevant questions prior to big news events. Before the arrest of Saudi businessmen and members of the royal family on November 4th, 2017, Q asked several questions, including why President Trump's son-in-law Jared Kushner, made an unannounced trip there and who he met. Weeks later, news stories reported he had met with Crown Prince Mohammad bin Salman. Sometimes Q's questions can seem confusing or irrelevant, but they hint at current or future events and must be re-evaluated after a news story breaks. Information contained in the questions when viewed after an event is reported, demonstrate Q's foreknowledge.

◆◆◆
Think mirror.
Look there, or [here], or there, truth is behind you.
◆◆◆

A mirror shows an image that is the opposite of reality. It may appear real, but it is false. This speaks to the use of disinformation. But it also illustrates how Q's questions and hints are intended to make us look back into the past to see the truth.

◆◆◆
What is a map?
Why is a map useful?
◆◆◆

A map provides information about where you are and it can help you find a destination. Q's posts, collectively, are called "the map."

◆◆◆
What is a legend?
Why is a legend useful?
◆◆◆

A legend helps interpret map symbols. Some of Q's posts contain symbolic meaning and they must be decoded. This message is a legend that helps interpret Q's posts.

◆◆◆
What is a sequence?

Why is this relevant?
♦♦♦

A sequence is a series of posts that cannot be correctly understood, individually. But when they are put together and analyzed, they reveal important information. For example, the series of posts related to "Bunker Apple Yellow Sky" and "Red Red" from November of 2017 can only be correctly understood by putting together posts over several weeks and connecting the dots.

♦♦♦
When does a map become a guide?
♦♦♦

The map (a collection of all posts) along with instruction from Q on how to decode them is our guide. The map provides information about current events (where we are) and future events (where we're going).

♦♦♦
What is a keystone?
♦♦♦

The answer to this question will be covered in a later chapter.

♦♦♦
Everything stated is relevant.
Everything.
♦♦♦

Everything posted by Q has relevance to someone, at some time. Whether we correctly understand the relevance of every post is a different matter. Many times, the significance is not appreciated until months or years later.

♦♦♦
Future provides past.
♦♦♦

News reports of future events provide insights into the full meaning of past posts by Q.

◆◆◆
Map provides picture.
◆◆◆

The map (a collection of all of Q's posts) provides a glimpse at the events happening on the geopolitical stage, or the "big picture."

◆◆◆
Picture provides 40,000ft. v.
◆◆◆

A complete and correct analysis of all of Q's posts gives us a look at the big picture, which Q refers to as the 40,000-foot view.

◆◆◆
40,000ft. v. is classified.
◆◆◆

The complete (40,000-foot) view of events happening on the global stage is classified. When we correctly interpret Q posts, we're given an understanding which would not be possible outside of a classified briefing.

◆◆◆
Why is a map useful?
Think direction.
Think full picture.
◆◆◆

Q's posts reveal details not reported by the mainstream media. They help us see the trajectory (direction) of global events, and they provide a glimpse of the big picture.

◆◆◆
Who controls the narrative?
Why is this relevant?
◆◆◆

A handful of powerful people have controlled the public narrative for years through a compliant and dishonest media complex. It's relevant because when we understand who controls the media, we can see through their agenda. Q intends to expose this false narrative and reveal the truth.

♦♦♦

What is a spell? Who is asleep?

♦♦♦

The mainstream media narrative has kept the public asleep as if under a spell. Think about how people spend their free time after work. They need to make dinner, maybe help their kids with homework, and prepare for the next workday. Many seek relaxation by watching movies, sports, or other television programs, including news media outlets telling them what to think about the stories they've chosen to print or broadcast. Media outlets disseminate a carefully scripted narrative. Today, even social media platforms create a narrative by silencing some viewpoints while amplifying others.

♦♦♦

Dissemination.

Attention on deck.

♦♦♦

Because the media bombard society with a biased and incomplete narrative, we (the anons, researchers, and citizen journalists) have been asked to help disseminate an accurate picture of current events in the hope of waking up a sleeping world.

♦♦♦

There is an active war on your mind.

Be [p]repared.

♦♦♦

Powerful people want to control society. They control society by controlling individuals. Controlling an individual is a matter of controlling their mind. Distorted facts presented by the mainstream media "program" the public to be compliant with an agenda intended to enslave them.

♦♦♦

Ope[r]ations underway.

Operators [a]ctive.

◆◆◆

Although it may seem as if nothing significant is happening, operations have been underway for years that are changing the world for the better. For example, since President Trump took office, human trafficking arrests by the Department of Justice have dramatically increased.

◆◆◆

Graphic is essential.

◆◆◆

A good way to stay informed is by focusing on Q's posts and using them to interpret daily events. Read them. Commit them to memory. Review them after big news events.

◆◆◆

Moves and countermoves.

◆◆◆

Q, the U.S. military, and President Trump are engaged in a war against corrupt people. Game theory strategies (moves and countermoves) are employed to defeat them.

Perhaps you've noticed several hidden messages in Q's post. By connecting the individual letters found in brackets, you'll find words like [C][I][A] and [p][r][a][l][y].

◆◆◆

They never thought she would lose.

◆◆◆

Corrupt people assumed Hillary Clinton would win the 2016 Presidential election. They thought things would continue as they had for decades. Q elaborated on the consequences of that assumption in this post.

Dec 14 2017

◆◆◆

Remember, they never thought she was going to lose.

Therefore, they never thought investigations and/or public interest

into their criminal acts would be exposed/investigated.
Therefore, they never thought they had anything to fear.
Therefore, they openly showcase their symbolism.
Therefore, they were sloppy.

Q

CHAPTER 4

The Great Awakening

TO DATE, Q HAS POSTED more than 4,800 messages. During the
first few weeks, it would have been easy to write them off as a childish
prank. But Q's persistence and willingness to search for and respond to
questions from followers leads me to conclude that he is on an enduring
mission to communicate an important message to a wide audience.

Q's thesis is that we have all been duped by the mainstream media,
politicians, Hollywood, and yes, even our history books. We haven't just
been bamboozled by the mesmerizing smiles of celebrities. Somehow,
a skewed view of history has found its way into our schools. Much of what
we believe to be true about history, about current events, about government
and its institutions is inaccurate—at least, according to Q. Fortunately
for us, Q has given us an opportunity to learn the truth if we're willing to
consider a different perspective.

This assertion is the hardest thing for me to accept about Q's mission.
I was perfectly content with the belief system I had. Then Q came along
and dared to tell me I was deceived. The paradox of deception is, of course,
that one may believe something to be true with every fiber of their being
and still be deceived. Truth is no respecter of sincerity. Although I've
generally accepted official explanations for significant events, I've never

trusted politicians. My distrust of them acted like a seed. If elected leaders couldn't be trusted, I wondered, who else is deserving of my skepticism? That question compelled me to consider Q's perspective.

Q presents information in the form of clues and hints for a reason. This presentation forces us to work if we want to learn the truth. It is the opposite of how most of us presently acquire information. The world I grew up in had a system for providing information. A bus picked me up every morning and whisked me off to school, where I passively learned the curriculum someone had created for me. A bus took me home at the end of the day, and TV news anchors informed me about the day's events. It was, in fact, more like a system of indoctrination. I never thought of public education this way until recently, but it is an apt description of how our education system works. Today, your phone or home device is ready and willing to provide the answer to virtually any question you ask; there's no need to bother doing your own research. And that is precisely the problem, according to Q.

Aug 27 2018
Think for yourself.
Research for yourself.
Trust yourself.
◆◆◆
FOLLOW THE FACTS.
SHEEP NO MORE.
Q

Q is like a school teacher, but he doesn't provide an easy path to learning. Unlike the passive model of government-run schools or artificial intelligence programs like Alexa, if we want to find the nuggets of truth contained in Q's messages, we must search for them. When you find a bit of truth on your own, something magical happens. You take ownership of it. No one is going to convince you something isn't true if you've spent weeks checking the facts and verifying the truth of it for yourself. Q doesn't provide a narrative for you to accept passively. He presents clues, and he expects you to determine what they mean.

Q discusses many subjects, but the main one is the corrupt use of power. Most people are aware that corruption exists in various parts of society, but few understand how pervasive it is or how seriously it affects us. According to Q, the way in which power has been used to enslave us has been hidden to such a degree that we would collectively exhibit symptoms of mental illness if we were to be suddenly confronted with the full truth.

Nov 5, 2017

◆◆◆

The complete picture would put 99% of Americans (the World) in a hospital.

◆◆◆

If the sudden revelation of the truth would cause harm to society, and if it is to be disclosed, it must be done gradually. Q is the mechanism by which the truth is being revealed to the world.

Q's operation has several parts with corresponding periods of time. The present time we're in, prior to the prosecution of corrupt people, can be described metaphorically as "the calm before the storm." The future prosecution of those who abused their power can be described as "the storm." As the truth is revealed about corruption, we will each awaken from the slumber of deception, and society will experience what Q refers to as "the great awakening."

The information contained in the chapters that follow will be just as hard for some of you to believe as they were for me to write. I've accepted the task of following Q's messages, researching them, and sharing what I've learned—despite the persistent fear that my own belief system will be destroyed in the process.

Apr 25 2018

Are you awake?

Do you SEE (for yourself) the MSM = propaganda tool of the LEFT?

Do you SEE FB/Twitter/GOOG censoring non LEFT POVs?

Do you SEE the corruption?

Do you SEE the EVIL?

Are you a SLAVE?

Are you CONTROLLED?

Are you a SHEEP?

ARE YOU AWAKE?

DO YOU THINK FOR YOURSELF?

LEARN THE TRUTH.

FACTS.

HISTORY.
THE GREAT AWAKENING.
THEY ARE LOSING CONTROL.
RESPECT OPINION OR ATTACK THOSE WHO DARE
CHALLENGE THE NARRATIVE?
IT'S RIGHT IN FRONT OF YOU.
WHO ARE THE TRUE FASCISTS?
WHO ARE THE TRUE RACISTS?
WHY DOES THE ANTIFA FLAG MIMIC THAT OF THE NAZIS?
COINCIDENCE?
FOR HUMANITY - WAKE UP - LEARN.
FIGHT FIGHT FIGHT
WHERE WE GO ONE, WE GO ALL!
Q

Awakening to the truth is an uncomfortable experience. Many people who have already awakened from their slumber soon felt frustrated, disappointed, and angry. These emotions are usually due to the perception of indifference to corruption by those responsible for setting things right. One might rightly ask: if amoral sociopaths run the world, why aren't they being arrested? Why are they allowed to continue committing crimes? Allow me to share an analogy that will explain this situation.

Imagine that ever since you were born, a fiendish creature had attached itself to you. Like a lamprey clinging to the side of a fish, it has lived off the nutrients it obtains from your circulatory system. Imagine that these creatures attach themselves to many people. Now imagine that some people can see these creatures, but you cannot. You go through life, year after year, ignoring comments from those who try to tell you about the beast. You get married and have children. And then one day—you're not sure exactly why—an uncomfortable feeling begins to gnaw at you. You wonder, what if there really *is* a creature attached to you? One night, in a moment of desperation before going to bed, you ask God to reveal the truth to you. In the morning, you awake and see the hideous creature in bed next to you. Surveying it, you notice that a long, slender tentacle is embedded in your body just below your armpit. You shake yourself to awaken from the nightmare, but you're not dreaming. You bound out of bed and run through the house in a panic. The creature effortlessly follows you. After calming down, you call your doctor and explain what you've found. He asks if you'd like to have the creature removed. "Of course,

I want it removed!" You reply sternly. "What sane person would want to live in this condition?" Your doctor tells you it will be two weeks before an appointment can be scheduled for surgery. Anger gushes from your mouth. You hurl profanities through the phone. "I can't wait for weeks for this thing to be removed. It has to be done now!" Your doctor takes a breath, and in a calm voice, warns you that the only safe way to remove the creature is by performing a very delicate procedure that detaches its tentacle from your circulatory system. If it is not removed carefully, you face certain death. Only a handful of surgeons are qualified to do the procedure, and they are booked for the next few weeks. You're simply going to have to live with this horrid thing until the next available appointment.

Awakening to the truth that you have been deceived will cause a flood of emotions. One emotion you're likely to feel is injustice. Another is urgency. When they meet, you'll develop a new sense of conviction; something must be done to bring corrupt people to justice, and it must be done immediately. Like the person with the parasitic creature, who suddenly became aware of its existence, you will demand that things be fixed now—despite that the fact that these problems had existed for decades before you became aware of them. Others knew. They tried to make you aware of the problem. But you weren't ready for the truth. And now that you are, the world needs your help.

Certain military leaders knew long ago that corrupt people were getting away with murder and that the general population was ignorant of it. They knew what needed to be done to remedy the problem. But they could not take action until the public woke up to the truth, lest they risk causing widespread panic, civil unrest, and war. Military leaders have been waiting. They've been waiting for just the right political leader to come along who would work with them to eradicate corruption—waiting to deploy traps that would provide the evidence needed to convict corrupt people—waiting for the justice system and our intelligence communities to be cleaned of criminal elements. They've been waiting for us to wake up to the truth and demand change. Now that you're awake, the first thing to understand is that centuries of rot and corruption which have infected every part of society aren't going to be removed in a few weeks. The process of removal has been ongoing for years. Much has been done already, but much more needs to be accomplished. You will be angry. But understand this—the most useful thing you can do right now is to help others awaken from their slumber. Once a critical mass of citizens has been awakened, the real work of exposing and removing corruption can begin.

Dec 7 2019
Knowledge is power.
Think for yourself.
Trust yourself.
Do due diligence.
You awake, and thinking for yourself, is their greatest fear.
Sheep no more.
THE GREAT AWAKENING.
Q

CHAPTER 5

The Rothschilds

Q HAS SUGGESTED THAT THE Rothschild banking family plays
a vital role in the way global events transpire. Publicly available information
on any topic is subject to the author's bias. Much of the information in the
public domain about the Rothschilds is too biased to be used in conducting
objective research. Count Egon Caesar Corti spent more than three years
scouring European libraries and museums in search of documents related
to the Rothschilds. The fruit of his labor was a two-volume set of books.
The first volume is titled *The Rise of the House of Rothschild;* the second
is *The Reign of the House of Rothschild.* The books trace the history of the
family from humble beginnings in 1770 to the financial dynasty they had
built by the start of the 20th century.

The books are filled with letters sent to and from members of the
Rothschild family to nobles, or other family members. Corti provides
an objective view of the Rothschilds, having little to say from a political,
religious, or philosophical perspective. In this chapter, I'll do my best to
summarize two and a half centuries of the family's history using Corti's
books as the primary reference.

Following the middle ages, a period of enlightenment came over Europe,
which led to a new way of viewing the role of government. In the 1770s,

American patriots revolted against the British monarchy and formed a constitutional republic, which would be governed by elected leaders. The French revolution soon followed, and led to similar uprisings in other parts of the world.

In the 18th century, Frankfurt, Germany, was a hub of commercial trade; people came from all over Europe to buy and sell there. To do so, they needed to convert their currency into the local coin. Into this scene was born Mayer Amschel Rothschild, whose father made a living exchanging currency and collecting valuable coins. The elder Rothschild taught his young son the family business. At the age of twelve, Mayer's parents died and left him a small inheritance. Feeling as though he was left with no other choice, the young Mayer Rothschild threw himself into his family's work.

Mayer Rothschild Meets a German Noble

Mayer soon became acquainted with a man who would have the greatest influence on his family's business. In 1760, the German ruler or "Landgrave" of Hesse-Cassel, William VIII, died. His son Frederick assumed rulership of the government at Cassel, Germany, and Frederick's son William became crown prince and the ruler of the small county of Hanau.

Prince William had a great interest in coin collecting. One of his military generals was also interested in numismatics and spoke to the Prince about Mayer Rothschild, who had bought coins for him. Foreigners visited Frankfurt's fairs every spring. Prince William was a regular attendee. Mayer Rothschild received notice of his journeys and sold to William not only rare coins but precious stones and antiques.

Unlike other princes, William was not driven to conquer nations. He was obsessed with making money. While other kings and princes waged war, William loaned his money to royals, including King George IV of Britain and the Duke of York. The interest gained from his lending made Prince William an extremely wealthy man. This fact did not escape the attention of Mayer Rothschild, who hoped to copy William's practice of lending money to monarchies.

Because Rothschild had no relationship with a royal family, he endeavored to become Prince William's financial agent. William didn't trust Rothschild at first. But a treasury official named Carl Buderus was given charge over the Prince's financial dealings. Rothschild became friends with Buderus, and later, became his confidential business partner.

In 1785, William's father, Frederick, died. William succeeded to the throne of Hesse-Cassel as Landgrave William IX. On reading his father's will, he learned that the country was free of debt and that he had inherited an enormous fortune.

At this time, titles and honors were of great practical importance. Unless one had a prefix or suffix attached to their name, the doors to upward social mobility and financial success were closed. Those who did not have a title of nobility by birth would try to obtain an office or title from a local count or prince. Mayer Rothschild, being a shrewd man with an intuitive understanding of human nature, focused his efforts on obtaining a title from William. In 1769, he was granted the title Crown Agent to the Principality of Hesse-Hanau.

It was common practice during this time for the postal service to open letters, note the contents, and then send messages on to their destinations. The House of Thurn and Taxis, which was based in Frankfurt, offered to give the emperor the information they obtained from private letters. Meyer Rothschild understood that it was critical for a banker and merchant to have early and accurate information regarding important events, especially in time of war. Mayer entered into a series of financial transactions with the House of Thurn and Taxis. He relied on these transactions when he applied for and was granted the title of Imperial Crown Agent.

The French Revolution Brings Opportunity

The French Revolution began in 1789, and from 1793 to 1815, France was almost continuously at war with Britain and other nations. French military successes led to the spread of revolutionary ideals into neighboring countries, which caused royals to take up arms. War was then—as it is today—an expensive undertaking. When a king launches a military campaign, they must provide food, clothing, lodging, ammunition, and other items for the invading army. Britain waged many wars, and although they had no equal at sea, they had limited ability to wage war on the European continent. Instead of sending *their* troops, they hired soldiers from other nations.

When a nation lost a war, they could be held financially responsible to pay for expenses incurred by their enemies. All of these war-related transactions were carried out by men with financial experience and a reputation for sound business practices—generally private banking firms, such as the Rothschilds.

Napoleon began his conquest of Europe in 1806, by declaring war against Prussia. William did his best to remain neutral, but by mid-October, Prussia had been defeated. Napoleon resented William's neutrality and ordered that Cassel and Hesse should be occupied, and that unless William left, he would be taken prisoner.

Mayer Rothschild Gains Influence

In October, 1806, Napoleon's army camped on the hills surrounding Cassel, while William made preparations to flee. William gave Buderus power of attorney to receive the interest payments due from a loan to Emperor Francis of Austria. Buderus transferred this power of attorney to Mayer Rothschild, who collected the payments through a friend in Vienna. As Napoleon's conquest of Europe progressed, William was forced to relocate several times, finally settling in Prague. German kings and princes suffered a shortage of cash, and many of them borrowed money from William.

In 1809, Buderus suggested to William that he should purchase British securities, and that Mayer Rothschild should oversee the transaction. William ordered 150,000 British pounds of the stocks to be purchased by Rothschild. Financial transactions in England were the most lucrative, but remittances from the royal family came in at irregular intervals and were often outstanding for long periods of time. William, however, wasn't worried about delayed payments. He regarded these investments as a means of putting the British royal family under obligation to himself. The royal family's uneasy feeling after failing to make payments on time sometimes led them to make amends in other ways, such as providing valuable information or political favors. These favors sometimes produced cash results that far exceeded the amount of debt they owed. Mayer Rothschild carefully observed how William dealt with nobility in these transactions.

Solomon Rothschild in Austria

Austria incurred massive debt during the reign of Emperor Francis, due mostly to fear of revolution. To keep from being removed from power, the Emperor spent a fortune sending armies to neighboring countries to quell revolutionary forces. William of Hesse extended many loans to the Austrian government. Mayer's son, Solomon, oversaw most of the transactions between the Rothschilds and the Austrian monarchy. In 1820,

Solomon moved to Vienna and set up a branch of the family's business there. He became a close confidant of Prince Metternich and extended credit to both the government and its ministers. In time, the Rothschilds would become the Austrian government's primary source of capital.

Carl Rothschild in Italy

Austria had, on several occasions, invaded the Kingdom of the Two Sicilies to put down revolution. In 1821, when the Austrian army occupied Naples, Carl Rothschild was sent from Frankfurt to manage the payment of war reparations. Carl gained influence with the local ruling families because he was able to extend them credit. He established a branch of the family business in Naples and made loans to King Ferdinand IV, the Dukes of Parma and Tuscany, and the Vatican.

Family Business Arrangements

On September 27th, 1810, a deed of partnership was drawn up between Mayer Rothschild and his five sons. For the purpose of sharing profits, the firm was divided up into 50 equal parts, the sons each having shares commensurate with their ages. The daughters and the children's in-laws were not allowed to see the company's books. A provision was made that required any brother wishing to bring a lawsuit against a partner to pay a penalty before going to court. This was to prevent disputes and keep the family's financial dealings out of court, where their books might be scrutinized. The Rothschilds valued secrecy and kept two sets of books. One was periodically examined by government authorities. The other was only seen by male members of the family.

Nathan Rothschild in England

The third oldest Rothschild son, Nathan, who, in 1798, was twenty-one, had an independent spirit. One day, an English traveler visited the family's business in Frankfurt, and was received by Nathan. English commercial travelers were sometimes perceived as arrogant and condescending. The man's demeanor annoyed Nathan. The encounter spurred him to ask permission from his father to go to England to become a merchant and to represent the firm of Rothschild there. His father and brothers supported his decision. Nathan took with him a sum of 20,000 British pounds, about a fifth of which was his own money, while the rest belonged to the family business.

Nathan settled in Manchester, England, and became a successful tradesman. After the required six years of residency, in 1804, he moved to London and applied to become a naturalized citizen. His citizenship was granted, and he began trading on the London stock exchange. He hired couriers to bring him messages and news across the English Channel. Having an early warning of important news is an advantage to financial traders. Nathan received news of Napoleon's defeat at Waterloo before anyone in England. The report allowed him to make extremely profitable trades on the London stock exchange. In addition to trades, Nathan oversaw frequent, large loans to European nobility.

Napoleon instituted a blockade of trade from England, but he understood that certain goods from England were desperately needed. He made a decree that permitted a limited number of items to be legally smuggled into the country, and Nathan took advantage of it. The British monarchy needed to send gold and silver across the English Channel to support their armies on the continent. Nathan wanted to be the agent who handled these transactions, but he needed a trustworthy person to oversee shipments arriving in France. He wrote to the Frankfurt office and requested his brother James to be sent to Paris.

James Rothschild in France

The oldest Rothschild son, Anselm, helped manage the family's original branch in Frankfurt, Germany. He was on friendly terms with France's local representative Karl von Dalberg, who arranged for James to receive a French passport. Though only nineteen years old at the time, James set off for Paris. Napoleon's finance minister received word of James' arrival and knew he would be receiving large sums of gold and silver from England. James and Nathan employed a disinformation campaign. They convinced French authorities that the British government was displeased with the shipments. Thinking it would harm Britain, Napoleon instructed his finance minister to allow the transfers to proceed. Nathan and James shipped vast amounts of gold and silver (at a substantial profit) through France to supply Wellington's armies, who were fighting the French in Spain.

James Rothschild took up permanent residence in Paris and opened a branch of the family business there. Being a gracious man, he made many acquaintances and rose in favor with the French aristocracy and brokered loans to French nobles.

Other Ventures

During the mid-1800s, the Rothschilds were the first to build a railroad on the European continent and were early adopters of steam-powered boats. Their ability to move freight and passengers using new technology greatly increased their wealth and influence. In the late 1800s, they provided capital to fund several mining companies, including DeBeers and Rio Tinto. During the Russo-Japanese war, the London branch issued bonds on behalf of Japan in the amount of 11.5 million British pounds. The London branch advanced Britain's Prime Minister, Benjamin Disraeli, 4 million British pounds to purchase Suez Canal shares.

During the 20th century, the Rothschilds assumed a less visible public profile. They continued expanding their financial empire through ownership of various banks, holding companies, insurance companies, and private equity groups.

Philanthropy

Like most wealthy families, the Rothschilds are known for their philanthropy. Although they've built some of the most exquisite mansions in the world, many have been donated to charitable causes. The family once possessed one of the largest private art collections in the world. Today, a significant portion of art in the world's public museums has been donated by the Rothschilds. In Frankfurt, Nathan's youngest child Louise and her seven daughters were responsible for many of the family's 30 charitable foundations in the city, including a dental clinic, a public library, a swimming pool, nursing homes, orphanages, soup kitchens, and hospitals. In Vienna, the family established hospitals, orphanages, and a municipal theater. According to the Rothschild Archives website, the family has been closely associated with the British Red Cross. In 1870, Nathan became one of the founding members of the committee of the National Society for Aid to the Sick and Wounded in War. He became chairman in 1901 and played a key role in the reorganization of the society into the British Red Cross. His son, Charles, was one of the first council members of the newly formed British Red Cross and helped establish their financial systems and policies.

Secrets to Success

The success of the Rothschilds seems to be attributable to several factors. Mayer Rothschild was exceptionally gifted at discerning people's motives, their needs, their abilities, and limitations. He instinctively knew how an individual might benefit him, and how he could benefit them. He often conducted business with influential people at a small loss to himself because he knew a short-term loss could be parlayed into a relationship that would profit him over time.

Mayer chose to make his sons his business partners at a young age and taught them his trade secrets as soon as they were able to grasp them. This gave his sons a strategic advantage in the marketplace and allowed them to outmaneuver people who were much older and more experienced. When the sons came of age, nearly every significant transaction made by the firm was done in consultation with and the agreement of all five brothers. This minimized the likelihood of a bad idea being approved.

Nathan's move to London gave the family access to news that was critical to their success. It also gave them a skilled investor in the world's most important financial district.

Likewise, James' move to Paris gave them access to valuable news on the continent and an ambassador inside the French government. Solomon's dealings in Vienna gave them access to a powerful monarchy and made them a handsome profit, albeit at great loss to Austrian taxpayers.

The Rothschilds always endeavored to ingratiate themselves to kings and emperors with an eye toward receiving titles of nobility. All five sons received titles that were passed on to their descendants, guaranteeing family members the social stature required for commercial success.

The family weathered financial storms that put others bankers out of business. Although they had many competitors, no financial entity in the world could compete with the combined resources of the family at their zenith.

The Rothschilds followed the practice of European nobility and often married within the family. For example, James married his niece, while his son Edmond, married his cousin, and Nathan's son, Lionel, likewise married his cousin. Such marriages minimized influences from outside the family and helped them keep certain facts hidden from the public. Mayer Rothschild studied the investment strategies of William of Hesse. He replicated them and improved on them. Like William, the Rothschilds amassed a fortune lending to nobles, but they gained influence with royal families that William couldn't. For more than two centuries, the kings and emperors of the world made decisions with consideration as to how those decisions would impact the Rothschilds.

Q's References to the Rothschilds

Now, we'll look at what Q has said about the family. On November 11th, 2017, Q posted a list of 165 banks he said are owned or controlled by the Rothschilds.

Nov 11 2017
ROTHSCHILD OWNED & CONTROLLED BANKS:
Afghanistan: Bank of Afghanistan
Albania: Bank of Albania
Algeria: Bank of Algeria
Argentina: Central Bank of Argentina
Armenia: Central Bank of Armenia
Aruba: Central Bank of Aruba
Australia: Reserve Bank of Australia
Austria: Austrian National Bank
Azerbaijan: Central Bank of Azerbaijan Republic
Bahamas: Central Bank of The Bahamas
Bahrain: Central Bank of Bahrain
Bangladesh: Bangladesh Bank
Barbados: Central Bank of Barbados
Belarus: National Bank of the Republic of Belarus
Belgium: National Bank of Belgium
Belize: Central Bank of Belize
Benin: Central Bank of West African States (BCEAO)
Bermuda: Bermuda Monetary Authority
Bhutan: Royal Monetary Authority of Bhutan
Bolivia: Central Bank of Bolivia
Bosnia: Central Bank of Bosnia and Herzegovina
Botswana: Bank of Botswana
Brazil: Central Bank of Brazil
Bulgaria: Bulgarian National Bank
Burkina Faso: Central Bank of West African States (BCEAO)
Burundi: Bank of the Republic of Burundi
Cambodia: National Bank of Cambodia

Came Roon: Bank of Central African States
Canada: Bank of Canada – Banque du Canada
Cayman Islands: Cayman Islands Monetary Authority
Central African Republic: Bank of Central African States
Chad: Bank of Central African States
Chile: Central Bank of Chile
China: The People's Bank of China
Colombia: Bank of the Republic
Comoros: Central Bank of Comoros
Congo: Bank of Central African States
Costa Rica: Central Bank of Costa Rica
Côte d'Ivoire: Central Bank of West African States (BCEAO)
Croatia: Croatian National Bank
Cuba: Central Bank of Cuba
Cyprus: Central Bank of Cyprus
Czech Republic: Czech National Bank
Denmark: National Bank of Denmark
Dominican Republic: Central Bank of the Dominican Republic
East Caribbean area: Eastern Caribbean Central Bank
Ecuador: Central Bank of Ecuador
Egypt: Central Bank of Egypt
El Salvador: Central Reserve Bank of El Salvador
Equatorial Guinea: Bank of Central African States
Estonia: Bank of Estonia
Ethiopia: National Bank of Ethiopia
European Union: European Central Bank
Fiji: Reserve Bank of Fiji
Finland: Bank of Finland
France: Bank of France
Gabon: Bank of Central African States
The Gambia: Central Bank of The Gambia
Georgia: National Bank of Georgia
Germany: Deutsche Bundesbank
Ghana: Bank of Ghana
Greece: Bank of Greece
Guatemala: Bank of Guatemala
Guinea Bissau: Central Bank of West African States (BCEAO)
Guyana: Bank of Guyana
Haiti: Central Bank of Haiti

Honduras: Central Bank of Honduras
Hong Kong: Hong Kong Monetary Authority
Hungary: Magyar Nemzeti Bank
Iceland: Central Bank of Iceland
India: Reserve Bank of India
Indonesia: Bank Indonesia
Iran: The Central Bank of the Islamic Republic of Iran
Iraq: Central Bank of Iraq
Ireland: Central Bank and Financial Services Authority of Ireland
Israel: Bank of Israel
Italy: Bank of Italy
Jamaica: Bank of Jamaica
Japan: Bank of Japan
Jordan: Central Bank of Jordan
Kazakhstan: National Bank of Kazakhstan
Kenya: Central Bank of Kenya
Korea: Bank of Korea
Kuwait: Central Bank of Kuwait
Kyrgyzstan: National Bank of the Kyrgyz Republic
Latvia: Bank of Latvia
Lebanon: Central Bank of Lebanon
Lesotho: Central Bank of Lesotho
Libya: Central Bank of Libya (Their most recent conquest)
Uruguay: Central Bank of Uruguay
Lithuania: Bank of Lithuania
Luxembourg: Central Bank of Luxembourg
Macao: Monetary Authority of Macao
Macedonia: National Bank of the Republic of Macedonia
Madagascar: Central Bank of Madagascar
Malawi: Reserve Bank of Malawi
Malaysia: Central Bank of Malaysia
Mali: Central Bank of West African States (BCEAO)
Malta: Central Bank of Malta
Mauritius: Bank of Mauritius
Mexico: Bank of Mexico
Moldova: National Bank of Moldova
Mongolia: Bank of Mongolia
Montenegro: Central Bank of Montenegro
Morocco: Bank of Morocco

Mozambique: Bank of Mozambique
Namibia: Bank of Namibia
Nepal: Central Bank of Nepal
Netherlands: Netherlands Bank
Netherlands Antilles: Bank of the Netherlands Antilles
New Zealand: Reserve Bank of New Zealand
Nicaragua: Central Bank of Nicaragua
Niger: Central Bank of West African States (BCEAO)
Nigeria: Central Bank of Nigeria
Norway: Central Bank of Norway
Oman: Central Bank of Oman
Pakistan: State Bank of Pakistan
Papua New Guinea: Bank of Papua New Guinea
Paraguay: Central Bank of Paraguay
Peru: Central Reserve Bank of Peru
Philip Pines: Bangko Sentral ng Pilipinas
Poland: National Bank of Poland
Portugal: Bank of Portugal
Qatar: Qatar Central Bank
Romania: National Bank of Romania
Russia: Central Bank of Russia
Rwanda: National Bank of Rwanda
San Marino: Central Bank of the Republic of San Marino
Samoa: Central Bank of Samoa
Saudi Arabia: Saudi Arabian Monetary Agency
Senegal: Central Bank of West African States (BCEAO)
Serbia: National Bank of Serbia
Seychelles: Central Bank of Seychelles
Sierra Leone: Bank of Sierra Leone
Singapore: Monetary Authority of Singapore
Slovakia: National Bank of Slovakia
Slovenia: Bank of Slovenia
Solomon Islands: Central Bank of Solomon Islands
South Africa: South African Reserve Bank
Spain: Bank of Spain
Sri Lanka: Central Bank of Sri Lanka
Sudan: Bank of Sudan
Surinam: Central Bank of Suriname
Swaziland: The Central Bank of Swaziland

Sweden: Sveriges Riksbank
Switzerland: Swiss National Bank
Tajikistan: National Bank of Tajikistan
Tanzania: Bank of Tanzania
Thailand: Bank of Thailand
Togo: Central Bank of West African States (BCEAO)
Tonga: National Reserve Bank of Tonga
Trinidad and Tobago: Central Bank of Trinidad and Tobago
Tunisia: Central Bank of Tunisia
Turkey: Central Bank of the Republic of Turkey
Uganda: Bank of Uganda
Ukraine: National Bank of Ukraine
United Arab Emirates: Central Bank of United Arab Emirates
United Kingdom: Bank of England
United States: Federal Reserve, Federal Reserve Bank of New York
Vanuatu: Reserve Bank of Vanuatu
Venezuela: Central Bank of Venezuela
Vietnam: The State Bank of Vietnam
Yemen: Central Bank of Yemen
Zambia: Bank of Zambia
Zimbabwe: Reserve Bank of Zimbabwe
The FED and the IRS
FACT: US Federal Reserve is a privately-owned company, sitting on
its very own patch of land, immune to the US laws.
Q

Notably, the list includes the Federal Reserve and the U.S. Internal
Revenue Service. On the same day, Q explained how people are controlled
on a global scale.

Nov 11 2017
Hard to swallow.
Important to progress.
Who are the puppet masters?
House of Saud (6+++) - $4 Trillion+
Rothschild (6++) - $2 Trillion+
Soros (6+) - $1 Trillion+
Focus on above (3).
Public wealth disclosures – False.

Many governments of the world feed the 'Eye'.
Think slush funds (feeder).
Think war (feeder).
Think environmental pacts (feeder).
Triangle has (3) sides.
Eye of Providence.
Follow the bloodlines.
What is the keystone?
Does Satan exist?
Does the 'thought' of Satan exist?
Who worships Satan?
What is a cult?
Epstein island.
What is a temple?
What occurs in a temple?
Worship?
Why is the temple on top of a mountain?
How many levels might exist below?
What is the significance of the colors, design and symbol above
the dome?
Why is this relevant?
Who are the puppet masters?
Have the puppet masters traveled to this island?
When? How often? Why?
"Vladimir Putin: The New World Order Worships Satan"
Q

Q explained that the majority of people in the world are under the indirect control of three families, whose real wealth is not reported publicly. The families are represented by plus signs, and Q estimated their true wealth. In a different post, the three families were illustrated with a triangle. One side of the triangle represented the Saudi royal family; one side represented the Rothschild banking family; and the third side, George Soros. According to Q, each plays a part in the control of the geopolitical landscape—the Rothschilds primarily control banks and financial institutions and through them, national governments as well as the Catholic Church. By controlling governments and the church, they control large numbers of people. According to Q, Saudi Arabia maintained economic control via its oil reserves and exerted control over some American and UK politicians through pedophilia and blackmail. Saudi princes like Alwaleed bin Talal have been major investors in the tech sector and the media, including social media platforms. Elitist investor George Soros funds left-leaning political activists and progressive organizations. As we learned, war is one way to make money. Taxes are remitted to governments who pay a substantial amount of it to banks owned by the Rothschilds. There is a hint from Q that family bloodlines help maintain power over successive generations.

Q mentioned the worship of Satan. It is my personal belief that Satan exists, but not everyone is convinced of that. Regardless, some people believe Satan exists, and they believe he can give them power if they obey and worship him. On April 6th, 2018, Q posted images related to Jeffrey Epstein's island and the sexual abuse that allegedly occurred there. Q takes the view that sexual abuse is part of the worship of Satan that is carried out by members of the three families, or as Q calls them, "the puppet masters."

On December 7th, 2017, Q posted photos of political leaders from around the world along with photos of George Soros, members of the Saudi royal family, and the Rothschilds. According to Q, American politicians like Hillary Clinton and Barack Obama were controlled by Saudi princes like Alwaleed bin Talal. The arrest of members of the Saudi royal family in November of 2017 removed their control.

Q then posted a follow-up message.

Dec 7 2017
Can you find a pic of Alwaleed and Hussein or Clinton or other US politicians?
L.
Heard you can't sleep anymore.
Don't come here again.
Q

Occasionally, Q will taunt the Rothschild family with messages like the one above, knowing they read them. "L" seems to be directed at Lynn de Rothschild—the chief executive officer of E.L. Rothschild, a holding company she owns with her husband, Evelyn Robert de Rothschild. The following message, posted a month earlier, also seemed to be sent to her. Note the bracketed initials [L][d][R].

Nov 13 2017
Distress cal[L]s to others will [d]o you/family no good at this
stage. We know whe[R]e you/the family are at all times and can
hear you breathing.
Q
_D7g^-_%19FZBx_decline

It's rare for Q to post anything *after* his signature, but he did so in the post above. Coded messages like this one are not necessarily meant for anons to decode. We assume they are intended for another purpose—perhaps for a military operation.

On March 20th, 2019, Q noted that Nicky Hilton, an heiress to the Hilton Hotel fortune married into the Rothschild family, suggesting that wealthy families marry members of other wealthy families to consolidate power.

Mar 20 2019
Who did Nicky Hilton (sister of Paris) marry?
James Rothschild.
Q

On February 5th, 2018, Q posted the following message.

Feb 5 2018
Why did the #Memo drop a Friday [& before the SB]?
Did this seem strange to you?
Watch the news.
Rothschild estate sale [Black Forest].
Stock market DIVE [666 - coincidence?].
Soros transfer of wealth.
Dopey FREED.
Marriage for POWER, not LOVE.
Hilton/Roth.
Soros/Clinton.
Etc.
News unlocks MAP.
Think Mirror.
Which team?
THEY don't know.
APACHE.

These people are EVIL.
Still don't believe you are SHEEP to them?
20/20 coming.
PUBLIC is VITAL.
RELEASE of INFO VITAL.
OUTRAGE.
JUSTICE.
Can we simply arrest the opposition w/o first exposing the
TRUTH?
FOLLOW THE LIGHT.
Q

Three days before this post, on February 2nd, two days before the Super-bowl (SB), a memo written by the staff of California Representative Devin Nunes was released. The memo alleged that the FBI, under Barack Obama, "may have relied on politically motivated or questionable sources" to obtain a Foreign Intelligence Surveillance Act (FISA) warrant on Carter Page, an advisor for Donald Trump's 2016 Presidential campaign. FISA surveillance is used when a person is suspected of being an agent of a foreign power. Everyone they come in contact with is a potential target for surveillance. Thus, the FISA surveillance of Carter Page allowed the Obama administration to spy on the entire Trump campaign.

On the same day the FISA memo was released, the Dow Jones Indus-trial Average dropped 666 points. Q implied that a powerful group of people caused the stock market to drop to that level as a veiled threat to President Trump.

A few days earlier, on January 31st, the Rothschild family auctioned off a large hunting estate in Austria that had been owned by their family for 143 years. One month prior, on December 21st, 2017, Donald Trump signed an executive order allowing the U.S. Treasury to seize the assets of people and organizations known to be involved in corruption, human rights abuse, or human trafficking. Q suggested the estate was sold to liquidate assets because the Rothschilds had fallen upon hard financial times after Trump issued his executive order. More information on the Rothschilds will be provided in the chapters that follow.

CHAPTER 6

Godfather III

Q'S GOAL IS TO MAKE the public aware of institutional corruption. Corruption in politics isn't hard for the average person to accept, but acknowledging it in other parts of society is more difficult. In areas where corruption is unexpected or where it has infiltrated trusted organizations, it is harder to swallow. In those cases, Q doesn't tell us plainly about the details of corruption. We're given hints, and we're encouraged to do our own research. If we do our own research, the evidence we find may be more believable.

Q sometimes hints at institutional corruption in the odd phrases found in the last few lines of a post. These phrases, which are often the titles of films, are called *signatures*. A signature at the end of a post contains a coded message.

Nov 5 2017
My signatures all reference upcoming events about to drop if this hasn't been caught on.
Snow White
Godfather III
Q

Q explained that his signatures are alerts of coming events. He provided one that we'll examine. This post contains the signature "Godfather III." Understanding the plot of the film or book indicated by the words that compose a signature will tell you something about the posts that contain that phrase. The film *Godfather Part III* is the final installment in the tale of the fictional Corleone crime family. Because the film closely mimics historical events, I'll first explain the movie's main plot, and then we'll look at its resemblance to real-life events. This will help us understand more about why Q uses this signature.

Godfather III, the Movie Plot

The film *Godfather Part III* opens with an aging Michael Corleone who, haunted by a life of sin, laments the fact that although he loved his father, he swore he wouldn't get involved in the family business. Michael never took religion seriously, but now, he is contemplating the possibility of redeeming his life and making something good of it. Trying to break away from his wicked past, he liquidates his casino holdings and informs other mob members that he will no longer do business with them.

He donates 100 million dollars to the Catholic Church in Sicily to aid the poor. The money is disbursed by his daughter, Mary, who he appoints as the chairman of the non-profit Michael Corleone Foundation. The recipient of the funds is Archbishop Gilday, who confesses to Michael that he's in a bind. He's responsible for 500 million dollars in missing Vatican money. A man named Don Lucchese has been stealing funds from the Vatican with the assistance of Gilday and a Swiss accountant named Frederick Keinszig.

Michael knows that the Vatican owns 25 percent interest in a real estate holding company called Immobiliare and that its assets are valued at 6 billion dollars. To help Gilday out of his predicament, Michael agrees to donate 600 million dollars to the Church in exchange for the Vatican's shares of Immobiliare. Michael intends to secure enough seats on the board of directors to control the company.

Michael travels to Sicily, anticipating the approval of his takeover of Immobiliare by Pope Paul VI. But the Pope becomes ill and is unable to ratify the deal before he dies. Michael then meets a Cardinal by the name of Lamberto, who persuades him to make his first confession in 30 years. During his confession, Michael reveals his mistaken belief that to receive salvation from his sins, he needs to atone for them. Lamberto rightly recognized that Michael would not change his ways unless he understood that his redemption came from God, rather than through good deeds of atonement. Cardinal Lamberto tells him that he is doomed to continue in his ways.

When Pope Paul VI dies, Lamberto becomes his successor, taking the title Pope John Paul I. Being a man of integrity, he calls for an investigation into the activities of the corrupt Vatican bank.

Lucchesi, Gilday, and Keinszig fear the new Pope will expose their crooked dealings, so they hatch a plan to murder him. Hours after approving Michael's takeover of Immobiliare, the new Pontiff is found dead in his bed, after drinking tea that had been poisoned by Gilday.

Keinszig prepares to leave Rome with a large sum of money and a briefcase full of documents. Michael Corleone passes the family's mantle to his nephew, Vincent, who immediately dispatches men to kill the family's enemies. Keinszig, the Vatican's accountant, is abducted by Vincent's men, who suffocate him and hang his body from a bridge, making his death look like a suicide.

Art Imitates Life

The character Keinszig appears to be loosely based on at least two real people. One is Nunzio Scarano, a senior Vatican accountant who was convicted of money laundering. Keinszig's death in the film resembles the real-life death of Roberto Calvi, the president of an Italian bank, who was convicted in 1981 of financial crimes.

The murder of the Pope in the film echoes a story told by Anthony Raimondi, the nephew of mob boss Lucky Luciano. Raimondi said that in 1978, he traveled to Italy with a team of men to kill Pope John Paul I. He alleges they poisoned the Pontiff with cyanide 33 days into his reign. The details are revealed in Raimondi's book *When the Bullet Hits the Bone.*

Raimondi claims he was recruited for the murder by his cousin, Cardinal Paul Marcinkus, who was the president of the Vatican bank at the time. Raimondi said Marcinkus sedated John Paul by spiking his nightly cup of tea with Valium, and after he was asleep, he was given cyanide. (Archbishop Gilday's character is based on Cardinal Marcinkus.)

Raimondi says the mob targeted the Pope because he threatened to expose a stock fraud scheme run by Vatican insiders. The scam involved a forgery expert at the Vatican who faked the Church's holdings in blue-chip American companies. The phony stock certificates were then sold to unsuspecting buyers. According to Raimondi, John Paul I vowed to expose the perpetrators, which included Marcinkus and several other cardinals and bishops.

The Holy See

In a post from August of 2018, Q pointed out that the Holy See's immunity from international law made it a safe haven for criminal enterprise. He included an open source link to the U.S. Department of State website.

> Aug 28 2018
> U.S.-HOLY SEE RELATIONS
> "The Holy See is the universal government of the Catholic Church and operates from Vatican City State, a sovereign, independent territory. The Pope is the ruler of both Vatican City State and the Holy See. The Holy See, as the supreme body of government of the Catholic Church, is a sovereign juridical entity under international law."
> https://www.state.gov/r/pa/ei/bgn/3819.htm
> Wealth?
> Power?
> Sanctuary against criminal prosecution?
> Recipe for ....
> Q

The Wealth of the Catholic Church

Next, I'll provide a brief history of the Catholic Church with an emphasis on its wealth. Some of the details in the section can be found in the book *The Vatican Exposed: Money, Murder and the Mafia* by Paul Williams.

The first three centuries of the Christian church were marked by severe persecution by the Roman Empire. The early church, as an organization, had no significant property or wealth. Constantine's conversion to Christianity and ascension to the throne as emperor forever changed the dynamic between church and state. Constantine donated the Lateran Palace in Rome and several large tracts of land on the Italian peninsula to the Church.

In the 5th century, the Byzantine Empire conquered Italy. The Lombards then invaded the Northern peninsula, and the Byzantines were unable to administer their rule over territories near Rome. Since the Church was the largest landowner, the Pope became the effective ruler of the region.

In 754, King Pepin defeated the Lombards and made a gift of land to the Pope, which became known as the Papal States.

In 1066, William the Conqueror gave over a quarter of the land in England to the Church. Landholdings increased over the next few centuries. By the 16th century, approximately one-third of the land in Europe was under the control of members of the clergy.

The Church Loses Real Estate and Influence

The Protestant Reformation of the 16th century brought significant changes to the land controlled by the Church. Under King Henry VIII, 825 monasteries throughout England, Wales, and Ireland were dissolved, and Catholic Church properties were confiscated. When Henry died in 1547, all monasteries, friaries, convents, and shrines were destroyed or dissolved.

In 1685, King Louis XIV of France assumed control of many of the Church's properties and threatened Pope Innocent XI with a military takeover of the Papal States. Emperor Joseph II of Austria likewise confiscated much of the Church's real estate.

In 1860, Victor Emmanuel II led an army of soldiers who captured the Kingdom of the Two Sicilies in southern Italy. In 1861, Rome was declared the capital of the reunited Kingdom of Italy; however, the Italian government could not establish its rule there because a French garrison guarded the city. In August of 1870, Napoleon III recalled his garrison from Rome. In September, the city was captured by Victor Emmanuel and what was left of the Papal States were annexed to the Kingdom of Italy.

Prior to the French Revolution of 1789, Roman Catholicism had been the state religion of France. In 1880, the French government began a gradual secularization process. Members of the clergy were removed from positions of influence, particularly in the fields of healthcare and education. In 1905 France ended state funding of the clergy and declared all church property and buildings to be state land, which could be used by religious organizations at no cost.

The Russian Revolution of 1917 created many problems for the Pope. The communist philosophy of Vladimir Lenin called for the surrender of private property, the redistribution of wealth, the rejection of Church dogma in general, and the infallibility of the Pope in particular. By 1919, Russian priests were being killed or imprisoned, and Church buildings were being turned into secular museums. By 1922, having lost most of its landholdings, the Catholic Church was hard-pressed to meet its financial obligations and was forced to take out loans, mostly from German banks.

Mussolini and the Catholic Church

At that time, a young, charismatic Italian named Benito Mussolini was speaking in meeting halls and market places in opposition to communism. He recruited a gang of thugs to enforce his ideology. Those who opposed Mussolini were silenced by his "black shirts." Mussolini needed the backing of the Catholic Church if he were to rule Italy. The Church needed money if it were to survive. In 1929, Pope Pius XI and Mussolini entered into the Lateran Treaty—a three-part agreement that benefitted both parties.

The first section of the treaty gave the Vatican jurisdiction over all Catholic organizations in Italy. These organizations, called "ecclesiastical corporations," were declared exempt from both taxation and audit. The Vatican could create as many organizations as it wanted. The second section established Vatican City as a sovereign state, consisting of 108 acres on Vatican hill in Rome and several properties outside of Vatican City. In return for these concessions, the Vatican agreed to renounce all claims to lands that were taken during the war of 1870 and agreed to establish diplomatic relations with the Italian government. The last section of the treaty stated that the Vatican would receive 90 million dollars as compensation for surrendering the Papal States to the Italian government. The government also agreed to pay the salaries of all parish priests in Italy.

Pope Pius XI created a new financial agency, the Special Administration of the Holy See, whose sole purpose was to generate income from the money that came from the Italian government. The Pope hired financial genius Bernardino Nogara to handle the Vatican's newfound wealth. Nogara agreed to take the position on the conditions that he not be restricted by religious or doctrinal considerations in his investment-making and that he would be free to invest the funds anywhere in the world without restriction.

Nogara purchased enough shares to gain control of Banca di Roma. Due to the depressed economic conditions of the day, the bank had many securities that were of little value. Nogara convinced Mussolini to include the bank in the Institute for Industrial Reconstruction (IIR). In doing so, the Italian government became the bank's guarantor. The IIR was Italy's solution to the economic devastation that followed World War I. The securities held by Banca di Roma gained value. Nogara then purchased shares of the bank on the open market, and by 1935, the Vatican was the largest holder of state-secured business in the country, including Italgas, a major supplier of natural gas. The Vatican also became the largest shareholder of Società Generale Immobillare, one of Italy's oldest construction companies that would, in time, grow into a powerful multinational corporation. The mafia's interest in Immobillare was a key element of the film *Godfather Part III*.

Adolf Hitler and the Catholic Church

Between 1928 and 1932, Germany's National Socialist Party grew rapidly. In response, the German clergy forbade Catholics from joining the Nazi party and precluded party members from receiving the sacraments and attending funerals or Church services.

In 1933, allies of Adolph Hitler pressured leaders of Germany's Catholic Center Party to unite with the National Socialist party. The result was the formation of a new government with Adolph Hitler as Chancellor. Hitler knew that gaining the support of the Catholic Church was critical to his success, so he proposed an agreement with the Vatican. The concordat, ratified in July of 1933, stipulated that Catholic social work would receive support from the government. Additionally, criticism of Catholic doctrine would be prohibited in schools and public forums, and a nine percent "Kirchensteuer" (church tax) would be levied on all practicing Catholics in Germany. The tax would, in time, funnel billions of dollars to the Vatican. The Catholic Center Party was dissolved, and its members joined the National Socialist Party.

In April of 1941, Adolph Hitler's army invaded Yugoslavia, and once conquered, the nation was divided into predominantly Catholic Croatia and Orthodox Serbia. Ante Pavelic became the ruler of the independent state of Croatia. The nation became the center of an ambitious experiment—the creation of a Catholic Aryan state. Croatia had a population of 6.7 million people, which included more than 2 million Orthodox Serbs, 700,000 Muslims, and 45,000 Jews. The Nazi utopia could not be realized without ethnic cleansing. Between December of 1941 and February of 1942, 40,000 Serbs were executed at the death camp at Jasenovac.

Between June and August of 1942, 60,000 more Serbs were killed there, including 2,000 children. Some of the commandants of the death camps were Catholic priests. Father Miroslav Filipovic, a Franciscan friar, served as commandant of the death camp in Jasenovac and was assisted by other members of the clergy.

Some Orthodox Serbs were able to escape execution by converting to Catholicism, but it came at a price. In some towns, a certificate of conversion could be purchased. Those who did not convert were killed. Their homes and many Orthodox Churches were looted. The spoils and the money made from the sale of conversions were deposited in accounts at the Vatican bank. Between 1941 and 1945, more than 500,000 Serbs, 80,000 Jews, and 30,000 gypsies were killed in the Independent State of Croatia. On a per-capita basis, it ranks as the greatest genocide of the 20th century.

By the end of World War II, 36 chests of gold had been collected from the bodies of those who were murdered. The gold came in the form of rings, watches, dentures, and fillings pried from the mouths of victims. The precious metal was collected and stored in a monastery in Zagreb. From there, it was moved to Rome, and then to Naples, where it was melted into bars. From there, it was transferred to the Vatican bank. After the war, the Holy See and the Vatican bank were accused of helping members of Germany's military escape to South America to avoid prosecution as war criminals.

Vatican Bank Scandals

The Vatican Bank was established by Papal decree in June of 1942. Formally called the Institute for Works of Religion (abbreviated IOR), it absorbed its predecessor, the Administration for the Works of Religion. According to some financial experts, the IOR is the most secretive financial institution in the world. It is located in Vatican City, and exists solely for the purpose of providing financial services to clerical members of the Catholic Church. However, the IOR does not fall under the jurisdiction of the Holy See. It exists as a sovereign financial institution. It is not subject to the oversight imposed on other banks, and has successfully dodged attempts by regulatory agencies to examine its books. For the sake of clarity, the scandals related to the Vatican bank that we'll look at next will be listed chronologically along with the names of the principal individuals involved.

Michele Sindona

Italian banker Michele (Michael) Sindona played a pivotal role in facilitating the Italian mafia's use of the Vatican Bank. Within a year of the Gambino family choosing him to manage their heroin profits, he had purchased his first bank. In 1963, his friend Giovanni Battista Montini had been named Pope Paul VI. By that time, Sindona had acquired many more banks. Sindona was a member of Propaganda Due (P-2), a lodge of Italian Freemasonry that operated in contravention of chapter 18 of Italy's Constitution, which banned secret societies. (Secret societies will be discussed in more detail in a later chapter.)

In 1974, Sindona's Franklin National Bank was declared insolvent due to mismanagement and fraud. The IOR was a major shareholder, and the collapse of the bank cost the Vatican 30 million dollars. By 1979, Sindona's banks had suffered even greater losses and had to be liquidated.

Giorgio Ambrosoli, the lawyer who was commissioned to liquidate the banks, was murdered. While under indictment in the United States, Sindona faked his own kidnapping and traveled to Italy, where he issued blackmail letters to allies in an attempt to rescue his banks and recover the mafia's money. The plot failed, and Sindona surrendered to the FBI. In 1980, he was convicted on 65 counts, including fraud, perjury, false bank statements, and misappropriation of bank funds. He was later extradited to Italy and stood trial for the murder of Ambrosoli. He died in prison after being poisoned with cyanide.

Paul Marcinkus

Paul Marcinkus was a Chicago-born Archbishop. In the 1960s, he served as an English translator for the Vatican. Michele Sindona was his mentor. In 1971, Pope Paul VI appointed Marcinkus Chairman of the Vatican bank. Sindona and Marcinkus set up a money-laundering operation where Marcinkus invested Vatican funds in Sindona's banks, and Sindona used the IOR for foreign currency transactions. During the 1960s and 1970s, large amounts of money generated by the mafia moved between Sindona's banks and IOR.

On April 24th, 1973, Marcinkus was questioned by U.S. law enforcement authorities about his involvement in the delivery of over 14 million dollars worth of counterfeit bonds to the Vatican. The investigation by a U.S. prosecutor and the Justice Department's Organized Crime and

Racketeering Section lends credibility to Anthony Raimondi's claim that the Vatican bank was involved in a stock counterfeiting scheme.

In the mid-1980s, according to a report in the *Arizona Republic,* Italian authorities tried to arrest Marcinkus in connection with crimes that included assassination financing, arms smuggling, and trafficking in stolen gold and counterfeit currencies. Italian police also wanted to talk to him regarding information he may have had about several murders.

Attorneys for Croatian holocaust victims wanted to know what Marcinkus knew about hundreds of millions of dollars that had been taken from Croatians by the Nazis during World War II. A 1998 U.S. State Department report confirmed that the Vatican bank had laundered Nazi gold valued at around 47 million dollars. It was "originally held in the Vatican before being moved to Spain and Argentina," the report said. Much of it passed through the Vatican Bank while Marcinkus was president. Whenever law enforcement agencies tried to question Marcinkus, Pope John Paul II protected him under the Vatican's sovereign immunity. Marcinkus resigned from IOR in 1990 and returned to Chicago and then moved to Sun City, Arizona.

Roberto Calvi

Roberto Calvi earned himself the nickname "God's Banker" because of his close association with Paul Marcinkus and the Vatican Bank. Calvi was the president of Banco Ambrosiano; the IOR was its largest shareholder. Michele Sindona had known Calvi since the late 1960s. Calvi was also a member of the Masonic lodge, P-2.

In 1981, Banco Ambrosiano came under investigation regarding illegal currency transactions. Calvi was convicted of transferring 27 million dollars out of the country, without alerting the Bank of Italy, as required by law. He was sentenced to four years in prison and fined more than 19 million dollars. He appealed the ruling and was released on bail. While awaiting appeal, he remained the bank's president.

During the next twelve months, Banco Ambrosiano fell deeper into debt. On June 5th, 1982, Calvi was compelled to write a letter to Pope John Paul II, warning that a collapse of the bank would "provoke a catastrophe of unimaginable proportions in which the Church will suffer the gravest damage."

When Banco Ambrosiano finally collapsed, its bad debt was estimated to be 1.5 billion dollars. Its largest shareholder, IOR, agreed to pay

224 million dollars to creditors as a "recognition of moral involvement" in the bank's collapse. Vatican Bank Chairman Paul Marcinkus officially denied any involvement in the collapse, but he was indicted in 1987 as an "accessory to fraudulent bankruptcy." Italy's highest court, however, ruled that he was protected from prosecution under the Vatican's sovereign immunity status.

Just before the bank collapsed, its president, Roberto Calvi, fled Italy. He traveled by boat from Italy to Yugoslavia; from there, he traveled by car to Austria and then, by plane to London. Calvi called his daughter, who, along with her mother, had moved to the United States. He planned to be reunited with them soon, but the next day, a young postal clerk made a grim discovery. He found Calvi's body dangling from an orange nylon rope tied to scaffolding under London's Blackfriar's bridge. Police initially ruled Calvi's death a suicide, but a later investigation determined that he was murdered. Investigators believed high-ranking members of the Italian mafia were concerned that Calvi might turn informant and arranged for him to be killed.

Emilio Colagiovanni

In 1999, the financial empire of American fraudster Martin Frankel came crashing down. After fleeing the country, the FBI tracked him down in Germany and extradited him. U.S. prosecutors said Frankel used aliases and shell corporations to drain hundreds of millions of dollars from eleven insurance companies that were under his control. Rather than investing their money in government bonds, as he claimed, he deposited it in off-shore accounts and used it to pay for furs, cars, mansions, and jewelry for his female housemates.

Frankel established the St. Francis of Assisi Foundation, a British Virgin Islands non-profit corporation. The foundation claimed to serve the poor, but in fact, it was one of many shell companies through which he laundered millions of dollars, much of it stolen from clients.

Monsignor Emilio Colagiovanni was a Catholic priest and president of the Monitor Ecclesiasticus Foundation. His foundation had an account at the Vatican bank. Colagiovanni allowed Frankel to use the account to make deposits and withdrawals, which could not be tracked by financial regulators. Frankel was convicted in 2004 and sentenced to 200 months in prison. Colagiovanni pleaded guilty to conspiracy to commit wire fraud and money laundering and was sentenced to five years' probation.

Vatican Bank Investigations

On September 21st, 2010, the Bank of Italy's Financial Intelligence Unit informed the Vatican bank that it was under investigation for money laundering. The IOR was suspected of using two Italian banks for illegal transactions. Notices were issued to IOR president Ettore Tedeschi and Roberto Cipriani, director-general of the IOR, for omission of procedures against money laundering. Nello Rossi, an Italian prosecutor, said about 23 million euros in IOR transactions were seized from the Italian bank accounts. Prosecutors charged the IOR with deliberately evading anti-money-laundering laws "with the aim of hiding the ownership, destination, and origin of the capital."

Vatican Reforms

The Vatican *officially* denied any wrongdoing, but in the following months, it took steps to address the problem of corruption. On December 30th, 2010, Pope Benedict XVI announced the establishment of Financial Information Authority (AIF), a Vatican agency whose purpose is to prevent the laundering of proceeds from criminal activities.

Two months later, in February of 2011, the Holy See requested an evaluation of Vatican finances by Moneyval, Europe's Committee of Experts on the Evaluation of Anti-Money Laundering Measures and the Financing of Terrorism. Their initial audit found that the Vatican had "come a long way in a very short period of time" and said they had met international requirements in nine out of sixteen core areas, but Moneyval requested further reforms to be made.

Pope Francis continued the efforts toward greater transparency, creating special commissions to address corruption. In 2014, he created the Secretariat for the Economy, which develops the annual budget of the Holy See and the Vatican. Cardinal George Pell was appointed as its first prefect and was granted authority to investigate financial irregularities inside the Vatican.

Because financial regulators can't access the IOR's transactions, they've applied pressure to the banks that do business with the IOR. In March of 2012, JP Morgan Chase, under pressure from the U.S. Treasury Department, notified the Vatican that it had closed an IOR account in its Milan branch. The account was closed because the IOR was "unable to respond" to requests for information about the origin of some deposits.

The account, opened in 2009, had processed a total of nearly 1.5 billion dollars in transactions. At the end of each business day, the account was zeroed with the balance being moved to other IOR accounts—mostly in Germany, according to financial documents published in Italy's financial newspaper *Il Sole 24 Ore*.

Nunzio Scarano

Nunzio Scarano was a senior accountant with the Vatican. In 2013, he was arrested after trying to smuggle 23 million euros in untaxed cash into Italy. Prosecutors said he was involved in a scheme that laundered money through the Vatican bank, from offshore companies that disguised it as donations to the Church. In 2016, Scarano was acquitted, but in 2019 he was convicted by an appeals court and sentenced to three years in prison.

Angelo Caloia

On March 3rd, 2018, Vatican prosecutors indicted Angelo Caloia, a former president of the Vatican bank, and his lawyer Gabriele Liuzzo for embezzlement and money laundering. Prosecutors accused them of transferring more than 57 million euros worth of IOR real estate assets into their personal accounts. The scheme involved the sale of 29 Vatican-owned buildings in Rome and Milan between 2001 and 2008. The outcome of the trial is pending.

Although the Vatican has made changes, it has not yet been able to decouple the IOR from the organized crime syndicates that have used it for their own benefit.

Q Posts about the Church

In the previous chapter, we examined a post by Q that suggested the Rothschild banking family exerts control over the Catholic Church.

Dec 7 2017
Rothschilds (cult leaders)(church)(P)
Banks / Financial Institutions
WW Gov Control
Gov Controls People
♦♦♦

According to Q, the Rothschilds are leaders of a cult. Other posts indicate that it is a Satanic cult. Q said the family also exerts a degree of control over the Catholic Church. The identity of (P) is the subject of much debate and is not the focus of this chapter. In April of 2018, Q elaborated on how the Rothschilds gained control over the Church.

> Apr 4 2018
> List the estimated wealth of religious organizations.
> Billions.
> Vatican bank.
> $229B.
> Board of Superintendence.
> Supervisory Commission of Cardinals.
> Clown connection.
> 1832 Rothschild loan to the Holy See.
> Q

On November 30th, 1831, James Rothschild signed an agreement with Pope Gregory XVI that provided a loan to the Holy See in the amount of 400,000 British pounds. His brother Carl, who managed the family's operation in Naples, assumed responsibility for the administration of the loan and met with the Pope in Rome in January of 1832.

Fourteen years later, Giovanni Ferretti was elected Pope Pius IX in 1846. He ruled the Papal States, which covered the central part of the Italian peninsula. Following the assassination of his Minister of the Interior, the Pope fled to Paris, where he remained for several years. While there, he began negotiating with James Rothschild to obtain a second loan for the Holy See. Like other powerful people, the head of the Catholic Church required the assistance of the Rothschilds to carry out his plans. After securing the loan, Pius IX returned to Rome, only to watch the Papal States dissolve, and the peninsula come under the rule of Italian nationalists.

In the above post, Q wrote "clown connection." Q sometimes refers to the CIA as "clowns" or "Clowns in America." The suggestion is that governing organizations of the Catholic Church are connected not just to the mafia but the CIA. The CIA is believed to engage in illegal covert operations. The problem for those who conduct illegal operations is depositing the money in an institution that can transfer it to other banks without the transactions being reported to banking regulators. As we've seen, the IOR is the perfect bank for conducting secret financial transactions.

Nov 6 2017
What is money flow disruption?
List the Billionaires.
What family history goes back pre_WW1/2?
Why is this relevant?
Why did the Bush family recently break silence and attack POTUS?
Coincidence pre SA arrests?
Who audits the billions paid for war?
Who audits the billions paid for environment policy (side note)?
Where do the funds go?
Offshore?
To who / which entity and/or org?
What slush fund was recently terminated by AG Sessions?
What is Fast & Furious?
What is the underlying theme?
MONEY.
Who controls the FED?
How did political leaders/'talking heads' accum assets in excess of $5mm+?
What was the net worth for each prior to taking office?
Reconcile.
Why is this relevant?
Snow White.
Godfather III.
Q

Q asked: What family goes back pre-World War I? The Bush family has had a significant influence on U.S. politics going back to the early 20th century. Samuel Prescott Bush was the patriarch of the Bush political family. He was the father of Senator Prescott Bush, the grandfather of former President George H. W. Bush, and great-grandfather of former President George W. Bush and Florida Governor Jeb Bush.

In 1901, Samuel Bush became general manager of Buckeye Steel Castings Company, which manufactured railway parts. The company was run by Frank Rockefeller, the brother of oil magnate John D. Rockefeller. In 1908, Rockefeller retired, and Bush became president of Buckeye, a position he would hold until 1927, becoming one of the top industrialists of his generation.

In the spring of 1918, banker Bernard Baruch was asked to reorganize the War Industries Board as the U.S. prepared to enter World War I. He appointed Bush to be the chief of the Ordnance, Small Arms, and Ammunition Section, with national responsibility for government assistance to and relations with munitions companies. Samuel Bush also served on the board of the Federal Reserve Bank of Cleveland. His sons and grandsons rose to positions of prominence in politics.

This post has two signatures—Godfather III and Snow White. In the first book of this *Q Chronicles* series, *Calm Before the Storm*, we learned that the signature "Snow White" pertains to the CIA. George Herbert Walker Bush was the only U.S. President to also serve as Director of the Central Intelligence Agency.

This post suggests that because there is no process for auditing money earmarked for things like war, environmental causes, and settlement funds, some of this money is diverted to slush funds to keep the world's elites in power and enrich elected officials.

The Lord's Prayer

On November 14th, 2017, Q posted the Lord's prayer.

Nov 14 2017

♦♦♦

"Our Father who art in heaven,
Hallowed be thy name.
Thy kingdom come.
Thy will be done
on earth as it is in heaven.
Give us this day our daily bread,
and forgive us our trespasses,
as we forgive those who trespass against us,
and lead us not into temptation,
but deliver us from evil."
Q

One month later, on December 9th, 2017, Q posted a follow-up message.

Dec 9 2017
News unlocks map.

Future proves past.
Why was the Lord's prayer posted?
Which version?
Why is this relevant?
What just came out re: the Lord's prayer?
What can be connected?
Do you believe in coincidences?
Re-review the map post relevant news drops.
Godfather III
Q

The version of the Lord's prayer that Q posted is from the Sermon on the Mount, found in Matthew chapter 6. This version of the prayer is said aloud during the Catholic mass. It is different from the Protestant version and is not found (as written above) in most Bibles. Q's December 9th post was in response to an announcement the previous day by Pope Francis that he desired a change to be made to the wording of that passage. "The current wording that says 'lead us not into temptation' is not a good translation because God does not lead humans to sin." He suggested changing the wording to "do not let us fall into temptation."

The news of the Pope's decision broke on December 8th, 2017, which was 25 days after Q posted the Catholic version of the Lord's prayer. Did Q know weeks in advance that the Pope was considering making a change to this passage? If so, how did he gain access to that information?

Corruption exists in many forms. One that has caused problems for the Vatican is the sexual abuse of children and the Church's attempts to cover it up. Recently, a number of state-wide investigations have been opened in the U.S. into sexual abuse of children in the Catholic Church. The investigations identified thousands of victims who had been sexually abused by priests over a span of decades. On December 5th, 2017, Q posted this warning about the signature Godfather III.

Dec 5 2017
Godfather III
Be prepared for what you find.
Q

On April 3rd, 2018, Q predicted that the Pope would have a terrible month of May and that those who supported him would be exposed.

Apr 3 2018
[Pope] will be having a terrible May.
Those who backed him will be pushed into the LIGHT>
Dark to LIGHT.
TRUTH.
Q

In May of 2018, bishops in Chile—31 were actively serving, and three retired—signed a letter to the Pope offering to resign en masse over the cover-up of a decades-long sexual abuse scandal. "We have put our positions in the hands of the Holy Father and will leave it to him to decide freely for each of us," they said. "We want to ask forgiveness for the pain caused to the victims, to the Pope, to God's people and to our country for the serious errors and omissions we have committed."

The move came after Pope Francis said the Chilean Church hierarchy was collectively responsible for "grave defects" in handling sexual abuse cases and the resulting loss of credibility suffered by the Church. He accused them of destroying evidence, committing sexual crimes, pressuring investigators to downplay abuse accusations, and showing "grave negligence" in protecting children from pedophile priests.

On May 9th, 2018, it was announced that Australian Cardinal George Pell would face two trials on sex crime allegations that spanned several decades. In March of 2019, Pell was convicted of sex abuse and was sentenced to six years in prison, but in April of 2020, his conviction was overturned by Australia's highest court. On October 5th, 2020, Italian news outlets reported that Cardinal Giovanni Becciu stands accused of using 700,000 euros of Vatican funds to bribe witnesses to secure a sex abuse conviction against Pell. Quoting leaked documents, the Italian newspapers *La Repubblica* and *Corriere della Sera* reported that Vatican investigators suspect that Cardinal Becciu hoped to use the money to sabotage Cardinal Pell's transparency program, which threatened to expose Becciu's allegedly corrupt management of Vatican cash.

Also, on May 9th, it was reported by the *National Catholic Reporter* that since the 1950s, the Vatican had paid 4 billion dollars to settle sex crime complaints against members of the clergy. In July of 2014, the Pope was quoted as saying that two percent of the Catholic clergy are pedophiles involved in abuse cases. "The Church fights in order for this vice to be eradicated...but even we have this leprosy at home." The quote was taken from an article published by the Italian newspaper *La Repubblica*.

Although the Vatican has never officially quantified the extent of the problem, in May of 2014, Archbishop Silvano Maria Tomasi said a total of 3,420 credible accusations of sexual abuse by priests had been referred to the Vatican in the previous ten years.

In August of 2018, Q posted a link to an article about an investigation into allegations of sexual abuse in Pennsylvania. Hundreds of priests are accused of having molested more than 1,000 children since the 1940s. A grand jury report alleged that senior Church officials covered up the abuse.

Aug 14 2018
https://www.foxnews.com/us/2018/08/14/stunning-findings-on-report-catholic-church-abuse-pa-priests-molested-more-than-1000-children.html
House of GOD?
Only the beginning.
Those who you are taught to trust the most....
Expect MANY MANY MANY similar reports to surface from around the world.
IT GOES A LOT DEEPER.
Connected.
The choice to know will be yours.
Q

On July 30th, 2019, Pope Francis tweeted the following message.

Pope Francis (from his Twitter account):
Let us pray that the Lord will free the victims of human trafficking and help us to respond actively to the cry for help of so many of our brothers and sisters who are deprived of their dignity and freedom. #EndHumanTrafficking
4:30 AM - 30 Jul 2019

That same day, Q responded on 8chan.

Godfather III
It's going to be BIBLICAL.
Q

CHAPTER 7

Secret Societies

CORRUPTION CAN BECOME INSTITUTIONALIZED WHEN it
is concealed. Many institutions and organizations are structured in
a way that hides their activities from the public. The Freemasons have
been mentioned several times by Q. I realize that many good people are
Masons, and they have no evil intent with their membership. However,
these organizations have levels of participation. New members are admitted to the lowest level, and they aspire to gain access to higher levels. The
activities within each level are compartmentalized. What happens within
one level is concealed from members of another. Thus, members may not
be aware of all the practices of their particular lodge.

In the previous chapter, we read that on May 20th, 1981, Italian banker
Roberto Calvi's body was found hanging beneath Blackfriar's bridge in
London. "Black Friars" happens to be the nickname of an Italian Masonic
lodge, also known as Propaganda Due or P-2, of which Calvi was a member.
The lodge was founded by Licio Gelli. A list of nearly 1,000 P-2 members
was found in one of Gelli's properties during an investigation of Italian
banker Michele Sindona.

A few days after Calvi's body was found, Italy's Justice Minister, Adolfo
Sarti, resigned his position when it was revealed that his name was on

the list of P-2 members. The list also included the names of cabinet ministers, members of Parliament, judges, army and police generals, bankers, journalists, and other influential Italian figures. The disclosure of nearly a thousand Masons in positions of power throughout Italy nearly caused the collapse of the government.

According to the police, members of P-2 had sworn allegiance to their grandmaster rather than to the nation. In a report to the government, the Milan magistrates wrote that "Gelli had constructed a very real state within the state," using blackmail, favors, promises of advancement, and bribes. "Lodge P-2 is a secret sect that has combined business and politics with the intention of destroying the constitutional order of the country and of transforming the parliamentary system into a presidential system," the magistrates wrote.

Secret societies like the Masons require members to swear allegiance to the lodge and the grandmaster rather than to God and country. When members occupy positions in government, this causes a conflict of interest. This conflict was highlighted in an exchange of letters between G.W. Snyder and George Washington. Snyder wrote to Washington to inquire about the activities of Masonic lodges in the United States. The following is an excerpt from his letter dated August 22nd, 1798:

Sir,

You will, I hope, not think it a Presumption in a Stranger, whose Name, perhaps never reached your Ears, to address himself to you the Commanding General of a great Nation...

It was some Time since that a Book fell into my Hands entituled "Proofs of a Conspiracy" by John Robison, which gives a full Account of a Society of Freemasons, that distinguishes itself by the Name "of Illuminati," whose Plan is to overturn all Government and all Religion, even natural; and who endeavour to eradicate every Idea of a Supreme Being, and distinguish Man from Beast by his Shape only. A Thought suggested itself to me, that some of the Lodges in the United States might have caught the Infection, and might cooperate with the Illuminati or the Jacobine Club in France... Upon serious Reflection I was led to think that it might be within your Power to prevent the horrid Plan from corrupting the Brethren of the English Lodge over which you preside.

Snyder assumed that Washington was a member of a Masonic lodge and asked if he might use his influence to steer the lodge in a direction that was best for the nation. George Washington replied:

"I have heard much of the nefarious, & dangerous plan, & doctrines of the Illuminati, but never saw the Book until you were pleased to send it to me. The same causes which have prevented my acknowledging the receipt of your letter, have prevented my reading the Book, hitherto; namely—the multiplicity of matters which pressed upon me before, & the debilitated state in which I was left after, a severe fever had been removed. And which allows me to add little more now, than thanks for your kind wishes and favourable sentiments, except to correct an error you have run into, of my Presiding over the English lodges in this Country. The fact is, I preside over none, nor have I been in one more than once or twice, within the last thirty years. I believe notwithstanding, that none of the Lodges in this Country are contaminated with the principles ascribed to the Society of the Illuminati.

With respect I am Sir Your Obedient, Humble Servant George Washington

Source: https://founders.archives.gov/documents/Washington/06-02-02-0435

Although Masons claim that Washington belonged to a lodge in Fredericksburg, Virginia, he plainly denied being a member and expressed his view that at that time, the lodges in the U.S. had not become infected with the corruption of European lodges.

On April 27th, 1961, President John F Kennedy addressed the problem of secret societies in a speech before the nation's journalists. Here is an excerpt:

The very word "secrecy" is repugnant in a free and open society; and we are as a people inherently and historically opposed to secret societies, to secret oaths and to secret proceedings. We decided long ago that the dangers of excessive and unwarranted concealment of pertinent facts far outweighed the dangers which are cited to justify it...

In time of war, the government and the press have customarily joined in an effort based largely on self-discipline, to prevent unauthorized disclosures to the enemy. In time of "clear and present danger," the courts have held that even the privileged rights of the First Amendment must yield to the public's need for national security.

Today no war has been declared—and however fierce the struggle may be, it may never be declared in the traditional fashion. Our way of life is under attack. Those who make themselves our enemy are advancing around the globe. The survival of our friends is in danger. And yet no war has been declared, no borders have been crossed by marching troops, no missiles have been fired.

If the press is awaiting a declaration of war before it imposes the self-discipline of combat conditions, then I can only say that no war ever posed a greater threat to our security. If you are awaiting a finding of "clear and present danger," then I can only say that the danger has never been more clear and its presence has never been more imminent.

It requires a change in outlook, a change in tactics, a change in missions—by the government, by the people, by every businessman or labor leader, and by every newspaper. For we are opposed around the world by a monolithic and ruthless conspiracy that relies primarily on covert means for expanding its sphere of influence—on infiltration instead of invasion, on subversion instead of elections, on intimidation instead of free choice, on guerrillas by night instead of armies by day. It is a system which has conscripted vast human and material resources into the building of a tightly knit, highly efficient machine that combines military, diplomatic, intelligence, economic, scientific and political operations.

Its preparations are concealed, not published. Its mistakes are buried, not headlined. Its dissenters are silenced, not praised. No expenditure is questioned, no rumor is printed, no secret is revealed. It conducts the Cold War, in short, with a war-time discipline no democracy would ever hope or wish to match.

Kennedy asserted that a powerful secret society had been created that controls the geopolitical landscape through covert means. Rather than assuming control of governments through military overthrow, it infiltrates and controls them through ideological subversion. Rather than allowing for dissenting opinions, it silences opposition and promotes its views through a controlled media complex. Kennedy described what many people today call the *deep state*—a monolithic entity that uses government and civilian institutions to bring the population of the planet under its control.

Q explained that the current attempts to infiltrate and subvert America's government are carried out by both domestic and foreign (D/F) assets. The remedy is the prosecution of those who committed these acts of treason and sedition.

Apr 10 2020
The credibility of our institutions [Constitutional Law that governs our Great Land [Our Republic]], and our ability to regain the trust and faith of the American people, all depends on our ability to restore [EQUAL JUSTICE UNDER THE LAW] by prosecuting those responsible [Blind-Justice].
Treasonous acts [sedition] against the Republic [the 'People'] of the United States [START - LEAD-IN].
Infiltration [rogue] at the highest levels of our gov, media, corps, etc.
Planned & coordinated [D/ F].
This is not about politics.
Something far more sinister [evil] has been allowed to flourish through all parts of our society.
It has been protected and safeguarded.
It has been camouflaged to appear as trusted.
It has been projected [normalized] by stars.
[CLAS 1-99]
One must only look to see.
[Symbolism will be their downfall]
This is not another [4] year election.
"Be on your guard; stand firm in the faith; be courageous; be strong."
You are not alone.
We stand together.
Q

On June 28, 2018, a mass shooting occurred at the offices of *The Capital* newspaper, near Annapolis, Maryland. The gunman, Jarrod Ramos, shot and killed five employees. Two others were injured while trying to escape. After the story broke, Q posted this.

Jun 28 2018
Law enforcement should interview the therapists.

Each shooter has one coincidentally.
Targets?
Relocation within 30 days of each shooting?
New name?
FBI doesn't know this?
Spooks are hard to find?
Dream to reality.
Q

Q noted that most perpetrators of mass shootings have therapists. I would imagine this is because they have pre-existing mental illnesses. Are they victims of mind control? Are they relocated and given new names? Are they merely assets of the deep state who carry out orders? When a man wearing a hat with a Freemason emblem showed up in news videos at the scene of the shooting, Q posted this.

Why are Freemasons on the scene of most shooting locations?
Openly giving interviews or in background shots?
Symbolism will be their downfall.
Q

CHAPTER 8

Symbolism Will Be Their Downfall

HUMAN LANGUAGE CONVEYS IDEAS THROUGH the use of arbitrary (though well-understood) symbols. Our first years of elementary school are designed to train us to understand and use the alphabet, numbers, and other symbols to communicate our thoughts. Q speaks to us through the use of these same symbols. The words used by Q sometimes convey their usual meaning, but in other cases, double meanings are intended. Q also employs the unconventional use of brackets, plus signs, and other characters to express certain ideas, symbolically.

Many spiritual concepts are best communicated through the use of symbolic imagery. The pages of scripture are filled with descriptions of bizarre creatures and frightening scenes that were intended to convey symbolic messages. According to scripture, God communicated to humanity through the figurative language of dreams and visions. There is nothing inherently evil in the use of symbolism. Nearly all religions use symbols to convey aspects of humanity, divinity, and the battle between good and evil.

It is the battle between good and evil that Q intends to highlight in his messages. He often reminds readers that the elites who crave wealth and power are obsessed with the use of symbolism.

A dictionary defines the elite as: *the choice part; the best of a class; the socially superior part of society; a group of persons who by virtue of position or education exercise much power or influence; a member of such an elite—usually used in the plural (elites).*

Elites exist across the globe. Many are connected to each other because of their wealth or status in government, politics, news media, entertainment, sports, business, technology, medicine, religion, and so on. Of course, being elite or wealthy does not make someone evil, but it brings opportunities to exert power and influence that ordinary people do not have.

Nov 21 2017
Their need for symbolism will be their downfall.
Follow the Owl & Y head around the world.
Identify and list.
They don't hide it.
They don't fear you.
You are sheep to them.
You are feeders.
Godfather III.
Q

Q describes the relationship of ordinary people and elites as one of parasitism. Elites control society. Our work and our resources keep them comfortable. We exist for their benefit, or as Q would say, we are "feeders" or "sheep" to them.

In researching the owl and the Y head, we find many images and descriptions regarding the history of these symbols. We'll cover some of that in this chapter. I wouldn't presume that everyone who is seen in a photo with an owl sculpture or tattoo is using them as symbols of darkness, but owls have been used in connection with the occult as well as ancient religions. The Y-shaped head of a goat is often associated with satanism. Do some of the world's elites openly display the owl and goat head as symbols of what they value most?

The single eye found on U.S. currency atop a pyramid hails back to ancient Egypt and the sun god, Ra. Many celebrity elites and performers are shown covering one eye or encircling one eye with their thumb and index finger in photographs. Is this a symbolic gesture—or merely an artistic expression that they have in common? Do they feel free to show these symbols publicly because they occupy positions of power and don't fear us catching on to the meaning? For centuries, they've flaunted their power—some even brazenly committed unspeakable crimes without fear of punishment. For example, Jimmy Saville was a pop icon in the UK and was knighted in 1990. Victim complaints of sexual assault brought while he was alive were investigated by police but never led to criminal charges. After his death, police investigated hundreds of allegations of sexual abuse by Saville spanning five decades. In 2014, investigations into his activities in 28 National Health Service hospitals—including a psychiatric hospital—concluded that he had sexually assaulted staff and patients between 5 and 75 years of age.

There has been one tier of justice for average citizens, and another lenient tier for elites. Consequences for elites have often been minor—or nonexistent. Famous Hollywood stars acknowledged the "casting couch" practices and sexual assaults of their celebrated producer, Harvey Weinstein, to the point of joking about it publicly. But he was not prosecuted until recently. Why did the justice system fail to stop him from offending much earlier? It seems his elite status gave him a pass—until now.

In recent years, the justice system in the United States has undergone many changes. William Barr explained why he came out of retirement to serve a second term as U.S. Attorney General. In his address to members of Congress, he noted that there is a two-tiered system of justice, and he feels he has an opportunity to restore equal justice for all. The Attorney General makes personnel decisions for the Department of Justice and the FBI. The two-tiered system of justice existed because corrupt people occupied positions of power in these agencies. In April of 2018, Q listed a few of the personnel changes that had recently occurred in the upper echelon of the FBI.

Apr 27 2018
Focus only on the FBI [for now].
Jim Rybicki, chief of staff and senior counselor - FIRED.
James Baker, general counsel - FIRED.
Andrew McCabe, deputy director - FIRED.
James Comey, director - FIRED.
Bill Priestap, Head of Counterintelligence and Strzok's boss - Cooperating witness [power removed].
Peter Strzok, Deputy Assistant Director of the Counterintelligence - cooperating witness [power removed].
Lisa Page, attorney with the FBI's Office of the General Counsel -

cooperating witness [power removed].
Conspiracy?
Think about the above.
Only the above.
Get the picture?
Q

On November 21, 2017, Q had more to say about the use of symbolism.

Nov 21 2017
Identify symbolism (Owl / Y).
Which performers/celebs supported HRC during the election?
Who performed during her rallies?
What jewelry and/or tattoos present?
What other events do they attend together?
What does HRC represent to them?
What celebrities have owl / Y head symbols?
What politicians have owl / Y head symbols?
What powerful people have owl / Y head symbols?
What powerful groups have owl / Y head symbols?
Why are they worn/shown openly?
Their need for symbolism will be their downfall.
MSM role?
Push conspiracy theory.
Social media role?
Push conspiracy theory and institute new rules allowing for ban.
Censorship.
The graphic is key.
Re-read graphic (ex: what family did Soros replace (Y)).
Part II – How were they 'adopted' into the cult (as children).
What were they provided for obeying and staying silent (brainwashed)?
All that you know to be right is wrong.
The 'cult' runs the world.
Fantasy land.
The world is fighting back (& destroying the cult).
20% public.
80% private.
The world would otherwise collapse.

40,000ft. v. (again) and need to decrease altitude to avoid 'conspiracy' label.
Was necessary.
GODFATHER III.
For God & Country.
Q

Let look at some of the most important points in the above post. The owl is associated with many ancient religions. Minerva, the Roman goddess of wisdom, and Athena, her Greek counterpart, are sometimes portrayed standing with an owl. Sometimes the owl itself symbolizes these deities. An owl represents the ability to see in the dark (to see what others do not) or to understand the mysteries of hidden wisdom and forbidden knowledge. The Y-shaped goat head, known as Baphomet, is a deity first revered by the Knights Templar. The icon later became associated with numerous occultic practices, including Satanism.

Hundreds of celebrities supported Hillary Clinton when she ran for President. Some performed at her campaign rallies in order to attract a crowd for her. By contrast, only a few supported Donald Trump, and those who dared to support him were ostracized by their Hollywood peers.

As someone who nearly became the first female American President, Hillary Clinton epitomizes a life committed to achieving personal success. Success itself isn't evil. It's how we achieve it that matters. But many believe history will show that Hillary gained hers through selling political favors, deceiving the public, and cleverly covering her tracks.

Public displays of symbolism can reveal an individual's core values and loyalties—but only to those who understand their meaning. If you're like-minded and familiar with the culture, you're treated with esteem by other members. If the average person isn't aware of the meaning of the symbols, there's little risk to celebrities in displaying them openly. What would happen if ordinary people were to become aware of the meaning and intent behind symbols of darkness and evil? Would there be a shift in public perception toward those who display these symbols? Rather than being idolized, would celebrities be despised?

The mainstream media's role is to confuse us. Factual information about symbolism is often labeled "conspiracy theory." The conspiracy theory label marginalizes those who seek the truth. The stigma of this news media label is intended to stop further discovery of the use, meaning, and purpose of these symbols.

It is human nature to believe that if an idea is popular, it must be correct. Social media helps establish cultural norms and enforces conformity of thought. Individuals who express views *supportive of* the official narrative are elevated. Those who express ideas *counter to* the narrative are suppressed. Social media platforms display trends that support the narrative while suppressing trends that oppose it. The highlighting of trends—whether actual or contrived—reinforces sanctioned thought patterns.

In addition to labeling alternative ideas "conspiracy theories," social media platforms label alternative ideas "hate speech." It's difficult to justify removing users for spreading a conspiracy theory, but easy to justify banning someone who promotes "hate."

A small but powerful group of people have managed over time to assume control over key politicians, Hollywood studios, broadcast and print media, influential academic institutions, pharmaceutical companies, multi-national corporations, social media platforms, government intelligence agencies, and some religious institutions. By controlling them, they effectively control many parts of society. Q wants us to research—and discover for ourselves—that these people are members (and leaders) of a cult. According to Q, the truth about how the world operates is so bizarre, the average person would not believe it.

Q claims to have access to information that reveals the truth about how the world's systems operate. At the time this message was posted, he indicated that 20 percent would be made public, while 80 percent would remain classified. To disclose the full truth would cause the complete collapse of society. In January of 2018, after lengthy discussions with anons, Q said 40 percent of their information would be disclosed while 60 percent would remain classified.

Jan 13 2018
[MONDAY]
Next Week - BIGGER.
PUBLIC.
We LISTENED [20/80 />/ 40/60].
Q

When we fly at a high altitude, we have a broad view of the land below us. When Q provides a behind-the-scenes glimpse of actions happening on the global stage, he refers to it as the 40,000-foot view. These disclosures provide critical information, but their highly controversial nature draws accusations from the media that the ideas are conspiracy theories. To minimize the damage from such claims, Q must limit those discussions, at least for now.

Dec 14 2017
Shall we play a game?
Find the spider(s) and build the web (the 'map').
Remember, they consider you to be the fly (specifically, the 'feeder').
Remember, they never thought she was going to lose.
Therefore, they never thought investigations and/or public interest into their criminal acts would be exposed/investigated.
Therefore, they never thought they had anything to fear.
Therefore, they openly showcase their symbolism.
Therefore, they were sloppy.
Hussein's last speech in Chicago re: 'scandal free'.
Why did he continually emphasize that phrase?
As a backup, they infiltrated and control the narrative (the 'MSM').
As a backup, they install only those on the team.
As a backup, they blackmail those that aren't.
As a backup, they defined 'conspiracy' as crazy/mentally unstable and label anything 'true' as such.
This works given most of what they engage in is pure evil and simply unbelievable (hard to swallow).
The 'fix' has always been in – no matter which party won the election (-JFK (killed)/Reagan(shot)).
This was always the promise made to those who played the game (willingly or otherwise) (i.e., they would never lose power).
Power of the (3) letter agencies.
Power over the US Military (WW dominance to push against other nations and install like-kind).
These people are really stupid.
◆◆◆
Q

As a general principle, only those who are compromised (and can be controlled) are given access to places of power in government. Elites fund the campaigns of those they want in elected positions and use bribery and extortion to control non-elected government officials. A promise is made to politicians that their embarrassing secrets will never be disclosed as long as they play the game. On the rare occasions when an outsider (who cannot be controlled) rises to a place of power, attempts are made to remove them. President John F. Kennedy was assassinated. The attempt to assassinate President Reagan failed. So far, the attempts to remove President Trump from office have likewise failed. These principles hold true for elected officials in both major political parties. The idea that liberal and conservative politicians are different in any meaningful way is an illusion. It allows people to believe they have a choice when, in fact, there is none. The entire political system is controlled by the elites. Or at least it was, until recently.

Because they've exerted control over the justice system, elites do not fear prosecution. Because of their connections inside the intelligence community (3-letter agencies), they don't fear having embarrassing or incriminating information made public. Because they controlled the media and large political donors, they were sure Hillary Clinton would win the election in 2016. Now that Donald Trump is President, he has control of the intelligence agencies like the NSA that store the secrets of corrupt politicians and their masters. Because the elites were careless, their criminality will be exposed. Because the justice system is being reformed, the guilty will stand trial for their crimes.

Apr 3 2018
Symbolism will be their downfall.
MONEY.
POWER.
INFLUENCE.
The BITE that has no CURE - NSA.
Q

CHAPTER 9

Titanic

Q HAS MADE SEVERAL REFERENCES to RMS *Titanic*, the cruise ship that sank in the North Atlantic on its maiden voyage in 1912. His questions suggest that the official story regarding the sinking of the ship is not true. The first order of business is to review the official account of the wreck and certain facts about the company that built it.

In the early 1900s, the transatlantic passenger trade was a profitable business. It was also highly competitive, with shipbuilders contending over the transportation of wealthy travelers and immigrants. Two of the largest shipbuilders were White Star Line and Cunard Steamship Company. Cunard hoped to increase its market share with the debut of two new ships, *Lusitania* and *Mauretania*, which were the fastest ships at that time.

White Star countered with liners that would deliver exceptional comfort. The company's president, J. Bruce Ismay, announced plans for a trio of the largest luxury ships ever built: in order of construction, *Olympic*, *Titanic*, and *Britannic*. The White Star Line was a wholly-owned subsidiary of the International Mercantile Marine Company (IMM), which was owned by J.P. Morgan. (This fact will become relevant later in the chapter.)

The *Titanic's* sister ship, *Olympic*, was built in Belfast, Ireland, by Harland & Wolff between 1908 and 1910. On September 20th, 1911, under the command of Captain E.J. Smith, *Olympic* collided with the British naval cruiser, HMS *Hawke*. Running in opposite directions in a narrow strait, the *Olympic* made a turn, and the *Hawke* suddenly veered into its side, being drawn in by suction from the larger ship's propellers. The *Hawke* was severely damaged. The metal side (hull) of *Olympic* was left with several large holes. *Olympic* was constructed with watertight compartments to give it buoyancy. Two compartments were damaged and became flooded. No lives were lost in the collision.

Government investigators blamed the crew of *Olympic* for the collision. The ensuing litigation left White Star with legal bills and an expensive ship sitting in drydock. Some have theorized that *Titanic* never actually sank. They believe that White Star Line switched the nearly identical ships as part of an insurance scam and sent the damaged *Olympic* to the bottom of the Atlantic while operating *Titanic* under the name *Olympic*. (That theory will not be explored in this chapter. Arguments for and against the switch can be found on the internet.)

White Star Line managed to use the collision to their advantage in one respect. They offered it as proof that their "watertight" compartment design made the Olympic class of ships unsinkable.

On March 31st, 1909, three months after work began on the construction of *Olympic*, the keel was laid for *Titanic*. The two ships were built side by side in a specially constructed gantry that accommodated their massive size. In addition to ornate decorations, *Titanic* featured an immense first-class dining saloon, a swimming pool, a gym, four elevators, Turkish baths, a photography darkroom, and three cigar rooms.

On April 10th, 1912, *Titanic* set sail on its maiden voyage, traveling from Southampton, England. The cruise nearly began with a collision, when backwash from its propeller caused the passenger ship *New York* to swing into its path. Swift action by a tug boat captain helped avert a collision.

On the evening of April 10th, the *Titanic* stopped at Cherbourg, France. The city's dock was too small to accommodate the liner, so passengers had to be ferried to and from it. After two hours, *Titanic* resumed its journey. On the morning of April 11th, it made its last scheduled stop in Queenstown, Ireland. At approximately 1:30 pm, it steamed toward New York City with 2,200 people aboard, 1,300 of whom were passengers.

During the voyage, wireless radio operators Jack Phillips and Harold Bride, who worked for the Marconi Company, received frequent warnings of icebergs from other ships. Most of the messages were passed along to the bridge.

On the evening of April 14th, the *Titanic* approached an area known to have icebergs. Captain Smith altered course slightly to the south but maintained the ship at its top speed of 22 knots. At 9:40 pm, the steamship *Mesaba* sent a warning of an ice field. The message was never relayed to the bridge. At 10:55 pm, *Californian* radioed that it had stopped because it was surrounded by ice. Phillips was handling passenger messages at the time and rebuffed *Californian* for interrupting him.

Two lookouts were stationed in the crow's nest. Their job of spotting icebergs was made more difficult because the ship's binoculars were missing, and the ocean was calm. Calm seas meant there would be little water breaking at the base of an iceberg, making them more difficult to spot.

At approximately 11:40 pm, an iceberg was sighted, and the bridge was notified. First Officer William Murdoch ordered the engines reversed, which slowed the ship's speed. He ordered the rudder "hard-a-starboard," which turned the ship to port (left). *Titanic* began its turn, but it was too close to the iceberg to avoid a collision. The ship's starboard (right) side rammed the ice, rupturing at least five compartments near the front of the ship. An assessment determined that the ship's forward compartments were quickly filling with water. The bow would drop deeper into the ocean, which would cause water from the ruptured compartments to spill over into adjacent ones. The *Titanic* would eventually sink.

Captain Smith ordered distress signals to be sent out. At around 12:20 am on April 15th, *Carpathia* headed toward *Titanic*, but it did not arrive for three hours. *Californian* was in the vicinity, but its wireless had been turned off for the night.

Titanic's lifeboats were launched, with orders for women and children to board first. Twenty lifeboats were available, the number required by the British Board of Trade, but they could only carry 1,178 people, far short of the total number of passengers and crew. Many lifeboats were launched below capacity. Lifeboat number 7, for example, carried about 27 people, though it could have held 65. Only 700 people were rescued in lifeboats.

The glamour associated with the ship, the fact that it sank on its maiden voyage, and its famous passengers magnified the significance and mystery of the tragedy. Rumors quickly spread about the night's events, those who had died, and those who survived.

Government inquiries were conducted in both the U.S. and Great Britain. They focused on the poor preparations of the crew for handling emergencies and conflicting testimonies about the location of ships in the area that did not render assistance.

In November of 2017, Q asked a number of questions about *Titanic*.

Nov 12 2017

♦♦♦

Who died on the Titanic?

What year did the Titanic sink?

Why is this relevant?

What 'exactly' happened to the Titanic?

What 'class of people' were guaranteed a lifeboat?

Why did select 'individuals' not make it into the lifeboats?

Why is this relevant?

How do we know who was on the lifeboats (D or A)?

How were names and bodies recorded back then?

When were tickets purchased for her maiden voyage?

Who was 'specifically' invited?

Less than 10.

What is the FED?

What does the FED control?

Who controls the FED?

Who approved the formation of the FED?

Why did H-wood glorify Titanic as a tragic love story?

Who lived in the movie (what man)?

Why is this relevant?

Opposite is true.

What is brainwashing?

What is a PSYOP?

♦♦♦

Why is this relevant?

What are sheep?

Who controls the narrative?

The truth would put 99% of people in the hospital.

It must be controlled.

Snow White.

Iron Eagle.

Jason Bourne (CIA/Dream).

Q

Q asked: Who died on the *Titanic*?

Although most of the dead were crew members and third-class passengers, many wealthy passengers perished. Among them were Benjamin Guggenheim, Walgreen's founder Isidor Straus and his wife Ida, and John Jacob Astor IV and his pregnant 19-year old wife. Astor was considered to be the richest man in the world at the time. Captain E.J. Smith went down with the ship as did *Titanic's* designer, Thomas Andrews.

Q asked: What class of people were guaranteed a lifeboat, and which specific individuals did not make it into one?

The suggestion here is that prior to the trip, wealthy people were assured there would be a place in a lifeboat for them, but these individuals were not allowed to enter one during the evacuation. White Star's chief executive J. Bruce Ismay was rescued in a lifeboat.

Q asked: What year did the *Titanic* sink?

The ship sank in 1912, two years before the founding of the Federal Reserve, which is mentioned in later questions. I would assume Q is connecting the two events.

Q asked: How do we know who was in the lifeboats, and who was dead or alive (D or A)?

The accounting of who survived and who did not was done by combining eyewitness accounts (for those who survived) with forensic reports for those who did not. *Encyclopedia-titanica.org* provides detailed accounts from witnesses and official reports that describe who made it into the lifeboats and who did not.

Q asked: How were the names and bodies recorded back then?

Upon recovery, each body retrieved was numbered and given as detailed a description as possible. The physical appearance of each body—height, weight, approximate age, hair and eye color, visible birthmarks, scars, or tattoos, were all cataloged. Some passengers had identifying information on their clothing (sewn monograms) or in their belongings. Personal effects found on the bodies were gathered and placed in canvas bags corresponding to their number.

Q asked: When were the tickets purchased for her maiden voyage?

In July of 1911, White Star announced a date for *Titanic's* maiden voyage of March 20th, 1912. Two months after the first announcement, on September 20th, 1911, a new announcement was made of a delay due to repairs to *Olympic.* (Some repairs required parts to be used from *Titanic.*) On October 11th, 1911, White Star announced the new date for *Titanic's* maiden voyage of April 10th, 1912. I assume that tickets could not be sold until after the announcement of the first voyage's date, since passengers would need to make their plans with April 10th, 2012, as the departure date. According to public records, tickets were still available in March of 2012.

Q asked: Who was specifically invited?

Guglielmo Marconi, the inventor of the telegraph, was offered free passage on *Titanic.* He initially accepted, but his plans changed. He needed to get back to New York earlier than expected, so he bought a ticket on the *Lusitania,* which departed three days before the *Titanic* sailed.

Emilio Portaluppi, a well-respected stonemason, received a telegram from the Astors inviting him to join them on *Titanic.* He traveled as a first-class passenger.

Bill Müller served as secretary to a Dutch traffic inspector. His job was inspecting ships for insurance and investment firms. He was invited as a guest of White Star Lines.

A few people did not make the trip who are worth noting. J.P. Morgan, the owner of White Star, had a ticket, but a last-minute change of plans caused him to miss the voyage. In the minds of some, Morgan's absence seems too convenient to attribute to good luck. It's one reason why they suspect foul play was involved in the sinking.

Robert Bacon partnered with J.P. Morgan to form the U.S. Steel Corporation and IMM. In 1909, Bacon briefly served as U.S. Secretary of State before being appointed Ambassador to France. He served in that role until April of 1912. He, his wife, and their four children booked tickets on *Titanic* but Bacon's replacement, Myron Herrick, was delayed arriving in France. Bacon stayed to help him transition into his new position and sailed instead on the maiden voyage of the SS *France* on April 20th, 1912.

Milton Hershey, the founder of Hershey Chocolate Company, spent the winter of 1911-1912 in southern France. He purchased a ticket on *Titanic,* but business called him back to the states earlier than he had planned, so he traveled on the German liner *Amerika.*

David Blair served as *Titanic's* Second Officer during her sea trials as well as the ship's journey from the shipyard in Belfast to Southampton's docks. He was slated to continue in that role for the duration of the voyage until there was a change of plans. *Titanic's* sister ship *Olympic* was laid up, and her Chief Officer, Henry Wilde, was transferred to *Titanic*, and Blair was moved to *Olympic*. The transfer happened so quickly that Blair accidentally took the key to *Titanic's* crow's nest telephone and left the binoculars of *Titanic* in his cabin without telling anyone; thus, no binoculars were available.

In his lengthy post on November 12th, 2017, Q asked a group of questions about the FED:

♦♦♦
What is the FED?
What does the FED control?
Who controls the FED?
Who approved the formation of the FED?
♦♦♦

The United States has a central banking system called the Federal Reserve System. The system—sometimes called "the Fed"— is comprised of 12 regional Federal Reserve Banks, each of which is responsible for a geographic area of the United States.

The Federal Reserve was established in response to repeated financial panics during the 19th and early 20th centuries. A financial crisis in 1907 was the precipitating event. The panic of 1907 was a six-week stretch where banks in New York City experienced a shortage of cash due to sudden withdrawals by depositors. Banks only keep on hand a fraction of the cash their customers have on deposit. On rare occasions, too many customers will withdraw cash, and a bank will run short of money. (This is known as a bank run.) The panic of 1907 was triggered when an attempt by F. Augustus Heinze and Charles Morse to buy up shares of a copper mining firm failed and resulted in a run on banks who funded the scheme. The panic was quelled when the federal government provided 30 million dollars in aid to troubled banks. Financiers like J.P. Morgan and John D. Rockefeller used their own money to bring confidence and liquidity back to the financial markets.

One difference between European and American banking systems at the time was the absence of a central bank in the United States. European countries could inject liquidity into the market during times of financial turmoil. It has been theorized that a central bank in the U.S. could have prevented the panic of 1907 by providing financial institutions access to liquid assets. To prevent such occurrences from happening again, in 1913, Congress established the Federal Reserve System.

After Democrats won control of Congress and the presidency in 1912 (the year *Titanic* sank), President Woodrow Wilson, Congressman Carter Glass, and Senator Robert Latham Owen led the passage of a central banking bill. The primary function of the Federal Reserve is establishing monetary policy.

Although the President appoints its board of directors, the Fed is not a government agency. It is a private entity. In recent years, Ron Paul and his son, Senator Rand Paul, have gained notoriety for insisting the Fed's financial records be audited.

In a previous chapter, I mentioned that Q provided a list of more than a hundred financial institutions that he said are owned or controlled by the Rothschilds. Among them is the Federal Reserve.

Let's look closely at this series of questions Q asked in that long post on November 12th, 2017:

◆◆◆

Why did H-wood glorify Titanic as a tragic love story?

Who lived in the movie (what man)?

Why is this relevant?

Opposite is true.

What is brainwashing?

What is a PSYOP?

◆◆◆

What are sheep?

Who controls the narrative?

The truth would put 99% of people in the hospital.

It must be controlled.

◆◆◆

In the 1997 film *Titanic*, a wealthy man named Cal Hockley survived the sinking of the ship while Jack Dawson, a poor artist, died. Q said the opposite is true, suggesting that select wealthy people were killed because they opposed the plans of other wealthy people. Were the deaths of the rich and poor reversed in the film to conceal the fact that the sinking eliminated those who opposed the creation of the Federal Reserve?

Q implied that false narratives are created to keep ordinary people (sheep) in the dark, which allows corrupt people to achieve their goals without the public's knowledge. Events on the global stage are carefully concealed, and they bear no resemblance to the ones we're shown by the media. An anon summarized his thoughts, and Q confirmed his observations by posting them on the board.

Anonymous • Nov 21 2017
My actual conclusion is probably what's delayed me the most as it's been mind blowing understanding our country now.... I totally get it.. Current conclusions?
so Titanic -> Rothchild screws America by making our money worthless -> crash of 29 -> Tons new government which doesn't fix the problem Rothchild created (but a war helps) -> cia -> everyone blackmailed with sex tapes -> media consumed cia -> Country forced hard left -> population to puppets -> Causes uprising by certain Patriots like Kennedy/Reagan/Trump and while they managed to kill Kennedy and outlast Reagan enough lessons were learned that we are now finally ready to clean house and become America again?

In December of 2018, an anon asked Q an intriguing question.

Anonymous • Dec 12 2018
Q: Do we have the gold?

Q replied.

Yes.
Gold shall destroy FED.
Q

9/11

IN THE YEARS THAT HAVE passed since the attacks of September 11th, 2001, many people have presented evidence that calls into question the official account of the disaster. Although I am not a fan of conspiracy theories, a review of videos taken at the time, combined with knowledge gained from other events, has caused even people like me to question the official narrative. This was the first post by Q that mentioned the 9/11 attacks.

Nov 1 2017
Note MI has the same SAPs as NSA, CIA etc as designated post 9-11. Why is this relevant?
Who can be held hostage and controlled?
CIA thinks its foreign offshore assets are strong enough to defend against the US executive (not accounting for military use on domestic soil).
Why does the Constitution explicitly grant this authority to the President and what is it to prevent?
They knew our agencies would grow in power so much so they could/can hold the executive hostage or engage with bad actors.

Trump nominated someone new to direct every agency but one. He controls the top.

Q pointed out that since the September 11th attack, Military Intelligence (MI) has had the same Special Access Programs (SAPs) as the other intelligence agencies—and the President, as Commander in Chief of the military, has full authority over military intelligence. Q asked: Why is this relevant?

Q proposes that the office of the President had been made subservient to the Central Intelligence Agency by virtue of the information and access to foreign power that the agency possessed. The President is elected by the people and is supposed to serve their interests. If a President wanted to be free of the influence of the CIA and foreign governments, they would need to battle the agency as well as their offshore assets. The CIA failed to properly assess the President's capability if he were to have the full support of the military, and the battle was waged on U.S. soil. The Constitution gives control of the military to the President partly to prevent the usurpation of power by other branches of government or intelligence agencies.

Barack Obama weakened the military during his eight years in office. Q has asserted that Obama appointed compromised people as heads of intelligence agencies. He fired at least one patriot, General Mike Flynn, who was the Director of the Defense Intelligence Agency. Donald Trump's first priority after taking office was to strengthen the military. It was a wise move since the military is one of the President's greatest assets. President Trump replaced the heads of all intelligence agencies except one, keeping Admiral Mike Rogers as head of the National Security Agency because he knew Rogers could be trusted. It was Rogers who uncovered abuses of government surveillance and shut down unauthorized access to the NSA's database by FBI contractors. The patriotism and courage displayed by General Flynn and Admiral Rogers in the face of adversity stands as a example for all of us to follow.

After members of the Saudi royal family were arrested on November 4th, 2017, Q posted the following message.

Nov 6 2017
Why was the arrest of Alwaleed and others important?
How is Alwaleed and BO tied to HUMA?
Why did Alwaleed finance BO pre-political days?

Why did Alwaleed finance BO pre-political days?
What is HUMA? Define.
What book was BO caught reading?
Why was this immediately disregarded as false?
What is 'Post-American World by Fareed Zakaria'?
Why is this relevant?
Why would the President of the UNITED STATES OF AMERICA be reading this book?
What church did BO attend as pre-POTUS?
Who was BO's mentor?
How is Alwaleed and HRC connected?
Who was HRC's mentor?
How is Alwaleed and Bush Sr./Jr. connected?
What occurred post 9-11?
What war did we enter into?
What was the purpose and disclosures given re: justification?
Who financed 9-11?
Why, recently, are classified 9-11 pages being released?
What just occurred in SA?
What FOIA docs are being publicly released (recently)?
Why is this relevant?
What information is contained within these c-releases?
Why is C Wray important with regards to these releases?
What does money laundering mean?
What is the single biggest event that can generate many nation states to payout billions?
Who audits where the money goes?
$15,000 for a toothbrush?
Reconcile.
Why did we attack Iraq?
Halliburton.
Who are they?
What do they specialize in?
What is oil field service?
Why is this relevant?
What 'senior' level political officials are affiliated w/ Halliburton?
What is the primary goal?
What is the primary mode of influence that drives corruption?
What does money buy?

How is this connected to SA?
How is this connected to Alwaleed?
How is this connected to LV?
Q

Q asked why the arrest of Alwaleed bin Talal and other Saudi princes was important. According to Q, the Kingdom of Saudi Arabia had amassed great wealth, and they've used it to control politicians in the United Kingdom and the United States—including Barack Obama. Q has implied that Alwaleed financed Obama's Harvard education. If the allegation is true, the investment paid off when he was elected President. Q has further suggested that Harvard University Muslim Alumni (HUMA) connects former Harvard grads with their Saudi financiers. Once the wealth of the Saudi princes was removed, the strings of control to U.S. politicians were cut.

Barack Obama was photographed holding the book *The Post-American World* by Fareed Zakaria. Obama may have been reading the book to get an understanding of how the global geopolitical landscape was changing (and not in favor of the United States). He attended Trinity United Church of Christ, which was pastored by the Reverend Jeremiah Wright, whose sermons seem to imply a belief that America deserved the terrorist attack on September 11th, 2001.

Alwaleed bin Talal and the Bush family have a long history involving oil production and wars in the Middle East. The partnership has enriched Saudi Arabia and has given them power over politicians. The September 11th attack led to American troop deployment in Afghanistan, which the Bush administration said was an effort to remove Osama bin Laden and the Taliban from power.

What is seldom reported is the effect that war has on people at the very top of the banking industry and the politicians they support. Protracted wars cause nations to borrow billions (in some cases trillions) of dollars, which must be paid back with interest to banks. Would ultra-wealthy bankers like the Rothschilds share some of that wealth with the politicians who decide which wars are fought and how long they last? Why do you suppose the war in Afghanistan became America's longest war? Who benefits? Why is President Trump planning to bring most U.S. troops home from Afghanistan?

Halliburton is one of the world's largest oil field service companies with operations in more than 70 countries. Former U.S. Vice President Dick Cheney was chairman and CEO of Halliburton from 1995 to 2000.

Cheney retired from the company during the 2000 U.S. Presidential election campaign with a severance package worth 36 million dollars.

The official story of the September 11th attacks was that 19 militants associated with the Islamic extremist group al Qaeda hijacked four airplanes and used them to carry out suicide attacks against targets in the United States. 15 of the 19 hijackers were Saudi nationals. Two of the planes were flown into the twin towers of the World Trade Center in New York City. A third plane hit the Pentagon just outside Washington D.C., and the fourth plane crashed in a field near Shanksville, Pennsylvania. Almost 3,000 people were killed during the attacks. Q has suggested the official story is not true and asked who funded 9/11. On February 17th, 2016, Donald Trump told the hosts of the *Fox & Friends* show that he believed Saudi Arabia was behind the attacks.

"Who blew up the World Trade Center? It wasn't the Iraqis, it was Saudi — take a look at Saudi Arabia, open the documents... because frankly, if you open the documents, I think you're gonna see that it was Saudi Arabia."
—Donald J. Trump

According to Q, politicians receive payments for political favors through a complex series of financial transactions. Those transactions require research by forensic financial investigators if they are to be exposed. Before becoming FBI Director, Christopher Wray specialized in prosecuting and defending white-collar crimes such as money laundering.

Osama bin Laden was a longtime friend of Alwaleed bin Talal. At the time of Q's post, Alwaleed owned the top five floors of the Mandalay Bay Resort and Casino, the location of the Las Vegas (LV) mass shooting in 2017. In other posts, Q suggested the official account of the Las Vegas shooting is not true. (The Las Vegas shooting was covered in more detail in the first book in this series, *Calm Before the Storm*.)

Nov 6 2017
What family was permitted to leave immediately after 9-11?
Who authorized the departure?
Why is this relevant?
Was anyone else permitted to leave?
Repeat.
Was anyone else permitted to leave?
Was it a private plane?

What can private planes carry v commercial?
What airport did they arrive/depart from?
What was carried on a private plane to Iran?
Why was the Bin Laden family here during 9-11?
Coincidence?
How does SA connect to the Bin Laden family?
Who in SA is connected specifically to the Bin Laden family?
What did they deliver?
To who?
Why?
What does money buy?
Why are the events in SA relevant to the above?
Who is the financial backer for human trafficking?
Who is the 'broker' for underage sex?
Think SA.
How does FB & Instagram play a role in capture?
Think 'Taken'.
Fantasy right?
Why do select senior political officials have foundations/institutes?
What is money laundering?
What does money buy?
Why is this relevant?
What other people were arrested in SA?
What are their backgrounds?
Are any connected to the Podesta Group?
Why is this relevant?
What do you need in order to prosecute senior political officials?
How do you avoid public misconception?
How do you justify counter-political attacks to the mass public?
Why is information so vital?
Is the country divided?
Why does the MSM portray the country as being divided?
Why is this relevant?
Q

Q asked what family left the U.S. immediately after the 9/11 attack, how they left, and who permitted their departure. According to a September 28th, 2009 article by Craig Unger in *Vanity Fair*, at around 1:30 pm on September 13th, private investigator Dan Grossi received a phone call from the Tampa Police Department (Tampa, Florida). The caller informed him that the department had been protecting a number of Saudi students in the two days since the attack. They wanted to know if Grossi would escort them on a flight from Tampa to Lexington, Kentucky. Grossi was initially skeptical of the request; private flights had been grounded by the FAA since the attacks, and the order was still in effect. Nevertheless, he was told the students would be delivered to Raytheon Airport Services, a private hangar at Tampa International Airport. What Grossi did not realize was that the Saudi Ambassador to the United States, Bandar bin Sultan, had been pulling strings behind the scenes to arrange the flights. Grossi accompanied the Saudi students on the plane, which made four stops to pick up passengers before flying to Paris.

According to documents provided to the 9/11 Commission, more than 140 members of the Saudi royal family and the bin Laden family left the country on chartered jets when private air travel was permitted only by approval of President George Bush. The records were released by the Department of Homeland Security in response to a Freedom of Information Act request by Judicial Watch. Documents report that FBI agents briefly interviewed some passengers and inspected some luggage. The flights picked up passengers in several states, including California, Texas, and Florida.

Q asked what private planes can carry that commercial planes cannot. At the time, private planes were not required to undergo a full customs inspection. Passengers vouched for goods on board rather than being subjected to inspection. This leaves open the possibility of smuggling weapons, money, drugs, or evidence of crimes out of the country.

Q asked why the bin Laden family was in the U.S. during the 9/11 attacks and how the family was connected to Saudi Arabia. My assumption is that the bin Laden family and the Saudi royal family conspired with the U.S. government to arrange the attacks, which would justify continued wars in the Middle East and Asia.

Osama bin Laden's father, Mohammed bin Laden was a wealthy Saudi businessman who made his fortune in the construction industry. He founded the Saudi Binladin Group and became the wealthiest Saudi citizen outside of the royal family. He was known as Saudi Arabia's "royal builder," due to his relationships with the royal family, particularly Prince Faisal, who issued a royal decree awarding all construction projects to bin Laden's construction company.

In his lengthy post from November 6th, 2017, Q asked:

♦♦♦

Who is the financial backer for human trafficking?
Who is the 'broker' for underage sex?
Think SA.
How does FB & Instagram play a role in capture?
Think 'Taken'.
Fantasy right?

♦♦♦

Saudi Arabia has been criticized for its unjust treatment of women and girls. Forced marriages had been common there, and for many years there was no minimum legal age for marriage. Girls as young as one year old have been married to much older men. Is this custom a cover to justify the trafficking of children for sex?

Q seems to have implied that social media platforms have been used to lure unsuspecting users who become sex trafficking victims. The film *Taken* is an action drama about a father who tracks down his estranged daughter's kidnappers. Some anons are not convinced that enough is being done to stop the trafficking of children. An anon posted a blurred image of the faces of missing children and asked Q about them.

Anonymous • Dec 19 2017
Q, where are the children?
Seriously. Where are the children?
Love,
TlinOKC

Q responded.

3,000+ saved by the raids in SA alone.
WW lanes shut down.
Bottom to TOP.
[HAITI].
[RED CROSS]
[CLASSIFIED]
High Priority.
Q

After he was appointed Crown Prince on June 21st, 2017, Mohammad bin Salman brought many reforms to Saudi Arabia. In December of 2019, he effectively banned child marriages. Under his direction, the Justice Ministry issued an order to the nation's courts with instructions that marriage applications for those under the age of 18 must be referred to a special court to make sure that "marrying those below 18-years old will not harm them and will achieve their best interest, whether they are male or female."

Q asked why some politicians have non-profit foundations. It is illegal for American politicians to receive donations directly from foreign governments. Because of that, some politicians have established non-profit foundations, which receive donations from foreign governments. For example, the Clinton Foundation has received somewhere between 10 and 25 million dollars from the Kingdom of Saudi Arabia. Why would a foreign government donate money to an American politician's nonprofit unless they expected a return on their investment? Although, technically, money donated to a nonprofit may not be used for personal expenses, some politicians violate the law, thinking they won't be held accountable. Making donations to the nonprofits of elected officials is one way that foreign governments buy power and influence.

Nov 14 2017
Who financed 9-11?
Who was Bin Laden's handler?
Why was the Clowns In America tasked to hunt/kill/capture UBL? Why not MI?
If we found UBL, eliminated his security, why would we immediately kill him and not take him alive?
Why wouldn't we want to capture UBL alive and extract other possible T-level events?
Perhaps someday people will understand 'they' had a plan to conduct 'another' mass extinction event.
WWI & II - orchestrated and planned by select families?
Fantasy land.
Remember, the more people there are, the more power the people have.
Why do D's push for gun control 'directly' after every tragic incident?
Why is this so very important to their agenda?

We, the people, are who they are afraid of.
We, the people, are who they fear will one day awake.
Our Father who art in heaven,
Hallowed be thy name.
Thy kingdom come.
Thy will be done
on earth as it is in heaven.
Give us this day our daily bread,
and forgive us our trespasses,
as we forgive those who trespass against us,
and lead us not into temptation,
but deliver us from evil.
Q

Q has suggested that the Kingdom of Saudi Arabia financed the 9/11 attacks, and the CIA masterminded the operation. Many media reports tell of the CIA tracking the terrorist Osama bin Laden, also known as Usama bin Laden (UBL). Is Q inferring that bin Laden was part of the 9/11 conspiracy and acted as an asset (or agent) of the CIA? The agency was tasked with tracking and capturing him—instead of the military—because they needed to keep bin Laden from disclosing sensitive information to the military. If this is true, perhaps capture was never the agency's intent. Did the CIA act as bin Laden's handler and order his execution (by Navy Seals) when he became a liability? As this book goes to print, more information is coming out that may shed more light on what really happened.

For the elites, control of the earth's population is the end game. It's easier to control a smaller population; thus, various mechanisms are used to limit population growth. World wars are one example. As long as the elites remain in power, mass extinction events will be planned at critical points in the planet's evolution. Fortunately, patriots in the U.S. military have put into operation a plan to remove the elites from power. Q acknowledged their service.

Nov 5 2017
US Military = savior of mankind.
We will never forget.
Fantasy land.
God save us all.
Q

CHAPTER 11

Jason Bourne – Deep Dream

JASON BOURNE IS A FICTIONAL character and the protagonist of a series of novels and films created by Robert Ludlum. A victim of the CIA's mind control program, Bourne became the agency's perfect killing machine until he turned against them. The plot of the 2016 film *Jason Bourne*, revolved around a social media platform called Deep Dream that was created by the CIA to covertly and illegally spy on private citizens. The fictional company Deep Dream is similar to the real-life company Facebook. That similarity is the subject of many posts by Q.

President Trump relies on his social media accounts to bypass the press and get his message out to the world. Recently, major social media platforms have interfered with that operation, sometimes by removing his posts and in other cases, placing warning labels on them. Earlier attempts at interference were less subtle. On November 2nd, 2017, President Trump's Twitter account was suddenly disabled. That day, Q posted the following warning.

Nov 2 2017 18:07 (EST)
Please refer back and collect my crumbs.
As discussed, we've anticipated the Twitter and other social

media blackouts.
Rogue agents/programmers.
Per sealed Federal orders, we quickly tracked and reinstated.
Expect outages periodically (infiltrated).
If this doesn't signal what I've been saying I don't know what will.
Q

An hour later, Q posted this.

Nov 2 2017 19:07 (EST)
:::::Flash Traffic:::::
Three letter agency embedded tracking/up-channel into POTUS'
Twitter to specifically target through specialized geo and send his
location.
We anticipated this (see post a few hours ago).
It has begun.
Perhaps more posts to follow as expected imminent departure.
Q

Q said a "three letter agency" (later identified as the Central Intelligence Agency) attempted to embed tracking software on the President's phone and send his location to others.

An anon responded.

Anonymous • Let's be clear - you're telling us POTUS is currently
under attack by our own intelligence agencies?

Q replied.

Let's be real clear.
The CIA just attacked the Command and Chief which was
immediately detected by NSA/MI and alerted to POTUS.
Re-review all my crumbs including today/yesterday/weekend.
What does this mean?
What actions are immediately occurring?
If this leaks, or the immediate action ongoing at Langley, you'll
have your verification ahead of schedule.
Q

The following day, November 3rd, President Trump wrote a tweet about his Twitter account malfunction.

Donald J. Trump (from his Twitter account):
My Twitter account was taken down for 11 minutes by a rogue employee. I guess the word must finally be getting out-and having an impact.
3:51 AM - 3 Nov 2017

Weeks later, Q provided more information about Twitter.

Nov 20 2017
Expand your thinking.
What are patterns?
How are patterns formed and isolated?
What are data sets?
What is a map?
Re: Twitter (repeat)(important).
What action is Twitter taking effective mid-Dec?
What is the purpose of this action?
Possible test to understand public / gov't response?
When was this announced?
When did events in SA transpire?
Who controlled a large portion of Twitter stock?
Why is this relevant?
Expand your thinking.
What is the real purpose of this action?
What is the SS?
Who is the primary person protected under the SS?
What action is Twitter taking effective mid-Dec?
Would POTUS be able to use Twitter post action?
Define the 'known' action.
Why is the MSM ignoring this action?
What transpired w/ POTUS' Twitter account a short time ago?
Re-read crumbs on this topic (necessary).
Two scenarios (lose/lose).
POTUS advised by SS to terminate use of Twitter due to new website tracking policy (cookies) amongst other spyware not disclosed (risk) – 1st time they failed (re-read).

POTUS silenced on Twitter due to new policy (re: SS / risk).
Direct message failure.
POTUS refuses to be silenced.
Bad actors gather metadata and targeting.
Small example of the ongoing silent war.
Options?
Regulate?
Problem: time to complete.
Solution?
Patriots, get the word out.
Jason Bourne (Deep Dream).
Q

Saudi Prince Alwaleed bin Talal was a major shareholder of Twitter stock before his arrest on November 4th, 2017. His control of the platform facilitated the suppression of some voices and the amplification of others.

Q asked about the actions Twitter planned to take in mid-December. Twitter announced that it would begin tracking the online habits of its users once they had left the site. CEO Jack Dorsey justified the move as part of an effort to crack down on what he called "hate speech." He claimed that by monitoring users' browsing habits, Twitter could better identify people who embrace dangerous ideologies. Q suggested there was a more nefarious purpose behind the announcement.

Twitter and other entities monitor the online habits of their users by inserting tracking cookies on their devices. Q suggested Twitter had deployed other (more dangerous) programs that are not publicly acknowledged. The Secret Service (SS) protects the President. They are aware of the malicious software Twitter uses and advised the President not to use his account because it comes with increased risk.

What kind of risk?

If a rogue agency wanted to physically harm the President, they would first want to know his location. The Secret Service often conceals the President's location for security reasons. If Twitter uses software that tracks a user's geographic location, it could give away the President's location. This puts him in a lose-lose situation. If he uses Twitter, he increases the risk to himself. If he doesn't use Twitter, he can't speak directly to the world, and the mainstream media take control of his message. Because the media misrepresent his message, POTUS is taking the risk and continuing to use Twitter.

Q said this was a small sample of an ongoing "silent war." The ultimate solution to the problem is the regulation of social media platforms. The drawbacks (in 2017) were: the time it would take to gather sufficient evidence to prove that regulation was warranted, and then convincing Congress and regulatory agencies to take the necessary steps. According to Q, the workaround is getting patriots on social media to help the President disseminate his message.

The following post contained a link to an article about how Google tracks our physical location, even when we tell them not to.

Aug 14 2018
https://apnews.com/828aefab64d4411bac257a07c1af0ecb/
AP-Exclusive:-Google-tracks-your-movements,-like-it-or-not
[SIRI]
FB listens [even after you remove app].
TWITTER GEO-T/L
You are under constant tracking/surveillance.
DARPA.
Q

According to Q, Facebook (FB) eavesdrops on users' conversations even after they uninstall the application, and Twitter tracks its users' geographic location. Artificial Intelligence programs like Siri and Alexa function as user-approved surveillance devices.

In the following post, Q compared the description of Facebook with that of LifeLog—a program developed by the U.S. Defense Department's Advanced Research Projects Agency (DARPA).

Mar 6 2019
◆◆◆
Define 'Lifelog' [DARPA].
"an ontology-based (sub)system that captures, stores, and makes accessible the flow of one person's experience in and interactions with the world in order to support a broad spectrum of associates/assistants and other system capabilities". The objective of the LifeLog concept was "to be able to trace the 'threads' of an individual's life in terms of events, states, and relationships", and it has the ability to "take in all of a subject's experience, from phone numbers dialed and e-mail messages

viewed to every breath taken, step made and place gone".
Define 'FB'.
The Facebook service can be accessed from devices with
Internet connectivity, such as personal computers, tablets and
smartphones. After registering, users can create a customized
profile revealing information about themselves. Users can post
text, photos and multimedia of their own devising and share it
with other users as "friends". Users can use various embedded
apps, and receive notifications of their friends' activities. Users
may join common-interest groups.
Compare & Contrast.
DARPA senior employees > FB?
DARPA TERMINATES PROGRAM FEB 4, 2004.
FB FOUNDED FEB 4, 2004.
DARPA = FB
Q

Q noted that the same day DARPA shuttered its LifeLog program, Facebook was launched (February 4th, 2004). Q suggested senior employees
with DARPA were hired by Facebook.

Mar 6 2019
Logical thinking.
Did DARPA complete build/code (tax-payer funded) 'LifeLog'
program?
After completion, was there fear the public wouldn't accept the
adoption if known it was DoD/C_A backed?
Do you believe people would join a platform knowing it was under the
control of the C_A and FED GOV?
No.
How do you lure the masses into entering all their personal info and
private messages (i.e. their LIFE LOG) onto a new platform?
Do you make it cool?
How did FB 'supposedly' start and launch?
Ivy league only?
Develop a trend and/or following?
How do you keep the project running w/o 'public' taxpayer funds?
[DoD reported LifeLog was TERMINATED to Congress/Senate OS]
Define 'Black Budget'.

Did HWOOD push?
Do people follow the 'stars'?
Competitors systematically attacked (myspace) to prevent comp?
THE LARGEST 'COLLECTIVE' SOCIAL MEDIA PLATFORM IN
THE WORLD (BILLIONS LOGGED) IS OWNED AND OPERATED
(COVERTLY) BY THE CENTRAL INTELLIGENCE AGENCY OF THE
UNITED STATES OF AMERICA.
The More You Know.
Q

Q explained that the government used taxpayer money to build the concept
for Facebook but realized no one would voluntarily use it if they knew the
CIA and the military ran it. An article found online at *wired.com* explains
some of the problems with public trust in DARPA's LifeLog.

The decision was made to close the program known as LifeLog
and transfer key people and the technology to a new civilian company called Facebook. Developers wanted to make Facebook more
alluring, so they limited enrollment to students at select colleges and
recruited celebrities to promote it. It is suggested by Q that funding
for Facebook came out of the CIA's black operations (off the books)
budget. Competitors like My Space were targeted for elimination to allow
Facebook to achieve market dominance. In the film *Jason Bourne*, Deep
Dream was a CIA project that allowed the agency to circumvent domestic
surveillance laws and spy on citizens without a warrant. Q indicated that
this is literally true of Facebook.

Mar 7 2019
Expand your thinking.
If covertly operated [data accessible to project designators]
would they attempt to prevent any type of GOV regulations from
being imposed?
Expand your thinking further.
Why was MZ chosen as CEO (public figure) tasked to expand
growth?
Family tree of MZ?
Who is the wife of MZ?
Family tree of wife?
Why won't CHINA allow FB?
Situational awareness?

Do they know it's an individual collection asset program being covertly operated by the C_A?
Do they know it's been expanded to tap into the microphone of any device for listening and bulk data collection?
Do they know it's been expanded to tap into the GPS router of the device for RT tracking?
Do they know it's been expanded to tap into the camera function of the device in order to view/record all target designators?
Q

Mainstream reports on the immediate family of Mark Zuckerberg (MZ) and his wife, Priscilla Chan Zuckerberg, can be found with a little research. Apparently, there's something that Q wants us to discover that is deeply hidden, and harder to find.

Priscilla's Family

Mark Zuckerberg's wife, Priscilla Chan is the eldest daughter of Dennis and Yvonne Chan. Dennis Chan—who was reportedly born in 1961—was said to have arrived in America by boat in the 1970s as a Chinese-born Vietnam war refugee. Some reports say his wife was also a refugee. After raising enough capital, Mr. Chan opened a Chinese restaurant in Boston at 47 years old. It's been reported that his daughter, Priscilla was born in 1985, and was raised primarily by her non-English speaking grandmother while her parents worked long hours in the restaurant.

Our research uncovered conflicting information about Dennis Chan. *Dailymail.co.uk* reported that Dennis was issued a social security number as an "Asian Refugee" between April 1975 and November 1979, when refugees came from Vietnam in boats. But another source reported that the U.S. Pacific Territories issued his social security number between 1993 and 1997 (many years later), and that his wife Yvonne had a social security number issued to her in 1993 (also by the Pacific Territories). It's hard to say with certainty which report is right.

We could not conclusively determine if (or how long) the family lived in Vietnam before moving to the United States. There is also some confusion over where the family lived in China. Some claim they lived in the eastern Chandong province, in the city of Xuzhou (which happens to be the home of Wendi Deng, *Fox News'* Rupert Murdoch's former wife). Other reports say the industrial town of Nanjing was their home.

Priscilla Chan Zuckerberg

Priscilla Chan was a high achiever in high school. She attended Harvard University and then the University of California, San Francisco, where she completed her pediatric residency before marrying Mark Zuckerberg in 2012.

All the daughters in the Chan family were high achievers. Priscilla's sister Elaine (born in 1987) graduated from Columbia University School of Nursing and works as a pediatric nurse practitioner. Priscilla's youngest sister Michelle was educated at Harvard in East Asian Studies and studied Mandarin Chinese at Harvard Beijing Academy.

Mark's Family

Mark Zuckerberg's father is Edward Zuckerberg. He had a dental practice located in his residence in New York state. According to the office's website, Dr. Zuckerberg is *retired*, and another dentist is currently treating patients at that office. Edward and his wife Karen Kempner Zuckerberg (a psychiatrist) have moved to California to be closer to their grandchildren. Dr. Zuckerberg currently teaches social media and marketing skills to help dentists grow their practice. Not surprisingly, he teaches dentists how to use Facebook. Mark has three sisters, Randi, Donna, and Arielle.

Open source reporting shows that Mark's sister Randi is an entrepreneur, a bestselling author, an award-winning producer, an investor, and the founder and CEO of Zuckerberg Media.

Mark's sister Donna is a writer. She has been highly critical of social media, claiming it has elevated misogyny to new levels of violence and virulence. She speaks out against what she calls the "manosphere," which includes the men's rights movement.

Mark's sister Arielle is a venture capitalist. Her interviews can be found online. In a *CNN Business* interview, she voiced disappointment and heartbreak that Hillary Clinton lost the 2016 election. Arielle said she was afraid minority entrepreneurs would be discouraged from starting businesses in the tech sector during a Trump presidency.

Mark Zuckerberg

An article on *biographymask.com* reports that Mark was an outstanding student; his parents enrolled him in programs that would help him advance.

As an example, he attended the Johns Hopkins Center for Talented Youth summer camp. The article delves into the many early accomplishments of the young Mark Zuckerberg, reporting that "On his college application, Mark Zuckerberg stated that he could read and write French, Hebrew, Latin, and ancient Greek."

My research also produced an article with a screenshot from Mark's Facebook page when he announced his goal of learning Mandarin Chinese. He noted on Facebook in January of 2010: "I have had a hard time learning languages in the past, so this seemed like a particularly good challenge." This seems like an odd statement coming from a man who has reportedly learned many languages.

The China Connection

Facebook once had operations in China, but in 2009, the platform was banned by China's government. In January of 2010, when Mark announced on Facebook a New Year's goal of learning to speak Mandarin Chinese, he said he wanted to communicate with Priscilla's family, who only speak Chinese. Priscilla reportedly speaks English, Spanish, and Cantonese, but not Mandarin Chinese.

In December of 2010, Zuckerberg traveled to China to meet with the CEOs of search engine Baidu, web services company Sina, and China Mobile (a Chinese state-owned telecom company). Mark's girlfriend at the time, Priscilla Chan, was with him on the trip. Notably, in 2011, Facebook claimed it had no plans to expand its operation into mainland China.

In 2012, Mark went to mainland China with Priscilla. *The New York Times* reported they were seen in Shanghai. That same year, Zuckerberg traveled to Russia to improve Facebook's market position there. He encouraged Russian engineers and programmers to apply for work at Facebook. Zuckerberg met with Russian President Dimitry Medvedev at the Russian leader's residence outside Moscow, on October 1st, 2012.

In 2014, Mark hosted a question and answer session at Tsinghua University in Beijing, China. During the event, he spoke only Mandarin Chinese.

In September of 2015, Mark posted that he had just met with China's President Xi Jinping at the 8th Annual US-China Internet Industry Forum in Seattle, Washington. Zuckerberg again spoke in a foreign language with Xi and other leaders.

In 2015, Mark posted a message on Facebook celebrating the Chinese New Year. In October, he returned to Tsinghua University and gave a 22-minute speech in Mandarin. Tsinghua's School of Economics and Management then named him to their advisory board. The school's website describes the advisory board this way: "Tsinghua SEM Advisory Board was established in 2000. Members of the Board are made up of elite business leaders, visionary government officials and renowned scholars from internationally renowned businesses and academic institutions."

In 2016, it was reported that Zuckerberg met with other Chinese officials—specifically the head of the Communist Party's propaganda wing, Liu Yunshan.

In October of 2017, according to the school's website *(sem.tsinghua.edu.cn)* Tsinghua's School of Economics and Management welcomed Mark back to Tsinghua again (as a member of their advisory board) to participate in a dialogue with students. The English version of the website says, "Facebook sent seven executives to lecture in the course, and industry coaches, mentors, and investors worked together with the students to facilitate the team projects."

Also, in October 2017, President Xi met with members of the Tsinghua SEM advisory board before meeting with President Trump in early November. Paraphrased from the website: Guests of the meeting were encouraged by Xi to give more guidance on China's advancement and to extend more help to China through cooperation and a greater introduction of China to the world. Mark Zuckerberg spoke at the meeting, as did Jim Breyer of Breyer Capital, Henry Paulson of Paulson Institute, Stephen Schwarzman of the Blackstone Group, and Tim Cook of Apple.

Zuckerberg and Facebook *did* have ties to mainland China, at least in an advisory capacity. President Xi openly recognized that role. The school's advisory board meets every year, but I found no mention of Facebook being represented at the October meeting in 2018. *South China Morning Post* reported that in 2018, Zuckerberg dismantled the team that was trying to gain entrance to mainland China. Facebook has been under scrutiny by the U.S. Congress. Mark Zuckerberg maintains that Facebook is the best alternative to global Chinese dominance in social communication. Ironically, he testified to Congress that Chinese companies like TikTok are exporting anti-American ideas like censorship and government surveillance to other parts of the world.

Q suggested that China's resistance to western social media platforms is due to their understanding of how users are surveilled for the CIA's benefit. In the film *Jason Bourne*, the CIA secretly developed the social media company Deep Dream and used it to their advantage. The CEO gave the company a pleasing facade. Those who work for the CIA sometimes have a past with missing or conflicting details. Zuckerberg's public history doesn't add up. Was it manufactured? If so, by who? Was he made the CEO of Facebook to hide the identities of the company's real controllers?

On February 18th, 2018, Q posted the following message.

Feb 18 2018
@SNOWDEN
WHERE ARE YOU?
NOT RUSSIA.
[EYES ON]
YOU ARE NOW A LIABILITY.
HELPING @JACK?
PROJECT DEEPDREAMv2[A]].
WE WILL NEVER FORGET.
ES FAILED.
WHERE IS ES?
JOHN PERRY BARLOW.
DEFINE THE END?
THE DAY OF RECKONING IS UPON US.
JOHN 3:16
Q

Edward Snowden (@snowden) has been living in Russia since leaking information about the NSA spy tools PRISM and XKeyscore to the press in 2013. Although he is broadly perceived to be a hero, Q has suggested his leaks were coordinated by the CIA in a effort to destroy public trust in the NSA, which would give the CIA a competitive advantage. In 2019, Snowden published the book *Permanent Record*. The Department of Justice sued and won a permanent judgment and injunction against him for violating the non-disclosure agreements he signed while working for the CIA and the NSA. A trust was established to receive all monetary compensation earned from the book. Q has indicated that Snowden will be extradited to the U.S. to stand trial, likely for espionage.

In the above post, Q asked, rhetorically, where Snowden was and then said he was not in Russia. [EYES ON] was a warning that he was being watched. Q asked if he was helping Twitter CEO Jack Dorsey and then mentioned Project Deep Dream. Q taunted Snowden by reminding him that former Google CEO Eric Schmidt (ES) failed. The mention of Eric Schmidt's failure is likely a reference to his attempt to set up an alternate communications network that Q alluded to in posts like this one.

Mar 7 2018
Who controls social media?
Who performs in a circus?
Who wrote the code to embed and censor across multiple platforms?
Why Russia?
Why China?
Why HK?
Why did ES (himself) arrange a C-link in multiple countries?
Learn.
Q

Clowns perform in a circus. Q is hinting that the CIA (Clowns In America) controls social media platforms and that a universal censorship algorithm is used on them. Eric Schmidt's visit to North Korea in 2013 had an objective different from its stated one. Q implied that Schmidt personally helped establish covert communication networks in North Korea and other countries. It's only a guess, but I suspect the purpose was to provide communications (for select people) that would be impervious to NSA collection.

In November of 2019, Q posted a link to an article where Google whistleblower Zach Vorhies explained the acquisition by Google of an artificial intelligence (AI) company called "DeepMind."

Nov 11 2019
GOOG whistleblower
Project DeepMind?
"AI Manhattan Project."
https://www.breitbart.com/tech/2019/10/14/whistleblower-google-is-developing-ai-for-planetary-surveillance/
[Feb 18 2018]
"Project DeepDream v2[A]?" – Q
Do you believe in coincidences?
Q

This post includes a repost of Q's mention of Deep Dream on February 18th, 2018. Here's a quote from the linked article:

"So Google bought this AI company called DeepMind," Vorhies replied. "Let me just put it in plain language what that is, DeepMind was creating a god-like AI system that is able to ingest the available public information on the internet and make sense of it. Think of it like Amazon Alexa except much, much, much, more intelligent. This AI system was moved out of the UK, I believe, and placed into China, and it's been dubbed the AI Manhattan Project."

Vorhies continued: "It's the most sophisticated and advanced AI project in the world made by an American company and placed in China. When people think of surveillance, they usually think of country surveillance. This is planetary surveillance of all information that is available on the surface web and also any sources that it can get in the deep web and utilizing Google's extensive deep analysis of its book scanning stuff. So think of the Library of Alexandria of all available websites that you can search for and all that data gets fused together and a decision-making process gets formed because of that. This is essentially what the Google DeepMind project is all about."

In May of 2020, Twitter applied a label to a tweet by President Trump, claiming it contained untrue information. The President accused Twitter of interfering in an election and signed an Executive Order directing Congress to consider modifying the laws that protect social media companies from legal liability. The order also instructed the Justice Department to review the way it investigates and prosecutes complaints of social media censorship. In addition to potentially risking billions in liability as publishers, Jack Dorsey, Mark Zuckerberg (MZ), Eric Schmidt (ES), and Reddit CEO Steve Huffman (SH) were warned that the cost for their personal involvement could be even higher.

Jan 21 2018
@Jack, MZ, ES, JB, EM, SH, MSM, etc.
Do you know that we know?
Do you know that we see all?
Do you know that we hear all?
FEAR the STORM.
NOBODY PLAYING THE GAME GETS A FREE PASS.
NOBODY.
Q

CHAPTER 12

Military Intelligence

MUCH OF WHAT THE MILITARY does can appear wasteful and redundant. For that reason, the term "military intelligence" has long been considered an oxymoron. As I've studied Q's posts, I've developed a newfound respect for military intelligence.

Q suggested that Donald Trump was approached by military leaders to run for President with assurances that they would minimize election rigging to give him a fair shot at being elected.

Oct 28 2017

♦♦♦

Why does Potus surround himself w/ generals?

What is military intelligence?

Why go around the 3 letter agencies?

What Supreme Court case allows for the use of MI v Congressional assembled and approved agencies?

Who has ultimate authority over our branches of military w\o approval conditions unless 90+ in wartime conditions?

What is the military code?

♦♦♦

Because senior leaders at the civilian agencies (FBI, DOJ, CIA, etc.) had been compromised, President Trump has relied on military intelligence to keep him updated on global events and matters of national security.

> Oct 31 2017
> Who did POTUS meet with yesterday?
> Was AG Sessions there?
> How many MI generals were on the WH list to attend a separate meeting?
> ◆◆◆

Q asked us to consider how many generals with military intelligence backgrounds had visited the White House.

> Nov 1 2017
> ◆◆◆
> Focus on Flynn.
> Background and potential role.
> What is the common denominator in terms of military backgrounds close to POTUS?
> ◆◆◆

After serving as Director of the U.S. Defense Intelligence Agency, Lieutenant General Mike Flynn served briefly as President Trump's National Security Advisor, before becoming a target of Robert Mueller's investigation into election interference. Q suggested that Flynn played a vital role in the Trump administration, albeit a behind-the-scenes one.

A few days later, Q provided more clues about General Flynn.

> Nov 5 2017
> Game Theory.
> Define.
> Why is this relevant?
> Moves and countermoves.
> ◆◆◆
> Flynn.
> What is Flynn's background?
> What was his rank?

Was he involved in intel ops?
What access or special priv?
Why is this relevant?
Set up..
Who wins?
Who becomes exposed?
Who knows where the bodies are buried?
Who has access?

♦♦♦

Although many people have perceived General Michael Flynn to be in a position of disadvantage with respect to his enemies, Q has asserted that he has the upper hand due to his background in military intelligence, his access to that information system, and the knowledge he has of his enemies' crimes. (Metaphorically speaking, he knows where the bodies are buried.)

Oct 29 2017
Key:
Military Intelligence v FBI CIA NSA
No approval or congressional oversight
State Secrets upheld under SC
Who is the Commander and Chief of the military?
Under what article can the President impose MI take over investigations for the 3 letter agencies?
What conditions must present itself?
Why is this so VERY important?
Who surrounds POTUS?
They lost this very important power _ the one area of the govt not corrupt and directly serves POTUS.

The U.S. civilian intelligence agencies (FBI, CIA, DOJ, etc.) are part of the government's executive branch. The President is the top-level administrator of all civilian intelligence agencies. Civilian agencies are subject to congressional oversight, Freedom of Information Act (FOIA) requests, and other regulatory measures. In theory, that should make them more accountable, but corrupt people have found ways to exploit sensitive information, and they've weaponized civilian agencies against their political opponents.

Military intelligence serves the various branches of the military. The National Security Agency (NSA or as Q sometimes calls them—No Such Agency) is part of the Pentagon. The NSA gathers and disseminates its intelligence products to civilian agencies as needed. The Defense Intelligence Agency provides intelligence information for use by the military. The military intelligence community answers to the Commander in Chief—the President. Military intelligence is not at the disposal of nor is it accountable to civilian politicians. According to Q, military intelligence has (for the most part) been able to keep free of corrupting influences.

Q asked what article permits the President to direct the military to take over investigations from civilian agencies. The insurrection act of 1807 (10 U.S. Code § 252) allows the President to use the military to put down lawlessness, insurrection, and rebellion. Some might think the Posse Comitatus Act would disallow such use of the military, but it does not. The Posse Comitatus Act restricts military enforcement of domestic law to that which is sanctioned by Congress or where it is otherwise permitted by law. Challenges to Presidential use of the military in this way have been upheld by the Supreme Court (SC). If, as Q claims, U.S. civilian intelligence agencies were acting contrary to the law, the President could use military intelligence agencies to accomplish their functions.

On October 31st, 2017, Q posted more questions.

Military Intelligence.
◆◆◆
Was TRUMP asked to run for President?
Why?
By Who?
Was HRC next in line?
Was the election suppose to be rigged?
Did good people prevent the rigging?
Why did POTUS form a panel to investigate?
Has POTUS *ever* made a statement that did not become proven as true/fact?
What is POTUS in control of?
What is the one organization left that isn't corrupt?
Why does the military play such a vital role?
Why is POTUS surrounded by highly respected generals?
◆◆◆

On September 30th, 2019, President Trump attended a ceremony where General Joseph Dunford stepped down as Chairman of the Joint Chiefs of Staff, and General Mark Milley became his replacement. In a speech he made at the ceremony, Trump explained that in 2015, at a dinner where he received an award from the U.S. Marines, General Dunford had a private conversation with him and encouraged him to consider running for President. This was the first time President Trump had revealed this detail in public. How did Q know about it two years earlier?

> Nov 1 2017
> Military Intelligence.
> No media.
> No leaks.
> How many MI generals have been in/out of WH in the past 30 days?
> ♦♦♦
> These are crumbs and you cannot imagine the full and complete picture.
> If Trump failed, if we failed, and HRC assumed control, we as Patriots were prepared to do the unthinkable...
> ♦♦♦

Q said military leaders were prepared to do the unthinkable if their plan failed. It appears as though they saw a succession of corrupt Presidents (both Republican and Democrat) over a period of time and how they were controlled by a handful of elites. They grew weary of the wars and resolved to find someone they could support as President who would not be controlled. This person would have to be immune to blackmail and would have to withstand the threats and intimidation that would come from the media, corrupt politicians, and rogue intelligence agencies. Standing in a firestorm is one thing, but this would require someone who would create a storm of their own—someone who could lay waste to the corrupt Washington D.C. swamp. The generals found their man in Donald Trump. It seems that a military coup was the other option. Donald Trump was their last hope for a peaceful transition of power.

Information Warfare

The military often wages war using weapons that cause physical injury or death. The military intelligence community engages in what could be called "information warfare." The Soviet Union was brought down by the U.S. government without firing a shot. The cold war was primarily a battle of information. Western intelligence operatives infiltrated the Soviet Union and disseminated information in a way that caused the empire to collapse. According to Q, military intelligence functions as the gatekeeper of all information.

Mar 27 2018

◆◆◆

Current censorship all relates to push for power [mid-terms].
LAST STAND.
Election FRAUD cases OPEN - DOJ [many].
Follow the FAMILY.
Follow resignations [Business/Gov't].
BIDEN/CHINA VERY IMPORTANT MARKER.
Who made it public?
Who really made it public?
Who is making it all public?
WE ARE THE GATEKEEPERS OF ALL [BY ALL WE MEAN ALL]
INFORMATION

◆◆◆

Q revealed details that were not common knowledge, hinting that the Department of Justice had multiple investigations open into election fraud and that the resignations of corporate leaders would prove to be highly significant. Joe Biden's connections to China are an important marker, and Q said he and his associates are the ones making it all public.

In a post from November 2017, Q touched on how information is disseminated and how it is used to control people.

Nov 20 2017
What is a key?
What is a key used for?
What is a guard?
What is a guard used for?
Who unlocked the door of all doors?
Was it pre-planned?
Do you believe in coincidences?
What is information?

Who controls the release of information?
WHO HAS ALL OF THE INFORMATION?
Who disseminates information?
What is the MSM?
Who controls the MSM?
Who really controls the MSM?
Why are we made to believe the MSM are the only credible news sources?
Who controls the MSM?
Who really controls the MSM?
Why are we made to believe the MSM are the only credible news sources?
Why is this relevant?
Why are non MSM platforms cast as conspiracy and/or non-credible?
Why are non MSM platforms cast as conspiracy and/or non-credible?
What happens when an entity and/or individual accumulates power?
Define corruption.
Wealth = power.
Power = influence.
Influence = control.
Rinse and repeat.
What power of influence was recently discovered (specifically re: 2016 election)?
How much power of influence does Twitter, FB, Reddit, etc. have in influencing the minds of people?
Has the stranglehold of the MSM been diminished?
What is open source?
What has become blatantly obvious since the election of POTUS?
Why would they allow this (visibility) to occur?
Were they not prepared to counter?
What miscalculation occurred?
What opposite impact did this generate?
How did POTUS recognize and invert?
What happens when an entity and/or individual accumulates power?
Define corruption.

Define censorship.
Define 'controlled' censorship.
What action is Twitter taking effective mid-Dec?
What is the purpose of this action?
Possible test to understand public / gov't response?

Q suggested that the mainstream media are controlled by a corrupt agency. In a 1977 article published in *The Rolling Stone*, Carl Bernstein claimed that more than 400 fellow-reporters were working for the CIA.

For decades, the mainstream press (and indirectly, the CIA) maintained a stranglehold on the information that ordinary people relied on for their understanding of world events. This information dominance was possible because they controlled radio and television technology, and they owned printing presses. Today, most people get their information from social media platforms like Facebook, Twitter, and YouTube. In 1970, you needed a broadcast studio to air a news program. Today, millions of people broadcast news and opinions using only their phones.

Q pointed out that social media platforms were supposed to keep Donald Trump from being elected, but their CEOs underestimated the influence people have when they collectively speak their minds. Trump supporters provided enough information to counter the mainstream narrative, giving him a victory.

Realizing their mistake, social media platforms have taken steps to silence dissenters. Censorship has increased, and many conservatives have had their accounts suspended. Silicon Valley CEOs justify censoring political views by labeling dissenting opinions "hate speech." In the lead-up to the 2020 election, social media platforms are censoring not just certain political views, but they're applying "election misinformation" warning labels to the posts of politicians—including the President.

In 2016, while addressing a group of young adults, General Flynn made an observation about the change that has occurred in the flow of information. He noted that because journalists had become arrogant, ordinary people "took over the idea of information... and they did it through social media."

Members of the press resent the assertion that they are controlled by the CIA. They also reject the notion that they could be displaced by untrained people like you and me, but the facts cannot be wished away. Since January of 2018, when I began broadcasting regular Q updates, my YouTube videos have garnered more than 40 million views with over

300 million impressions. There are hundreds, if not thousands, of people like me publishing broadcasts on YouTube and other social media platforms. Some have many times more viewers than I do. At present, our collective influence dwarfs that of the mainstream media.

As this book was about to go to print, YouTube removed many influential Q-related accounts from its platform—including ours. Twitter recently locked the account of White House Press Secretary Kayleigh McEnany, and Twitter is currently blocking links to a *New York Post* exposé about Joe Biden's son, Hunter. In response to the recent censorship blitz by "big tech," the FCC is looking into clarifying the Section 230 immunity protections that were given to tech giants like YouTube, Facebook, and Twitter.

Nov 21 2019

♦♦♦

THE GREAT AWAKENING.
You are the news now.
Handle w/ care.
Q

Q's operation is designed to aid us in developing a more accurate understanding of current news and historical events by encouraging us to conduct our own research. If the complaint against mainstream reporting is dishonesty or inaccuracy, citizen journalists must hold themselves to the same standard they expect of others. In a movement numbering in the millions, there will be some who miss the mark, but Q's admonition to handle this responsibility with care should be taken to heart by anyone who wants to be taken seriously.

Oct 5 2018

♦♦♦

This movement challenges their 'forced' narrative.
This movement challenges people to not simply trust what is being reported.
Research for yourself.
Think for yourself.
Trust yourself.
This movement is not about one person or a group of people.
WE, the PEOPLE.

♦♦♦

After we do the research necessary to arrive at the truth, Q encourages us to trust ourselves. This is not, by the way, to be taken as an instruction *not* to trust God. It's specific to how we view current and historical events. Rather than relying on the press to inform us, Q asks us to trust our own research. If we do, we can share our findings with others to counter the narrative of the mainstream media.

In the leadup to the 2018 mid-term elections, those who opposed President Trump began a campaign that stirred up racial tension. Q posted a photo of a group of black Americans wearing MAGA hats (an icon of President Trump's Make America Great Again campaign). The young people were listening attentively to President Trump's address during the 2018 Young Black Leadership Summit held at the White House.

Nov 2 2018
Ask yourself a very simple question.
Why is the FAKE NEWS media continually expending resources to defame, debunk, and cast as a conspiracy, for, as they say, a nobody who started on 4chan?
Why did the FAKE NEWS media attempt to cast blame of recent events on the 'Q' movement?
Was it an attempt to silence?
◆◆◆
Attempts to label all those who challenge their narrative as 'racists' 'white supremacists' will fail [predictable].
Q

The attacks against Q suggest that the media have lost control of the narrative. Because the movement is non-violent, the press falsely attributed acts of violence or hatred to Q's followers. Q has highlighted that the flag used by the anarchist group Antifa is based on the one used by the militant wing of the German Communist Party of the 1930s (Antifaschistische Aktion). In the summer of 2020, Q pointed out similarities between the violent tactics of present-day members of Antifa and those used by Hitler's brown shirts. Predictably, the media immediately accused Q followers of being modern-day Nazis.

Jun 24 2020
This has never been attempted.
Use of general public to counter the narrative [propaganda] push

by controlled media.

Analysis [start-to-now] indicates situational awareness [decoupling of MSDNC control of information (channels 1-99)] of general public expanding at massive pace.

Attacks indicate [can be defined as] loss of generalized information control.

Need to expend ammunition [muster network to defend and coordinate attacks] to counter.

MIL-CIV Alliance.

Q

Since his first post, Q has rapidly gained followers, which today number in the millions. Because he has dared to defy the press, they've published thousands of articles attacking him or his followers. Multimillion-dollar news corporations would not expend vast amounts of time, effort, and money attacking Q unless they perceived him to be a threat. Q explained that he is part of an alliance of civilians and military members working together to highlight the truth that opposes the narrative disseminated by the press.

In June of 2020, Q offered an opportunity to join this military-civilian alliance in the digital information battle. Then he gave the first set of instructions to those who would like to accept the assignment, which I'll explain line-by-line following the post.

Jun 24 2020

You have been selected to help serve your Country.

Never retreat from the battlefield [Twitter, FB, etc.].

Use other platforms as a form of centralized command and control.

Organize and connect [bridge through linking].

Source meme(s) material from battlefield and/or garage [highlight & share][take & drop]

Mission 1: Dispute [reject] propaganda push through posting of research and facts

Mission 2: Support role of other digital soldiers [one falls another stands (rises)]

Mission 3: Guide [awaken] others through use of facts [DECLAS 1-99 material and other relevant facts] and memes [decouple MSDNC control of info stream] _ask 'counter' questions to initiate 'thought' vs repeat [echo] of MSDNC propaganda

Mission 4: Learn use of camouflage [digitally] _primary account suspended-terminated _use of secondary

Mission 5: Identify strengths / weaknesses [personal and designated target(s)] re: Twitter & FB [+other] example re: meme(s) failure to read through use of ALGO [think Tron (MCP_master control program)] _dependence on person-to-person capture [slow response time unidentified user(s)]

Game theory.

Information warfare.

Welcome to the Digital Battlefield.

Together we win.

Q

Here's my breakdown of Q's instructions to those who want to join the information warfare mission:

Never retreat from the battlefield [Twitter, FB, etc.]. — We are in the midst of a war over the control of information. The battlefields are the social media platforms where people get their information. If you choose to become a soldier in the digital war of ideas, you might consider setting up accounts on several social media platforms. Q's instruction is that when your account gets suspended, you should create another one. If that one gets suspended, start another. Keep creating new accounts. Keep posting, and don't quit.

Use other platforms as a form of centralized command and control. Organize and connect [bridge through linking]. — Many of us have become active on the platforms Parler, CloutHub, and Gab. Unlike Twitter and Facebook, these platforms are not under the control of bad actors. We use them as a safe venue for communicating ideas, strategizing with leaders, and meeting other digital soldiers in a friendly environment. Safe social media platforms are not the battlefield; they're more like command centers and communication networks. Twitter, Facebook, YouTube, and Reddit are the battlefields.

Source meme(s) material from battlefield and/or garage [highlight & share][take & drop] — Visual memes convey profound truths and reach the subconscious in a way that a written article does not. Social media platforms do not have the technology to read and censor images. Find memes wherever you can, i.e., Twitter and Facebook (the battlefield), or create them yourself (garage). Share the ones you have with others and grow your collection. In a recent post, Q explained that social media platforms are now using advanced Artificial Intelligence (AI) programs to find and remove certain memes, making it necessary to alter them slightly to avoid censorship.

Mission 1: Dispute [reject] propaganda push through posting of research and facts. — Engage politicians and members of the press on social media. Do not blindly accept their narratives. Present the facts from your research, but be respectful.

Mission 2: Support role of other digital soldiers [one falls another stands (rises)] — Digital soldiers are not loners. They must collaborate to be effective. Support the work of other digital soldiers by sharing their content when appropriate. As fellow digital soldiers leave a platform or take breaks, fill in the gaps with your work.

Mission 3: Guide [awaken] others through use of facts [DECLAS 1-99 material and other relevant facts] and memes [decouple MSDNC control of info stream] _ask 'counter' questions to initiate 'thought' vs repeat [echo] of MSDNC propaganda. — As information is declassified, present it and other relevant facts that counter the mainstream narrative. Ask thought-provoking questions instead of echoing the opinions of others.

Mission 4: Learn use of camouflage [digitally] _primary account suspended-terminated _use of secondary. — Learn how to avoid being de-platformed on social media. Some specific strategies can be helpful: Avoid using certain words that others can report to get your account suspended. Avoid engaging with agitators. Often, their goal is to elicit a response from you that can be reported to get your account suspended. When your account is suspended, know how to create a new one and avoid taking the same actions that caused the suspension. In a later post, Q suggested omitting direct references to "Q" and "Qanon" on social media. Reporters don't tell you about their sources; they give you the information their sources provide. Q is a source. The key is the information, not the source. Thus, if mentioning Q will put you at risk of having your account suspended, don't mention Q, but continue reporting the information he provides.

Mission 5: Identify strengths/weaknesses [personal & designated target(s)] re: Twitter & FB [+other] example re: meme(s) failure to read through use of ALGO [think Tron (MCP_master control program)] _dependence on person-to-person capture [slow response time unidentified user(s)] — Know your strengths and learn how to use them. Know your weaknesses and learn how to avoid them. Know the strengths and weaknesses of social media platforms. Leverage them to your advantage. One weakness of social media platforms is their inability to read and interpret memes and images. Therefore, use memes to convey powerful messages that bypass censorship algorithms.

Digital soldiers need leaders. Q provides leadership as a distributor of information. General Flynn has been silent on social media for three years due to the Robert Mueller investigation, but as his case approaches its conclusion, he's become more active on Twitter and now has an account on Parler. Current NSA Director Paul Nakasone created a Twitter account in June of 2020. It appears as though leaders in the military intelligence community are preparing to assist the digital soldiers they're recruiting.

Those who research Q's posts have accepted an offer never before made to civilians. We've agreed to work with an entity that we believe to be part of a military intelligence operation without knowing exactly who we are working with. In turn, the military has agreed to provide a level of information never before given to civilians, despite the fact that we have no security clearances, and we might make poor use of the information. That is how important this mission is to members of the military intelligence community.

CHAPTER 13

What Is the Keystone?

IN THIS CHAPTER, WE'LL FOLLOW a trail of crumbs to answer a question that was asked by Q: "What is the keystone?" The first mention of the "keystone" was in a post on November 9th, 2017.

Nov 9 2017
Trip added.
[C]oordinated effort to misdirect.
Guide to reading the crumbs necessary to cont[I]nue.
◆◆◆
What is a keystone?
◆◆◆
Find the ke[y]stone.
◆◆◆
Q

On November 20th 2017, Q asked again about the keystone.

Nov 20 2017
POTUS opened the door of all doors.

Expand your thinking.
What is the keystone?
Q

On December 5th, 2017, Q began to explain the keystone.

Dec 5 2017 16:01 (EST)
Key - unlocks the door of all doors (info)
Stone - the force / strength capable of yielding power to act on info
Key+Stone=
Q

Q's keystone has two parts. The "key" is information. Metaphorically, it opens the door to possibilities. The "stone" is the strength or power to act on that information. Five minutes after the above post, Q provided more information.

Dec 5 2017 16:06 (EST)
Adm R/ No Such Agency (W&W) + POTUS/USMIL =
Apply the Keystone.
Paint the picture.
Q

Q reposted this message by an anon, confirming he had the correct decode.

Anonymous • Dec 5 2017 16:05 (EST)
Military Intelligence, No Such Agency = key
POTUS and Patriots = stone

Intelligence collected by the National Security Agency is the "key." (The NSA's former Director was Admiral Rogers.) The power of President's office combined with the might of the U.S. military and the networking capabilities of patriots is the "stone." When combined, they form the "keystone." The information provided by the military helps *us* understand events that are happening on the world stage (they reveal the big picture). We help *them* by disseminating the information they provide.

The word "keystone" has at least one other application. In architecture, a keystone refers to a trapezoidal-shaped building stone found at the apex of some arches and doorways. This stone plays a role in distributing weight down the side support blocks in the columns. Without the keystone, the arch in this sort of design would collapse. The temple-like building on Little St. James Island, formerly owned by Jeffrey Epstein, had a door with a keystone at the top of its arch. On July 18th, 2018, Q posted a photo of an ancient building in Syria, which had doorways and design themes strikingly similar to the temple on Little St. James island.

CHAPTER 14

Speed

IN THIS CHAPTER, WE'LL DECODE the signature "Speed," which, at the time this book was published, appears in only three posts. As is often the case, this signature presents a real-world situation that mimics the plot of a film.

The 1994 film *Speed* was an action thriller featuring Sandra Bullock as the unwitting driver of a public transit bus that had been rigged with a bomb by a disgruntled former cop. The bomb was set to detonate if the speed of the bus dropped below 50 miles per hour. To make matters worse, the bomber threatened to detonate the device if any of the passengers were removed from the bus. Keanu Reeves played the hero. His task was to either defuse the bomb without slowing the bus down or remove its occupants without the bomber's knowledge. The film presents a thorny conundrum; how does one defuse a bomb without stopping the bus?

The first appearance of the signature "speed" was on November 5th, 2017, the day after the arrest of corrupt Saudi princes.

Nov 5 2017
Social media platforms.
Top 10 shareholders of Facebook?

Top 10 shareholders of Twitter?
Top 10 shareholders of Reddit?
Why is SA relevant?
MSM.
Controlling stakes in NBC/MSNBC?
Controlling stakes in ABC?
Controlling stakes in CBS?
Controlling stakes in CNN?
Investor(s) in Fox News?
Why is this relevant?
What is Operation Mockingbird?
Active?
Who is A Cooper?
What is A Cooper's background?
Why is this relevant?
Snow White.
Godfather III.
Speed.
Q

As previously mentioned, prior to their arrest, Saudi princes like Alwaleed bin Talal were major shareholders in social, print, and broadcast media companies. In Operation Mockingbird, the CIA infiltrated the mainstream media for the purpose of controlling the public narrative on key issues. CNN anchor Anderson Cooper interned for the CIA after he graduated from college. Although the CIA claims it ended Operation Mockingbird decades ago, Q suggests the agency has strengthened its control over media companies in recent years. If you're unfamiliar with the CIA's alleged covert operations, a basic internet search will give you plenty of information to consider.

On the same day, Q posted a second message with the signature "speed."

Nov 5 2017
Who is the Queen of England?
How long in power?
With power comes corruption.
What happened to Diana?
What did she find out?

Why was she running?
Who did she entrust to help her flee?
What was the cover?
Why is this relevant?
Why now?
Old.
Connection.
News.
Bad actor.
London Mayor.
Background?
Affiliation?
Connection to Queen?
British MI6 agents dead.
When?
How?
What was reported?
What really happened?
Why is this relevant?
Wealth.
Corruption.
Secret society.
Evil.
Germany.
Merkel.
Migrants.
Why are migrants important?
Assets.
What are assets?
Define assets?
Why are migrants so important?
What are assets?
Why are migrants so important?
What are assets?
Why are migrants so important?
Operations.
Satan.
Who follows?
What political leaders worship Satan?

What does an upside down cross represent?
Who wears openly?
Why?
Who is she connected to?
Why is this relevant?
Spirit cooking.
What does Spirit Cooking represent?
Cult.
What is a cult?
Who is worshipped?
Why is this relevant?
Snow White
Godfather III
Speed.
Q

The world is awakening to the reality of government corruption. For centuries, the money we've given to our governments has been funneled into the pockets of malevolent people whose only desire was to keep us under their control. In the above post, Q alluded to a secret discovered by Princess Diana that put her life in jeopardy.

Sadiq Khan is the mayor of London because he is willing to advance the agenda of globalists. The UK, Germany, and other European nations were flooded with migrants from Africa because it advances the globalist agenda. Those who desire a one-world government are opposed to national identities and borders between nations. The importation of millions of migrants, over time, has the effect of erasing national identities.

Who wears an upside-down cross?

Most people understand that the cross represents the power of God. They also comprehend the symbolism of the pentagram and similar icons. Does an upside-down cross represent the inverse of God's power—the power of Satan? Do corrupt leaders worship Satan? Do their lives portray works of darkness and evil? It may be valuable for you to research these questions on your own. Your search may uncover images of well-known people.

The upside-down cross is used as a symbol of atheism, humanism, and the demonic. In some cases, it conveys an anti-Christian belief system, but the intended meaning is determined by the context in which it is displayed.

The upside-down cross has been used in Christianity. It is connected to the belief that the Apostle Peter was crucified upside down. According to *Wikipedia*: "It is believed that Peter requested this form of crucifixion as he felt he was unworthy to be crucified in the same manner that Jesus died. As such, some Catholics use this cross as a symbol of humility and unworthiness in comparison to Jesus."

In this same post, Q brought up the topic of Spirit Cooking. Marina Abramovic is a performance artist who helped create a Spirit Cooking book in 1996 that incorporated body fluids as ingredients. She then turned that idea into an art installation in Rome with her recipe instructions painted on white walls in pig's blood. Her Spirit Cooking art later evolved into a form of "dinner party entertainment" that Abramovic sometimes puts on for her collectors, donors, and celebrity friends.

In 2015, Spirit Cooking became a topic of discussion on social media after *WikiLeaks* published the Podesta emails and posted tweets of them on their Twitter account. One of the emails was from Abramovic, who sent dinner party invitations to Washington D.C. lobbyist Tony Podesta and his brother John Podesta, who managed Hillary Clinton's 2016 campaign. Citizen researchers (many of whom had never heard of Abramovic) were suddenly faced with images of celebrities participating in "spirit cooking" events that mimicked cannibalism.

In April of 2020, Microsoft produced a product ad video featuring Abramovic, referring to her as "the most legendary artist working now." Due to public backlash (24,000 dislikes on the video in three days), Microsoft removed the ad from its YouTube channel. Abramovic uses symbolism like pentagrams, skeletons, and blood rituals—and she was photographed holding a bloody Baphomet-like goat's head. The art world and media outlets downplay the occult imagery used in her performances, and then accuse the outraged public of engaging in "satanic-panic." Marina Abramovic later publicly defended herself, stating she's not a Satanist. Are the media and celebrity elites simply more sophisticated in their artistic tastes than the rest of us? Do they really view this art as worthy of their time and attention? Or is there more to the fascination?

Downsizing Darkness and Corruption

Once citizens become aware that their government is riddled with corruption, they may wonder how it could be removed without destroying the necessary services government provides. This conundrum is illustrated by the signature "speed." The CIA is as corrupt as any government agency, but it provides services that are essential for maintaining national security. How can the unethical and illegal aspects of the CIA be removed without compromising national security? This matter was addressed by Q in the following post.

Nov 9 2017
[C]los[I]ng [A]ct:
Dismantled.
Impossible to clean.
Operations --> [N]o [S]uch [A]gency
Q

Is Q suggesting the CIA is being dismantled—including a long-term plan to transfer its intelligence operations to the National Security Agency? If so, it would seem CIA Director Gina Haspel has been tasked with minimizing the agency's damage while it is being downsized. Gradual downsizing would allow it to continue providing essential functions while bad actors are being removed, and operations are transferred to the NSA. At some point, will the CIA be eliminated? (I've noticed that under President Trump, the CIA has lost agents and analysts in large numbers, while the NSA has hired new employees or contractors on an almost continual basis.)

A similar downsizing has happened in the National Security Council. During the Presidency of John F. Kennedy, the National Security Council had only about a dozen members. Over the last 70 years, it became a bloated bureaucracy. In January of 2020, after his impeachment was facilitated by members of the National Security Council, President Trump decided it was time to downsize. In a matter of weeks, staffing at the NSC was cut nearly in half.

Dec 22 2017
We are moving fast.
Remember, not all within the C-A, D-J, F-I are bad apples.
House cleaning (TOP).
Restructuring (1 to 2).
Operations 24/7.
Speed.
Q

Q explained that not all employees in the CIA, DOJ, and FBI are corrupt. The biggest problems were employees occupying positions at the top of these agencies. Bad actors are being removed and replaced. At the time of this post, Q seems to have indicated that it would take one to two years to restructure these agencies. Later posts revealed that corruption was more widespread and harder to remove than anticipated.

Just before this book was published, Sean Davis of *The Federalist* wrote two articles based on information he had received from sources working inside the government. These sources told him that both FBI Director Christopher Wray and CIA Director Gina Haspel were blocking the declassification of documents that would prove embarrassing to their respective agencies or themselves personally. Q included a link to one of the articles in this post.

Sep 30 2020
https://thefederalist.com/2020/09/30/davis-cia-director-gina-haspel-is-blocking-declassification-of-remaining-russigate-documents/
Some believe the protection of Agency is what matters most.
Some believe the declassification [public exposure of truth] and rebuilding of Agency is what matters most.
Apply same to FBI.
Apply same to State.
....
Any attempt to buck the system, no matter severity of crime, and they will fight back [self-preservation].
SHADOW GAME.
Prevent public exposure of truth.
Why?
PEOPLE [UNITED] HAVE THE POWER.
◆◆◆
Q

CHAPTER 15

Red Red

SOMETIMES Q WILL POST A message that contains coded text, which he calls a stringer. In this chapter, we'll examine messages by Q that include variations of the stringer RED_RED. On November 25th, 2017, Q posted a message that was deleted from the board less than 30 minutes later. (Websites that aggregate Q's posts are generally able to display them even after they've been deleted.) A few of the abbreviations in this message can be understood, but it's impossible to know with certainty the full meaning without a decryption key. For the purposes of this discussion, I would draw your attention to the line below the second timestamp that reads: RED_RED_.

Nov 25 2017 13:30 (EST)
Deleted: Nov 25 2017 13:56 (EST)
RED_RED_
_FREEDOM-_v05_yes_27-1_z
_FREEDOM-_v198_yes_27-1_b
_FREEDOM-_v-811z_yes_27-1_c
_FREEDOM-_vZj9_yes_27-1_y
_FREEDOM-_v^CASOR-T_yes_27-1_87x

_FREEDOM-_v&CAS0R-T2_yes_27-1_t
_FREEDOM-_vEXh29B_yes_27-1_ch
_FREEDOM-_v_stand
_FREEDOM-_v_stand
_FREEDOM-_v_stand
_FREEDOM-_v_stand
_FREEDOM-_v_stand_CAN
_FREEDOM-_v1_stand
_FREEDOM-_v1_stand
_FREEDOM-_v1_stand
_FREEDOM-_v2_stand
_FREEDOM-_v3_stand
_FREEDOM-_v4_mod_D092x
_FREEDOM-_v4_mod_CAS80^
_FREEDOM-_vv1_stand
_FREEDOM-_vv2_stand
_FREEDOM-_vSHAz1EVCB_yes_27-1
_FREEDOM-_vSA_US_yes_DC08vC_EX_y_AW_Conf-go
_FREEDOM-_vSA_US_yes_DC09vC_EX_y_AW_Conf-go
_FREEDOM-_vSA_US_yes_DC10vC_EX_y_AW_Conf-go
_FREEDOM-_vSA_US_yes_DC11vC_EX_y_AW_Conf-go
_FREEDOM-_vSA_US_yes_DC12vc_EX_y_AW_Conf-go
_FREEDOM-_vSA_US_yes_DC13vC_EX_y_AW_Conf-go
_FREEDOM-_vSA_US_stand_DC14vC_EX_y_AW_Conf/stand
_FREEDOM-_vSA_US_yes_DC15vC_EX_y_AW_Conf-go
_FREEDOM-_vSA_US_yes_DC16vC_EX_y_AW_Conf-go
_FREEDOM-_vSA_US_yes_DC17vc_EX_y_AW_Conf-go
_FREEDOM-_vSA_US_yes_DC18vC_EX_y_AW_Conf-go
_FREEDOM-_vSA_US_yes_DC19vC_EX_y_AW_Conf-go
_FREEDOM-_vSA_US_yes_DC20vC_EX_y_AW_Conf-go
_FREEDOM-_vSA_US_yes_DC21vC_EX_y_AW_Conf-go
_FREEDOM-_vSA_US_yes_DC22vc_EX_y_AW_Conf-go
_FREEDOM-_vSA_US_yes_DC23vC_EX_y_AW_Conf-go
_FREEDOM-_vSA_US_yes_DC24vC_EX_y_AW_Conf-go
_FREEDOM-_vSA_US_yes_DC25vC_EX_y_AW_Conf-go
_FREEDOM-_vSA_US_stand_DC26vC_EX_y_AW_Conf/stand
_FREEDOM-_vSA_US_yes_DC27vc_EX_y_AW_Conf/term/
zJ&bY028739478-g
_FREEDOM-_vGER_US_yes_000BVx_LO_yes_[... + 1]_Conf_y

```
_Conf_4_3_good_EXT-TVB7xxj_ALL_FREEDOM_#[1-43]_
EX_27-1
Q
```

After this post was deleted, Q indicated that the 4chan board /pol/ had become unsafe due to infiltration by bad actors, and he began posting on the 8chan board /pol/. This was his first post on that board.

```
Nov 25 2017 13:54 (EST)
Test
Test
4Chan infiltrated.
Future posts will be relayed here.
Q
```

About a half-hour later, Q tried to post again on 4chan /pol/, but the message (shown below) was deleted by someone 16 minutes after it was posted.

```
Nov 25 2017 14:22 (EST)
Deleted: Nov 25 2017 14:38 (EST)
T: B, F, J, 1,5,11-20, ^
_Conf_d-ww_CON_off[dark]_
_Conf_SIL-_EX
COMM_Castle_Active_7ZbV-WT9
RED1_RED2_
SAT_40k_se_c_[30m]
Godspeed.
P_pers: WRWY
Q
```

There are two things I'd like to highlight in this post. The first is the last line, where Q wrote, P_pers: WRWY. The stringer P_pers is Q's way of indicating that a personal message has been sent from the President to the board. WRWY is an acronym that stands for "we are with you." Again, this is a personal message from the President. Another detail to note in the above post is the stringer RED1_RED2_.

A few minutes later, Q posted on 4chan /pol/ for the last time. Again, the message was deleted. Note that the stringer RED1_RED2_ appears in the post.

Nov 25 2017 14:35 (EST)
Deleted: Nov 25 2017 14:49 (EST)
_Conf_goTWIT_P_act-small#_
RED1_RED2_
Q

At this point, our discussion branches in two different directions. I'd like to first look at what seems to be evidence of Q's coordination with President Trump and his Twitter account. Observe in the above post, the stringer: _Conf_goTWIT_P_act-small#_. I want to suggest a decode for that stringer: Confirm go Twitter POTUS account "small" with #. Also, note the timestamp of 14:35, which is 2:35 pm in non-military time.

Five minutes after Q's post, the President tweeted this:

Donald J. Trump (from his Twitter account):
Happy #SmallBusinessSaturday!
A great day to support your community and America's JOB creators by shopping locally at a #SmallBiz. #ShopSmall
2:40 PM - Nov 25, 2017

Q appears to have predicted that the President would tweet about the word "small." His tweet had three hashtags containing that word. Also, Q's post contained the stringer RED1_RED2_. The President's tweet included four clipart images. One of them had a storefront with two red doors.

Now, we'll check out crumbs that lead in a different direction. On December 4th, 2017, Q posted the following message.

Dec 4 2017 22:12 (EST)
#FLYROTHSFLY#

A name with hashtags is typically used by Q when someone is about to be removed from power. "Roths" is a reference to the Rothschilds.

Twenty-six minutes later, Q posted about RED_RED, but this message had a different context than what we've discussed.

Dec 4 2017 22:38 (EST)
RED_RED
Remember?

Hussein AIDS Video.
Hidden message?
Response?
Twitter.
Roles.
Actions.
Expand your thinking.
News unlocks meaning.
Q

In November of 2017, dozens of retailers participated in a Christmas shopping promotion called "RED." On November 28th, the show *Jimmy Kimmel Live!* featured an advertisement for the RED program that benefitted the Red Cross and AIDS research. Barack Obama was featured in the show's promotional video. Notably, Obama mentioned people reacting negatively to posts on Twitter. Q suggested the video by Obama was a response to the RED_RED stringer that he posted three days earlier on November 25th. Here's a link to the video: https://www.youtube.com/watch?v=eoqYd39wkZs

Q wanted anons to make the connection between the date of his RED_RED stringer and the AIDS video by Obama.

Dec 4 2017 22:50 (EST)
Re-review RED_RED stringer.
Focus on Hussein AIDS Video.
Cross reference.
Date of stringer vs video?
Learn to decider.
News unlocks message.
Find the keystone.
Q

Eleven minutes later, Q posted again.

Dec 4 2017 23:01 (EST)
Red Cross is corrupt and used as a piggy bank.
Future topic.
Diseases created by families in power (pop control + pharma billions kb).

Think AIDS.
Future topic.
Relevant.
#FLYROTHSFLY#
Q

Q indicated that this topic would not be discussed fully until a later time but did provide some information about the Red Cross. There are many good people who volunteer their time or are employed by the Red Cross. We should be careful not to judge them unfairly. According to Q, the Red Cross is a corrupt organization, but as is often the case, the corruption is likely at the top and many people inside the organization may not be aware of it. Q implied that much of the money donated serves as a piggy bank for the world's elites. The Red Cross and agencies like it claim to fight diseases. Q said the diseases themselves are manufactured to reduce the world's population, and the medicines developed to treat them bring in billions to pharmaceutical companies and families like the Rothschilds. Q mentions this family with the hashtag #FLYROTHSFLY#. The inclusion of the Rothschilds in this post suggests that when corruption related to the Red Cross is fully exposed, it will uncover their involvement. If elites have a plan to control the world's population, an excellent way to implement it would be through organizations like the Red Cross, which the public would never suspect.

An anon posted an image of a woman holding a sign that said, "MEET ME IN SEOUL." The image appeared on the main page for the RED website.

Anonymous • Dec 4 2017
On main page of Red website.
>COINCIDENCE?

Q reposted the anon's message and replied.

Expand your thinking.
When did Hussein travel to Asia?
When was the stringer released?
When was the RED video taped?
Do you believe in coincidences?
Q

An anon replied.

Anonymous
Q pointed out the picture on the RED.ORG site with the Korean woman pointing to "Meet Me In Seoul" Obummer goes to China, did he go to Seoul too?

In the post below, an anon included a link to an article dated October 3rd, 2017, which explained the difficulties South Korea has had in discussing unification with North Korea. The anon included a quote from the article that mentioned the Red Cross.

Anonymous • Dec 4 2017
South Korea calls North Korea daily:

"The ministry has to keep pestering Pyongyang over the military and Red Cross talks," he said. "It has to keep placing calls on the Panmunjom telephone. The situation can quickly change and North Korea could feel the need for dialogue. When they do return, they will likely want to deal with the United States first, but let them try to accomplish anything in talks with Washington without the involvement of Seoul — it won't work."

https://www.bloomberg.com/news/articles/2017-10-03/north-korea-tension-sidelines-south-s-unification-ministry

Q responded.

RED CROSS RED RED.
NK.
Hussein.
ASIA.
Why was that STRINGER sent out?
Decode.
News unlocks message.
Future proves past.
Where is the RED CROSS?
Runs deep.
Children.

Pray.

Q

The next day, Q posted again about Red Red.

Dec 5 2017
RED RED 9/11.
Funds raised vs distributed?
Oversight?
7/10 plane crashes are targeted kills.
Those in the know never sleep.
Q

Some may have a hard time believing the Red Cross is corrupt. But an online search for "Red Cross fraud," "Red Cross corruption," or "Red Cross scandals" brings up numerous results from a variety of news outlets. For example, the Red Cross made an apology for losing 5 million dollars in donor funds due to fraud and corruption during West Africa's Ebola epidemic.

Q suggested the Red Cross does not properly distribute the money it receives and lacks financial accountability and oversight. In November of 2001, the U.S. House Energy and Commerce Committee's oversight panel held a hearing where it questioned outgoing Red Cross President Dr. Bernadine Healy about the agency's finances. The Red Cross raised more than 564 million dollars for its Liberty Fund, which was set up in response to the attacks on the World Trade Center and the Pentagon. Although the Red Cross stated on their website that they spent more than any other relief agency responding to the terrorist attacks, at the time, they had distributed only 154 million dollars of the money they received. Some of the money intended by donors to go to the relief of victims was put in a long-term fund.

Senator Chuck Grassley has been battling the Red Cross for decades over its unwillingness to provide required financial information to Congress. The more he tries to uncover the details of the Red Cross's inner workings, the more roadblocks they erect to obtaining information. The post above contains an ominous message—the suggestion that 70 percent of plane crashes are targeted kills of people who need to be silenced.

John Perkins' book, *Confessions of an Economic Hitman*, spent 70 weeks on *The New York Times* bestseller list. In a recent interview, Perkins said,

"Private plane crashes are the best way to assassinate someone if you ever decide you want to do that." Perkins claims to have played a role in the alleged economic colonization of Third World countries on behalf of a cabal of corporations, banks, and the U.S. Government.

> Dec 5 2017 00:31 (EST)
> RED Haiti.
> Children.
> $
> Since POTUS elected what changed w/ RED?
> Since POTUS elected what changed w/ CF?
> Since POTUS elected what changed w/ Mc_I?
> These people deserve ....
> Q

Q seems to have suggested that the Red Cross operations in Haiti covered up child trafficking, from which corrupt people profited. After Donald Trump was elected, according to Q, the operations of nonprofits like the Red Cross, the Clinton Foundation, and the McCain Institute have changed.

A few minutes later, Q posted again.

> Dec 5 2017 00:45 (EST)
> RED RED stringer 25th.
> Hussein RED video 27th (response).
> Hussein in Asia on 28th post stringer.
> Analyze.
> Coincidence?
> More than one meaning.
> Hussein RED Indictments variables.
> Think circle.
> Expand your thinking.
> Take multiple paths.
> One connects to another.
> Learn to read the map.
> The map is the key.
> Find the keystone.
> What holds everything together?
> Q

Q posted the RED_RED stringer on November 25th. The RED video aired on the 27th; Obama visited Asia on the 28th. It seems that the stringer posted on the 25th was a shot across the bow—a warning that criminal activity in Asia related to the Red Cross had been uncovered. The phrase "Hussein RED Indictments variables" makes me wonder if sealed indictments exist pertaining to Obama and the Red Cross. If so, his trip to Asia may have been to conduct damage control.

Q indicated that this topic would be discussed in more detail at a later time. If and when more information is provided, it will be examined in a future volume.

CHAPTER 16

DEFCON

IN THIS CHAPTER, WE'LL PULL together a handful of cryptic posts by Q and see if they communicate a coherent message. I would like to warn readers that understanding the details provided in this chapter will require more than the usual amount of focus. Before we begin, a little background information will be helpful.

As mentioned previously, President Trump visited Asia in November of 2017. On November 3rd, 2017, Air Force One departed for Japan and landed at Joint Base Pearl Harbor-Hickam in Hawaii to refuel. According to the White House Press Pool and local news agencies, the President stayed overnight on the island. The following day, he received a classified briefing with U.S. Pacific Command leaders before visiting the USS Arizona Memorial at Pearl Harbor. He then departed for Japan. Ten days later, on November 14th, as his trip to Asia concluded, according to news reports, the President skipped a session of the 18-nation East Asia Summit at the last minute. He instead headed to Air Force One—leaving from the Philippines. Air Force One lifted off from Ninoy Aquino International Airport more than 30 minutes earlier than scheduled. While en route to Washington D.C., Air Force One landed in Hawaii for a refueling stop. That day, Q asked a few questions about the President's trip home.

Nov 14 2017 12:51 (EST)

♦♦♦

Why did POTUS depart Manila 30 min ahead of schedule?

Why is AF1 landing in Hawaii?

Does AF1 have in-air refueling ability?

Nothing is as it appears.

♦♦♦

Q hinted that a significant event happened in Hawaii, but anons did not understand the reference.

On December 23rd, 2017, Q posted the following message.

Dec 23 2017 15:22 (EST)

SEARCH crumbs: [#2]

Who is #2?

No deals.

Q

"No deals" was a promise from Q that people who occupied high places in government would not be offered plea bargains when their crimes are prosecuted. When we search posts for #2, we find that Q used that term on December 4th, 2017, to refer to former FBI Deputy Director Andrew McCabe. #2 indicates that he was second in command at the bureau.

Dec 4 2017

Have you been watching the news since Friday?

Who is Peter Strzok?

How was he compromised?

How was he paid?

Who is Melissa Hodgman?

Company?

Title?

Date of promotion?

Focus on the date.

What events re: Peter recently occurred that you now know?

Think HRC emails, Weiner laptop, etc.

Dates?

Date of promotion of wife?

How do they stack the deck?
Who do they want inside the gov't?
What are puppets?
How do you control a puppet?
#2 in FBI?
Wife connection?
What is a pattern?
Follow the wives.

♦♦♦

As the Mueller investigation of Donald Trump and his associates progressed, members of Mueller's team, like FBI agent Peter Strzok, were removed from the investigation when it was revealed that they had conflicts of interest. Strzok's wife, Melissa Hodgman, worked for the Securities and Exchange Commission and was promoted in 2016 to associate director around the time Strzok participated in the Bureau's investigation of Donald Trump. Q implied that corrupt FBI employees are controlled (and sometimes compensated) through their wives.

Virginia Governor Terry McAuliffe is an influential Democrat with longstanding ties to Bill and Hillary Clinton. Campaign finance records show that McAuliffe's political-action committee donated $467,500 to the 2015 state Senate campaign of Jill McCabe, the wife of Andrew McCabe. The Virginia Democratic Party—over which Mr. McAuliffe exerts significant control—donated an additional $207,788 worth of support to her campaign. That adds up to more than $675,000 donated by entities either directly under Mr. McAuliffe's control or influenced by him. There is a hint by Q that McCabe may have been compensated for his efforts to investigate President Trump through donations to his wife's campaign.

Looking at the timestamp of Q's December 23rd post about #2 (Andrew McCabe), we find that the President tweeted about McCabe five minutes after Q posted.

Donald J. Trump (from his Twitter account):
How can FBI Deputy Director Andrew McCabe, the man in charge, along with leakin' James Comey, of the Phony Hillary Clinton investigation (including her 33,000 illegally deleted emails) be given $700,000 for wife's campaign by Clinton Puppets during investigation?
3:27 PM - 23 Dec 2017

An anon posted the text of the President's tweet on the board and Q responded.

> Who posted first?
> [#2].
> Q

Based on the timestamps, Q posted about Andrew McCabe (#2) five minutes before the President tweeted about him. Q then posted the following message, which included reposts of his previous message about #2 and the President's tweet about McCabe.

> Dec 23 2017
> Side-by-side graphic?
> Locate and create.[:22]
> SEARCH crumbs : [#2]
> Who is #2?
> No deals.
> Q
> [:27]
> How can FBI Deputy Director Andrew McCabe, the man in charge, along with leakin' James Comey, of the Phony Hillary Clinton investigation (including her 33,000 illegally deleted emails) be given $700,000 for wife's campaign by Clinton Puppets during investigation?
> [5]
> Previous also logged in graphic form [10] + others?
> Timestamps important.
> Countdown?
> Markers.
> Q

In the above message, where Q copied his previous post and the President's tweet, he asked anons to create a side by side graphic showing the timestamps of the two posts as visual proof. At [22] minutes after the hour, Q posted about #2 (Andrew McCabe). At [27] minutes after the hour, the President tweeted about Andrew McCabe. The time interval between their posts (sometimes called a "delta") was five [5] minutes. Q noted that previous posts had graphics with an interval of ten [10] minutes. The time intervals of 5 and 10 serve as a countdown. Thus, we might expect shorter and longer time intervals in the future. (For ease of reference, timestamps for the posts that follow in this chapter will be displayed in non-military format and in the Eastern time zone of the U.S.)

In the early morning hours of January 7th, 2018, Q posted the following message.

> Jan 7 2018 3:28 am
> We will never lose again win this is finished.
> Q

Note that the word "when" was misspelled "win." At 9:21 pm, President Trump tweeted a quote from *New York Post* columnist Michael Goodwin. Note that Goodwin's name ends in "win."

> **Donald J. Trump** (from his Twitter account):
> "His is turning out to be an enormously consensual presidency. So much so that...there has never been a day that I wished Hillary Clinton were President. Not one. Indeed, as Trump's accomplishments accumulate, the mere thought of Clinton in the W.H., doubling down on Obama's.....
> 9:21 PM - 7 Jan 2018

Trump misspelled the word "consequential" in his tweet and instead wrote "consensual." Note that the misspelling omitted the letter "q."

Fifteen minutes later, the President posted a second tweet to finish the quote by Goodwin.

> **Donald J. Trump** (from his Twitter account):
> ....failed policies, washes away any doubts that America made the right choice. This was truly a change election, and the changes Trump is bringing are far-reaching and necessary.' Thank you Michael Goodwin! (Please read entire column) mgoodwin@ nypost.com"
> 9:36 PM - 7 Jan 2018

Shortly after 10:00 pm, Q posted again. Note the name Goodwin and the number 15 in brackets. Also, note the word "win" is in brackets twice.

Jan 7 2018 10:05 pm
Good[win]
[win]/when
[15]
Q

Four minutes later, Q posted again. Note the word DEFCON and 15-10-5. Also, note the number 1 is in brackets with the abbreviation SIG.

Jan 7 2018 10:09 pm
LOCK: 15-10-5
DEFCON [1]
[1] SIG
Q

Using what we've learned from the previous post and Q's hint at a countdown, we might expect to see one, five, ten, and 15-minute intervals related to this post by Q and the President's tweet. And in fact, there was a 15-minute interval between the President's two tweets about Michael Goodwin's article and a five-minute interval between Q's post and the President's tweet about Andrew McCabe.

DEFCON is an acronym for Defense Condition. It's a rating used by the U.S. military to rate perceived threats. It prescribes an alert condition on a scale from 1 through 5, with DEFCON 5 being the lowest state of alert and DEFCON 1 being the highest. In some cases, it's used to assess the relative threat of nuclear war.

An anon responded and noted the 15-minute interval between the first and second tweets by the President. The anon also noted the addition of the letter "Q" in the misspelled word.

Anonymous • Jan 7 2018 10:09 pm
time btw trump tweets today 15

conseQuential —> consensual

Q replied a minute later.

Jan 7 2018 10:10 pm
Do you believe in coincidences?

[2] Q Chapters.
Q

Eight minutes later, Q posted again.

Jan 7 2018 10:18 pm
DEFCON 1
4-10-20
FIRE & FURY
(9) states of CLAS-ready go-live.
(34) commands LIVE.
CODES command ACTION.
[non-nuclear].
[1] OWL [1]
Q

Let's look at a few points mentioned in the above two posts. "[2] Q chapters" refers to an unauthorized copy of the book *Fire and Fury* by Michael Wolf, which was posted by *WikiLeaks* on their Twitter account the same day. The PDF version of the book had two chapter title pages with spelling errors. In both cases, the letter Q was inserted where it did not belong.

Note in the second above post, Q wrote DEFCON 1 (the highest state of alert) but also indicated the subject was non-nuclear. It seems, in this instance, the word DEFCON was intended to draw attention to something important. The numbers 4-10-20 suggest that this post was related to Donald Trump, whose initials are DJT. (When numbers are substituted for letters, the result is 4-10-20.)

Five minutes later, at 10:23 pm, after deleting his first tweet about Michael Goodwin's article, the President posted another tweet with the correct spelling of the word "consequential," along with a second tweet, one minute later, that finished the quote.

Donald J. Trump (from his Twitter account):
"His is turning out to be an enormously consequential presidency. So much so that, despite my own frustration over his missteps, there has never been a day when I wished Hillary Clinton were president. Not one. Indeed, as Trump's accomplishments accumulate, the mere thought of...
10:23 PM - 7 Jan 2018

Donald J. Trump (from his Twitter account):
...Clinton in the WH, doubling down on Barack Obama's failed policies, washes away any doubts that America made the right choice. This was truly a change election — and the changes Trump is bringing are far-reaching & necessary." Thank you Michael Goodwin!
10:24 PM - 7 Jan 2018

Three minutes later, Q posted again.

Jan 7 2018 10:27 pm
P_pers: [1] Confirmed.
_ACTION_DBF5Cz-BSY-1_y
FOR GOD & COUNTRY.
SKY FORTRESS ENGAGED>
Q

As mentioned previously, P_pers is Q's way of indicating that a personal message has been sent from the President to anons on the board. In this post, note that the number 1 is in brackets, and Q indicated that it is confirmed. This is a reference to the one-minute interval between the President's second set of tweets. Q often reminds anons that this operation is for God and country. What do you suppose "SKY FORTRESS ENGAGED" might mean?

Q then posted this message.

Jan 7 2018 10:44 pm
Original [15] min
DEFCON [1] CONF
Revised [1] min
Coincidence?
Q

As we decode Q's shorthand, we find that he pointed out that the original time interval between the President's two tweets about Michael Goodwin was 15 minutes. The interval between the second pair of corrected tweets (after anons were alerted to them) was one minute, which seems to have been predicted by Q.

A minute later, Q posted again.

Jan 7 2018 10:45 pm
Original missing "Q"
Revised including "Q"
Coincidence?
Q

Q then posted the following messages.

Jan 7 2018 10:46 pm
WE ARE TALKING DIRECTLY TO THIS BOARD.
LEARN OUR COMMS.
Q

Jan 7 2018 10:49 pm
Marker [1] Confirmed.
Confirmed: 15, 10, 5, 1
[0]
Q

Jan 7 2018 11:01 pm
IMPORTANT:
Do you understand what just occurred?
POTUS Tweets [15 min] between.
POTUS missing "Q" in select word.
DEFCON [1] POST HERE
POTUS mods Tweets [1 min] between.
POTUS adds "Q" in select word.
This was not meant to signify AUTH / established.
This is to train you how to understand the correlation between posts and Tweets.
Future proves past.
Wind the CLOCK.
The CLOCK and the GRAPHIC are ESSENTIAL.
Feel privileged - POTUS just spoke to this board [P_pers]
We serve at the pleasure of the President.
Q

An anon responded.

Anonymous • Jan 7 2018
Thank you for confirmation so that we may move fwd with
established comms.

Q replied.

Graphic form for each correlation a MUST.
This will be the AUTH tool you use when all of this becomes public
to provide friends, family, others.
Do you think POTUS re-tweeted MAGA PILL for no reason?
We chose this BOARD for a very specific reason.
We believe in you.
Q

Q told anons that creating graphics was important for disseminating
information to others. He asked why would POTUS retweet the MAGA
PILL Twitter account. The retweet in question contained a link to a website that lists the President's accomplishments, along with information
about public corruption. After Trump retweeted this account, media
outlets published articles accusing him of retweeting a conspiracy theory
website. Because Q mentioned DEFCON in this post, some people were
concerned about the possibility of a nuclear attack. The following day,
Q posted this.

Jan 8 2018
DEFCON does not refer to Defense r Condition w/ regards to prev
post.
Thought clear.
Now crystal clear.
Q

In the context of Q's posts and the President's tweets, DEFCON did not
refer to defense condition. It was Q's way of bringing anons to attention.
However, less than a week later, on the morning of January 13th, 2018,
a missile alert was issued by Hawaii's Emergency Alert System over television, radio, and cellphones. The alert stated that there was an incoming
ballistic missile threat to Hawaii, it advised residents to seek shelter, and

stated: "This is not a drill." For 38 minutes, millions of people thought their world was coming to an end. The alert turned out to be false. There was no incoming missile, at least according to authorities who spoke on the record. The alert was attributed to an operator who was said to have been confused about whether the alert was for a drill or for a real threat.

The day after the missile alert, Q posted this.

Jan 14 2018
Side_by_Side (graphic form):
BDT/False Flag posts vs actual news of bomb attempt (NYC)_
DEFCON 1 posts vs H scare_
[2] above represent PRIMARY indicators.
SEC indicators = Posts:Tweets:Time
REMAINDER below.
START HERE.
WILL GUIDE.
Q

Q mentioned two events and his advanced warnings about them. He asked anons to create side by side graphics showing his posts with dates and timestamps along with news articles about the related events. "BDT/false flag" refers to an event foreshadowed by Q in December of 2017.

Dec 10 2017
Blunt & Direct Time.
Adam Schiff is a traitor to our country.
Leaker.
NAT SEC.
EVIL.
Tick Tock.
Hope the $7.8mm was worth it.
Enjoy the show.
Q

On its face, the post appeared to be about California Representative Adam Schiff, and Q listed several accusations against the congressman. The following day, Q posted again, suggesting that the phrase "Blunt & Direct Time" had a double meaning.

Dec 11 2017
Do you believe in coincidences?
"Blunt & Direct Time"
BDT.
Think currency.
Think fireworks.
Thwarted.
Message delivered.
These people are sick!
Q

The day of this post, a pipe bomb was detonated in a New York tunnel by a Bangladeshi terrorist. The phrase "Bangladeshi terrorist" could be abbreviated BDT. The currency of Bangladesh is the taka, which can also be abbreviated BDT. In the same way that "Blunt & Direct Time" had more than one meaning, Q's warning about DEFCON had at least two meanings. The immediate application was to the January 7th tweets by the President quoting Michael Goodwin and the corresponding posts by Q. Another application related to the following week's missile alert for Hawaii (H scare). One reason Q uses double meanings is to frustrate enemies who use artificial intelligence (sniffer) programs to interpret his posts.

Feb 11 2018
Double meanings work well against sniffers.
Q

On March 8th, an anon asked why Air Force One stopped in Hawaii on the President's return trip from Asia.

Anonymous • Mar 8 2018
Why the stop in Hawaii after? That still makes me wonder!

Q replied.

DEFCON, No Such Agency.
We knew.
How did we know?
Who did WE meet?

Need to know kept to 5 people + special SEC detail.
Future proves past.
Q

It seems that on his return trip from Asia in November of 2017, the President stopped in Hawaii to be briefed by the NSA about the missile incident that would not happen until January of 2018. That leads me to wonder whether there actually was an inbound missile and the threat was neutralized by the military. Perhaps that's what Q referred to by SKY FORTRESS ENGAGED on January 7th when he posted that message six days prior to the Hawaiian missile alert .

CHAPTER 17

North Korea

NEXT, WE'LL EXAMINE WHAT Q has said about North Korea. A number of factors make this subject tricky to understand. Because North Korea has isolated itself from the rest of the world, it is hard to find reliable information on its history or current events through open source publications. (I suspect the limited availability of information is by design. I'll share more thoughts on that shortly.) A second reason for the difficulty is that Q's hints are obscure, and they pertain to many separate but related subjects. All of them must be collected and analyzed together if we are to take in the big picture. At first glance, some of these posts and some of my observations may not seem relevant, but I would ask you to read them through as the relevance will become apparent in time.

I deliberately left out of this chapter many clues I had uncovered because I wanted to focus on the most important subjects and avoid unnecessary rabbit trails. If all the clues and proofs about North Korea provided by Q were fully examined, they would fill an entire book. I would suggest paying close attention to the minutiae of the posts in this chapter. If you do, you may find a few surprises of your own.

On November 3rd, 2017, President Trump departed for Asia. According to the authorized White House biography written by Doug Wead, Barack

Obama warned Trump that his greatest challenge as President would be North Korea. Obama all but assured him he would face the prospect of nuclear war with the hermit kingdom. When Trump asked Obama if he had attempted to communicate with North Korea's leader, Kim Jong-un, Obama said he had not, adding that Kim wouldn't listen even if he had tried to reason with him. Rather than avoid confrontation with North Korea, President Trump chose to open a communication channel with Chairman Kim. Much to the dismay of pundits and the media, Trump incited a war of words with Kim through his Twitter account.

Donald J. Trump (from his Twitter account):
North Korean Leader Kim Jong Un just stated that the "Nuclear Button is on his desk at all times." Will someone from his depleted and food starved regime please inform him that I too have a Nuclear Button, but it is a much bigger & more powerful one than his, and my Button works!
5:49 PM - 2 Jan 2018

Two days prior to President Trump's departure, Q posted this about his visit to Asia.

Nov 1 2017

POTUS will be well insulated/protected on AF1 and abroad (specific locations classified) while these operations are conducted due to the nature of the entrenchment. It is time to take back our country and make America great again. Let us salute and pray for the brave men and women in uniform who will undertake this assignment to bring forth peace, unity, and return power to the people.

It is our hope that this message reaches enough people to make a meaningful impact. We cannot yet telegraph this message through normal methods for reasons I'm sure everyone here can understand. Follow the questions from the previous thread(s) and remain calm, the primary targets are within DC and remain at the top (on both sides). The spill over in the streets will be quickly shut down. Look for more false flags – stay alert, be vigilant, and above all, please pray.

"For God so loved the world that he gave his one and only Son, that whoever believes in him shall not perish but have eternal life. Love is patient, love is kind."

God bless my fellow Americans.
4,10,20

Apparently, an adversary had made plans to harm the President while he was overseas, but Q indicated that security measures were in place. This post closed with a signature composed of the numbers 4,10,20. Anons weren't sure what it meant, so Q gave them a hint.

Nov 2 2017
4,10,20
A,b,c,d,e......

When each number is replaced with its corresponding letter, the signature is DJT—the initials of Donald John Trump. Q posted about North Korea and Barack Obama (BO) the following day.

Nov 2 2017 01:14 (EST)
Would it blow your mind if I told you BO has been to NK and perhaps there now?
Why did his administration do little to slow their nuclear and missle capabilities?
Who feeds NK w/ strategic intel? Iran?
What deal was done with Iran under BO?
Why was the deal sealed under a top secret classification?
Why wasn't Congress notified?
Why after BO left office all of a sudden NK has nukes and the tech to miniaturize for payload delivery within the US?
What about NSA CIA DI etc all confirming tech won't be in place for 5+ years (statements made in 2016).
Why is all of this relevant and what does it tell you?
Big picture is rare.

In 2016, U.S. intelligence agencies assured us that North Korea was at least five years away from having the capability of launching a nuclear weapon that could reach a target in North America. Suddenly, after

Donald Trump was inaugurated, North Korea was believed to have that capability. Q suggested that North Korea obtained intelligence from Iran and that the Obama administration assisted with the development of Iranian and North Korean nuclear weapons programs while denying they had that capability. (In the post above, please note that the word "missile" in the second sentence is missing the letter "i." It will become relevant later in the chapter.)

Thirty-three minutes after posting the previous message, Q posted this:

Nov 2 2017 01:47 (EST)
What a coincidence the mountain that housed NK's nuclear weapons and testing collapsed. Unbelievable timing. I wonder if critically important materials as well as scientists aka the bomb makers were inside when it happened. Shocking no global news agency suspects we had nothing to do with it. Enjoy the crumbs.

Did President Trump use a classified technology to destroy North Korea's weapons facility? Why didn't previous Presidents do more to impede their development of nuclear weapons?

On November 2nd of 2017, Q posted the following message.

BIG DROP:
How did NK obtain Uranium?
How did Iran obtain Uranium?
Why did BO send billions (in cash and wire) to Iran?
Why the cash component?
Was the hostage component a cover?
For what?
Could any of the cash component be handed off to other people?
How many planes carried the cash into Iran?
Did all land in Iran?
Did all land in the same location?
Why is this relevant?
Who controls NK?
Who really controls NK?
Don't think of a single person.
Think of a powerful entity.

Why is this important?
Why are wars so important?
Who benefits?
What does hostage refer to?
Who can be held hostage and controlled by NK having miniaturized nuclear weapons?
Where is BO TODAY?
Where is VJ?
Alice & Wonderland.

Q has suggested that the bulk of the money supposedly sent to Iran was actually distributed to European leaders as bribes for their cooperation with the Joint Comprehensive Plan of Action (JCPOA), more commonly known as "the Iran deal." (This subject is covered in more detail in the first book in this series, *Calm Before the Storm.*) According to Q, North Korea and Iran obtained uranium as part of the Iran deal.

Who Controls NK?

In the above post, Q hinted that a shadowy entity secretly controlled North Korea. On November 11th, 2017, more information was provided about their identity.

Nov 11 2017
◆◆◆
Who controls NK?
Who really controls NK?
Who controls several agencies within the US, EU, and abroad?
Why is No Such Agency so vital?
Enormous scale of events currently ongoing.
Why is Russia helping to kill ISIS?
This is not easy to accept nor believe.
Crumbs make bread.
Operations active.
Joint missions underway.
The world is fighting back.
Refer back to graphic.
The Great Awakening.
Snow White.

Iron Eagle.

Jason Bourne (2016)(Dream/CIA).

Q

Q asked (twice) who controls North Korea. When a question like this is asked twice, it implies that an entity is in control that has not been revealed to the public. (Most often that entity is the CIA.) This post closes with four signatures, including the phrase "Snow White." When Q helped anons decode that signature, a *Chicago Tribune* article was found that explained that the CIA had seven supercomputers named after the seven dwarves. Q confirmed that Snow White signified the CIA. We will tentatively assert that prior to Trump's Presidency, the CIA controlled North Korea.

In the following post, Q implied that North Korea had greater nuclear capabilities than what had been publicly disclosed, including the ability to launch intercontinental ballistic missiles (ICBMs).

Nov 30 2017

What if NK had miniature nuke payload delivery in 2004?

What if NK had ICBM capability since 2009?

What if the previous tests that failed were staged?

Why would this be relevant?

Who is involved and why?

Biggest cover up in our history.

U1 - CA - EU - ASIA\NK.

Iran deal.

Russian reset.

Q

Q suggested that previous Presidents concealed North Korea's nuclear technology and that their so-called "missile failures" were staged incidents that hid their true capabilities. The goal of prior administrations was the creation of an environment favorable to nuclear war. That statement may sound irrational, but there is a logical explanation.

Many people believe the near-constant state of war around the world is a direct result of the existence of independent nation-states. They argue that nations must wage war to maintain national sovereignty. The solution they propose is to have all independent nation-states surrender their sovereignty to a single global government. Their goal is the eradication of borders between nations and the creation of a global community. That goal necessitates either the willing submission or the forced subjugation of individual nation-states. The United States has been a persistent thorn in the side of globalists. According to Q, a plan was developed to force the U.S. to surrender its sovereignty.

Barack Obama and Hillary Clinton's 2009 "Russian reset" was a necessary precursor to the sale of the North American company Uranium One to Russia. According to Q, past Presidents allowed rogue nations like North Korea and Iran to acquire nuclear weapon technology covertly. The sale of Uranium One to the Russian energy company Rosatom provided cover for the secret delivery of uranium to these nations. At a future time, a nuclear war would take place involving the U.S. that would reduce the planet's population, making control of the population easier. The devastation of war would be blamed on the existence of sovereign nations. It would provide the final argument for the elimination of borders and the creation of a global community controlled by a single entity.

Q has suggested that some American companies receive taxpayer subsidies for nefarious reasons. The following series of exchanges over several days led to the realization by anons that technology developed by SpaceX was being provided to North Korea. On December 11th and 18th of 2017, Q had mentioned the word "shutdown." On December 22nd, an anon replied.

Anonymous • Dec 22 2017 00:51 (EST)
No SHUTDOWN it seems.

Q replied.

Dec 22 2017 00:58 (EST)
Define Shutdown.
Was ATL shutdown?
Will NK be shutdown?
Who controls NK?
Leverage?
Remove leverage to capture the flag?
Capture the flag to end the rule?
End the rule of who?
Who controls NK?
TRUST.
Q

Q asked if the Atlanta International Airport (ATL) had been shut down. The answer is yes; the airport was shut down on December 17th, 2017 due to a power outage.

Four minutes later, Q posted again.

Dec 22 2017 01:02 (EST)
How did NK suddenly have miniaturized nukes upon POTUS taking office?
What was stated during Hussein's term by agencies?
How did NK suddenly obtain missle guidance cap?
What is leverage?
Define hostage.
Their last hope!
Q

Q asked how North Korea acquired missile guidance capability (cap) and suggested it was used as leverage against the United States.

An anon responded, repeating what Q said.

Anonymous
Q just said this:
How did NK suddenly have miniaturized nukes upon POTUS taking office?
What was stated during Hussein's term by agencies?
How did NK suddenly obtain missle guidance cap?
What is leverage?
Define hostage.
Their last hope!
Q

In the above post, the word "missile" was missing the second letter, "i." Also worth noting, is a missing letter "i" from the same word in a post we looked at from November 2nd. Q replied to the anon.

Why is the 'i' missing?
Q

An anon responded with a guess, and asked Q if it was correct.

Anonymous
Missile tech/guidance cap is SpaceX tech, methinks. Via Obama possibly?
Amirite q?

Q replied.

Why is EM provided BIG WW subsidies?
No subsidies = ?
Clown contribution in exchange for access code?
Why relevant?
Amazon Echo?
Google Home?
Clown contributions?
Apple Face ID Tech?
FB Face ID Tech?
Catching on?
Bombs Away.
Q

Q implied that companies like Google, Amazon, Facebook, and Elon Musk's (EM) Tesla, receive money from taxpayers, and in exchange, the CIA receives access to the data they collect.

An anon replied to Q.

Anonymous
we already knew this though.

Q responded.

Dec 22 2017
What do Clowns do w/ the access codes and tech?
Who controls NK?
Who really controls NK?
What families are protected using leverage?
Bank / Financial leverage?

NUKE strike package leverage?
Why is IRAN protected?
Why is IRAN funded by the US?
What news about IRAN broke?
Drugs?
What about WMDs?
Why did Brennan / others provide false intel re: NK capability +
IRAN Tech / NUKE DEV?
Plate full.
Have faith.
Q

Q suggested that the technology developed by tech companies and the data they collect helps the CIA operate an unlawful domestic surveillance program. Former CIA Director Brennan concealed the capabilities of rogue nations because the weapon systems of these nations were controlled by the CIA and held American presidents hostage to the agency.

Later that morning, President Trump tweeted about signing a missile defense bill.

Donald J. Trump (from his Twitter account):
Will be signing the biggest ever Tax Cut and Reform Bill in
30 minutes in Oval Office. Will also be signing a much needed
4 billion dollar missile defense bill.
10:07 AM - 22 Dec 2017

Q posted, and drew attention to the difference between two spellings of the word "missile." In the first instance provided by Q, the spelling was correct. In the second instance, the second letter "i" was omitted.

Dec 22 2017 11:12 (EST)
MISSILE.
MISSLE.
FOX THREE.
SPLASH.
AS THE WORLD TURNS.
RED_OCTOBER>
Q

The following day, an anon posted a photo of a movie set from the James Bond film *You Only Live Twice*.

Anonymous • Dec 23 2017
james-bond-you-only-live-twice-ken-adam-set-design1.jpg
Just imagine North Korea like a James Bond film, their own little bit of hell, can you imagine with the cash they have stole what they could have built on NK paychecks (they work or die, sort of free)

Q responded.

2011 Shuttle Program terminated by Hussein.
US loses space dominance.
http://www.foxnews.com/opinion/2017/08/09/obama-administration-knew-about-north-koreas-miniaturized-nukes.html
IRAN Nuke deal.
NK Nuke/Missile Tech.
SpaceX.
NASA Tech to ?
HRC SAPs (private server).
Connected.
$$$,$$$,$$$.00 (pockets).
◆◆◆
EVIL.
STUPID.
JUSTICE.
Q

Q implied that U.S. space programs were ended for a nefarious reason, and that NASA technology was supplied to rogue nations to benefit corrupt people.

There is also the mention of Hillary Clinton and SAPs. In other posts, Q suggested that Hillary, as Secretary of State under Barack Obama, sold highly classified information in the form of Special Access Programs to foreign governments, which allowed them to kill American intelligence operatives.

An anon speculated as to why the letter "i" may have been missing from Q's December 22nd missile post.

Anonymous
Q posts missing letter "i" are markers?

Q responded.

What rocket fired today?
[i]
Message sent.
Q

Q confirmed that the missing letter "i" was a marker—something that marks a detail that will become clear at a later time. An anon noted that the SpaceX Iridium rocket had launched that day.

Anonymous
Iridium?

Q confirmed the anon's guess and said further information was coming.

Future news will unlock more of the message.
Missing [i] confirmed.
Q

An anon shared his disgust at the way the Obama administration allowed the space shuttle program to languish.

Anonymous
I'm from SoCal, everybody worked their ass off to win in space, so many people that made a lot of money in the 70s till 80s, it was a dream to make your country the greatest on earth, so many dreams destroyed, a fountain of talent squashed and sold out, it really hurts, we really cried when we watched each shuttle launch and knew we did that

Q predicted the space program would make a big comeback.

Dec 23 2017
It's coming back in a big way.
Space is critical to our NAT SEC.

Was terminated for a specific reason.
Godspeed, Patriot.
Q

Q hinted that the space program was terminated to weaken the defenses of the United States. It wasn't until six months later, on June 18th, 2018, that President Trump first publicly announced his plan to create a sixth branch of the military called "Space Force." How did Q know the Trump administration would prioritize space exploration?

Later that day (December 23rd), Q posted a photo that had accompanied a news story about Eric Schmidt's visit to North Korea in January of 2013. The photo showed Schmidt and former New Mexico Governor Bill Richardson looking over the shoulders of two Korean men in uniforms who sat at a desk in front of computers. All of the men in the photo were dressed in heavy coats, and one wore a winter hat as if they were in a cold building. There was no text included with the image. A month later, on January 19th, 2018, Q posted again about Eric Schmidt and North Korea.

Jan 19 2018
♦♦♦
Who just resigned from GOOG?
Why was ES in NK?
Why was ES in NK?
What private network did ES set up in NK?
What private network did ES set up in NK?
Who else was in NK during this time?
What private email address did Hussein use while in office?
Why would the Chairman of GOOG travel to NK?
WHY WOULD NK ALLOW ACCESS TO ES?
Nothing is ever truly erased/deleted.
These people are STUPID.
DECLASS-POTUS_
THE SHOT HEARD AROUND THE WORLD.
Q

I have no direct evidence to substantiate these assertions, but here is my current theory on who controlled North Korea: Before the election of Donald Trump, it seems North Korea was under the control of the CIA, which served as a secure location where the agency could conduct its off the books (black budget) operations. Kim Jong-un was under the CIA's control. Did he force his people to complete the work the agency needed? Members of the western press may have been refused entry into the country unless they agreed to align their reporting with the agency's views. North Korean citizens had no internet access, perhaps, because much of what the CIA did there was illegal, and information about their activities had to be contained.

The National Security Agency has been the CIA's nemesis. Their ability to eavesdrop on the CIA's communications has been a persistent problem. Was Eric Schmidt acting as a CIA asset? Was he tapped to build a communications network in North Korea that would be impervious to surveillance by the NSA? What was Barack Obama's role? Did he also make trips to North Korea? Did his departures and arrivals happen in secure locations, facilitated by the CIA to avoid media coverage? Elon Musk and Tesla received taxpayer subsidies courtesy of Obama. Was SpaceX rocket technology covertly used by the CIA in their quest for space dominance? Was missile technology provided to North Korea to advance the agenda of nuclear war? If Musk had been serving the interests of the CIA under Obama, it seems he is no longer cooperating with them. President Trump has endorsed the use of private companies for space exploration and SpaceX is leading the way. That leads me to conclude that Elon Musk is now working with President Trump.

The CIA's plans came crashing down when Donald Trump was elected President. The December 21st, 2017, Executive Order on human rights abuse, human trafficking, and corruption coincided with Eric Schmidt's resignation as executive chairman of the board of Google's parent company Alphabet. Mike Pompeo's one-year term as CIA Director may have been an attempt by the President to rein in rogue agents and their black budget operations.

On February 10th, 2018, when the winter Olympic Games were being held, Q confirmed that the CIA's operations in North Korea (and other locations in Asia) had been halted.

Feb 10 2018
Clown black op sites.
Asia.
Goodbye.
Q

The following day, Q asked anons to analyze recent events to see the big picture. A notable story in the news at the time was the appearance of Kim Jong-un's sister, Kim Yo-jong, at the Olympic Games. During the opening ceremony, she stood silently next to Vice President Mike Pence.

Feb 11 2018
Ask yourself, why is NK participating in the O-games this year?
Ask yourself, why is the 'sister' w/ Pence?
Ask yourself, if controlled, how might you protect yourself and look for a way out?
Ask yourself, what is a distraction?
Ask yourself, why did Korea come together as a country v N&S?
Ask yourself, what occurred in Asia (ref pics) just prior to the O-games?
Ask yourself, what does FREED mean?
Ask yourself, do we want a WAR?
Ask yourself, who is trying to start a WAR?
Ask yourself, if a missile was launched by rogue actors, what would be the purpose?
Ask yourself, what would/should immediately start a WAR?
Ask yourself, would the PUBLIC understand the following statement: "Rogue actors (Clowns/US former heads of State) initiated a missile launch in order to 'force' the US into a WAR/ conflict against X?"
Be the autists we know you are.
Those who cannot understand that we cannot simply start arresting w/o first ensuring the safety & well-being of the population, shifting the narrative, removing those in DC through resignation to ensure success, defeating ISIS/MS13 to prevent fail-safes, freezing assets to remove network-to-network abilities, kill off COC to prevent top-down comms/org, etc etc. should not be participating in discussions.
Q

North and South Korea's participation as a unified nation in the Olympic games signified the loss of the CIA's control. The appearance of Kim's sister served as confirmation. Q noted that although Kim Jong-un had been set free from the grip of the CIA, the agency had not abandoned its plan to initiate a war. Rogue agents might set off a false flag operation and launch a missile, making it appear as if it had been launched by North Korea (or another country) in an attempt to start a war. Q closed with one of his most important exhortations to date. Evil people could not be arrested without first assuring the safety of citizens, forcing (some) corrupt politicians into retirement and replacing them, freezing the assets of power brokers, disrupting their chain of command (COC), and removing their support networks.

Watch the Water

On February 5th, 2018, Q posted a photo of Kim Jong-il (Supreme Leader of North Korea from 1994-2011) sitting next to former President Bill Clinton. The mural on the wall behind them depicted turbulent waves. The carpet they stood on had a floral design. Q discussed the details of the photo with anons and then provided clues to their symbolic meanings.

Feb 12 2018 11:35 (EST)
Flowers & Gardens.
Learn the hidden symbolism.
http://www.encyclopedia.com/humanities/applied-and-social-sciences-magazines/slave-gardens
What does a 'Flower' represent?
What does 'Deflower' represent?
Q

Four minutes later, Q responded to his previous post.

Feb 12 2018 11:39 (EST)
Think children.
Think slaves.
Think sheep.
Q

Q suggested that the scene with Kim and Bill Clinton symbolically portrayed what amounts to modern-day slavery—the abuse of children and human trafficking. One month later, Q posted the following message.

Mar 5 2018
BOOM

BOOM
     BOOM
          BOOM

An anon posted a photo of Kim Jong-un (the current Supreme Leader of North Korea) standing among five South Korean officials. Behind the men was a mural of a serene seascape at sunset. The photo was taken when South Korean officials met for the first time with Kim since his rise to power as North Korea's leader. The meeting was considered to be an important first step in establishing diplomatic relations between the United States and North Korea. Q reposted the photo and made a few observations.

Mar 6 2018 00:02 (EST)
Water.
Why is this event BIG?
What does it signify?
Why is NK out of the news?
As The World Turns.
Q

Three minutes later, Q added this comment.

Mar 6 2018 00:05 (EST)
WATCH the water.
Q

Q instructed anons to "watch the water." This statement has never been clarified by Q though many people have since tried to assign meaning to it. I suspect it was simply an admonition to expect a future event related to this meeting. An anon replied.

Anonymous
Calm. Tranquil. Setting sun. Dusk
Peaceful end to the 70 year old nightmare. No more division, no more fuse.
Setting sun of the fake half of the hermit kingdom in a tranquil manner.
Kim boy looks beaten, puffing out chest in last act of defiance.

Another anon posted a side-by-side graphic. It contained the photo of Kim Jong-il and Bill Clinton next to the newer picture with Kim Jong-un and the South Korean officials. Under it was the caption "Watch the Water."

Q responded.

> Future proves past.
> You have so much more than you know.
> Biggest intel drop in our known history.
> Q

Asia Live

In November of 2017, Q posted a photo taken from the window of Air Force One during President Trump's trip to Asia and asked anons what was below. An anon reposted the photo and asked if it was North Korea.

> **Anonymous** • Mar 6 2018
> also 111 days before monday was this
> did we decide it was north korea?

Q confirmed the anon's guess.

> Do you think the Asia live OP posted was for nothing?
> =
> Q

The abbreviation OP sometimes refers to "original post." In this instance, I believe OP stands for "operation." The "Asia live OP" was depicted by a series of photos posted by Q on February 7th, 2018. The first post contained an image of the King Tower building in Shanghai, China.

> Feb 7 2018
> :We see you (live).
> Q

Other images followed that showed cars arriving in a parking lot. Later photos of the same building showed a slightly open window with a white powder on the edges and adjacent windows. Q hinted that the powder was residue from a blast and that the images, posted in real-time, were taken while bad actors were being apprehended.

Feb 7 2018
People asked for arrests.
Gave one example.
Just because you can't see doesn't mean it's not ongoing.
Trust the plan.
Q

An anon posted a theory of what transpired in the building.

Anonymous
Q we love you. Trying to keep everyone positive. Someone in that building was arrested. The door was breached (hence the residue). Blew the window open.

Q replied to the anon's theory.

Window opened ahead of time to prevent pressure blast.
Think intel.
[Last discussion on this subject].
Q

This concludes our evaluation of the Asia live OP from February of 2018. Now we turn our attention back to the posts about North Korea.

Strings Cut

In response to Q's March 6th post about the "Asia live Op," an anon posted a news headline reporting that North Korea was willing to discuss denuclearization. Q warned anons that the issue was far from settled.

Mar 6 2018 11:30 (EST)
Wait & see.
Re_read drops - you have more than you know.
Eyes in the SKY.
SUM of ALL FEARS //\\
Q

Twenty-three minutes later, Q responded again.

Mar 6 2018 11:53 (EST)
Big news week?
Not over yet.
Q

Two days later, on March 8th, news outlets reported that President Trump would begin making plans to meet with Chairman Kim to discuss denuclearization.

An anon responded to the news.

Anonymous • Mar 8th 2018
ok here we go Anons WOW HUGE !!!!!!!! NK will meet with 45 !!!
MAGA !!

A few minutes later, Q informed anons that the President had already met with Kim.

He already did.
Think back _ NK pic(s).
Everything has meaning.
This will break the MSM.
Q

An anon posted a photo showing a window view from Air Force One that was pulled from a video that President Trump tweeted on November 14th, 2017, as he concluded his trip to Asia.

Donald J. Trump (from his Twitter account):
THANK YOU ASIA! #USA
10:39 AM - 14 Nov 2017

Q replied.

Mar 8 2018
Thank you Kim.
Deal made.

Clowns out.
Strings cut.
We took control.
Iran next.
Q

Q explained that the removal of the CIA from North Korea ended the control they exerted over Chairman Kim—metaphorically speaking, the "strings of control" were "cut." In the last line of the post, Q implied that a similar situation exists in Iran and that it is the next problem to be addressed.

An anon asked when the President first met with Kim.

Mar 8 2018
Think FORBIDDEN CITY.
POTUS never crossed the line (ground).
Do not glorify us.
We work for you.
Promises made.
Promises kept.
Q

Apparently, President Xi Jinping had arranged for Kim Jong-un to meet in secret with President Trump during his visit to the Forbidden City in China. Two days later, on March 10th, President Trump tweeted about North Korea's missile testing.

Donald J. Trump (from his Twitter account):
North Korea has not conducted a Missile Test since November 28, 2017 and has promised not to do so through our meetings.
I believe they will honor that commitment!
11:38 AM - 10 Mar 2018

An anon posted an image of the tweet.

Anonymous
I swear Trump is killing me here. HAHA He keeps putting out clues he has already talked to Kim

Q responded.

> You are learning.
> How many coincidences before it becomes mathematically impossible?
> Wait until you learn who has been talking to you here.
> Q

On March 27th, 2018, news outlets reported that Kim Jong-un had traveled by train to Beijing, China, to meet with President Xi Jinping. Regarding that trip, Q posted the following message.

> Mar 27 2018
> Why did Kim travel to China?
> Why was travel impossible in the past?
> What changed?
> What constitutes the need for a F2F meeting v. secured call?
> What US publicly traded co. previously N. Korea to establish comms?
> Think logically.
> WHY DID GOOG VISIT N KOREA?
> WHY WOULD THE FORMER CHAIRMAN & CEO [HIMSELF] OF GOOG/ALPHABET PERSONALLY ATTEND?
> Who is Sergey Brin?
> Where was Sergey born?
> Track the 'FAMILY' - IMPORTANT.
> Think COLD WAR.
> Think KGB.
> US, China, N Korea [3].
> FACEBOOK data dump?
> Who made it public?
> Who sold shares -30 days from announcement?
> You can't imagine the magnitude of this.
> Constitutional CRISIS.
> Twitter coming soon.
> GOOG coming soon.
> AMAZON coming soon.
> MICROSOFT coming soon.
> +12

Current censorship all relates to push for power [mid-terms].
LAST STAND.
Election FRAUD cases OPEN - DOJ [many].
Follow the FAMILY.
Follow resignations [Business/Gov't].
BIDEN/CHINA VERY IMPORTANT MARKER.
Who made it public?
Who really made it public?
Who is making it all public?
WE ARE THE GATEKEEPERS OF ALL [BY ALL WE MEAN ALL]
INFORMATION.
U1>CAN>EU>RUSSIA>IRAN>NK>SYRIA>PAK>>>
IRAN NEXT.
$700B - MILITARY [THIS YEAR].
WHY IS THE MILITARY SO IMPORTANT?
RE_READ ALL.
NATIONAL SECURITY.
NATIONAL SECURITY.
These people are STUPID.
Art of the Deal.
TIDAL WAVE INCOMING.
BUCKLE UP.
Q

I have no direct knowledge or evidence from which to answer all of Q's questions, but here is my hypothesis: Chairman Kim wasn't able to travel to China in the past because he was under the control of the CIA. Since the agency had North Korea's communications (set up by Eric Schmidt) under continual surveillance, Kim would need to travel to China to say anything that he did not want the agency to know.

Sergey Brin was born in the Soviet Union (Moscow) and emigrated to the U.S. with his Jewish parents in 1979. Both his mother and father were graduates of Moscow State University. Some Soviet Jews were refused exit visas during the Cold War, but the family applied in 1978 and received permission to leave the USSR in 1979. Sergey Brin was a co-founder of Google and became the president of Google's parent company, Alphabet Inc., but stepped down from that role in December of 2019. He remains a co-founder, board member, employee, and controlling shareholder of Alphabet.

Brin is a donor to Democratic Party candidates and organizations. He donated $5,000 to Barack Obama's reelection campaign and $30,800 to the Democratic National Committee (DNC). *Forbes.com* shows Brin's real-time net worth at over 65 billion dollars and reports, "The richest immigrant in America, Brin has been an outspoken critic of Trump's immigration ban." Brin was married to Anne Wojcicki, the CEO of the genetic testing company 23andMe. They separated in 2013, finalized their divorce in 2015, but still jointly run The Brin Wojcicki Foundation. Anne Wojcicki's sister Susan is the CEO of Alphabet's subsidiary YouTube.

Ann and Susan's father, Stanley Wojcicki, was a physicist. He worked at the Lawrence Berkeley National Laboratory and was a National Science Foundation fellow at CERN. He served as chair of the Stanford University Department of Physics. He headed the High Energy Physics Advisory Panel, which advises the United States Department of Energy and the National Science Foundation on particle physics matters.

Q has suggested that Facebook monitors its users' communications and location data, and supplies that information to the CIA, circumventing domestic surveillance laws. In a number of posts, Q has indicated that this illegal arrangement will eventually be exposed (which may be why Facebook executives sold large amounts of the company's stock). Twitter, Google, Facebook, and other tech companies are currently under investigation by the Department of Justice.

Election fraud is a necessary tactic for bad actors who hope to remain in power. Q said the DOJ has many current open investigations into election fraud (at the time of this post in 2018). The discovery that former Vice President Joe Biden facilitated his son Hunter's relations with the Chinese government may expose a pattern of corrupt practices by politicians and their families. Ukrainian law enforcement officials and the U.S. Congress are currently investigating allegations of corruption involving the Biden family.

It is my belief that Q's team is comprised mostly of military personnel, including NSA staff. If so, that would explain Q's claim that they are the gatekeepers of all information, since the NSA gathers virtually all electronic communications on the planet. Now that the strings of control have been cut between the CIA and North Korea, other nations that were under their control—like Afghanistan and Iran—can be freed next.

The fact that a country has been set free of the influence of the CIA does not automatically mean that the nation's leaders will make the best decisions. It means they have the *freedom* to make choices different from the ones they've made in the past, but some leaders will continue making poor choices.

After years of declining spending, it was critical to get America's military back to its former state of readiness. President Trump's negotiation with Congress to approve a 700 billion dollar military budget gave patriots the resources they needed to combat bad actors around the globe and maintain national security. Later the same day, Q provided more information about North Korea.

Mar 27 2018
What does the house cleaning represent?
We always knew.
Final stage.
What does NK represent?
Threat.
Safeguard.
Insurance.
POOF!
KIM TO CHINA REPRESENTS SOMETHING VITAL [KEY].
Many will be buried before exposed [them/self].
FF / DISTRACTIONS.
Q

Once North Korea had the capability of successfully launching and targeting a nuclear warhead, the CIA's ability to control them gave the agency leverage over the entire world. That leverage suddenly vanished when the CIA's control of North Korea was removed. The removal of control was evidenced when Kim boarded a train to Beijing, China, as reported by news agencies on March 27th, 2018.

Singapore

On May 10th, 2018, Q posted an image without text on the board /patriotsfight/. The post was a photo taken from a distance of the Gardens by the Bay Hotel in Singapore. The hotel has a 2.5-acre observation deck called the SkyPark located above the 57th floor. The SkyPark bridges all three towers of the hotel, and one segment is cantilevered off the northernmost tower. It features gardens, an infinity pool, and a public observation deck. The filename of the image was: NKSINGSEC.png.

File names sometimes contain important clues. We'll discuss the relevance of the file name shortly. I would not normally highlight the post number, but in this case, it's worth remembering. This was post number 72 on Q's read-only board /patriotsfight/.

An anon reposted Q's Singapore picture and asked a question.

Anonymous • May 10 2018
Marina Bay sands, Singapore.
IS THIS THE SKY EVENT?

That question was in response to this post from April 2018, where Q mentioned a "SKY Event."

Apr 19 2018
EO.
Treason.
Update.
Read.
Study the EOs.
Follow the 'pen'.
EOs post 'pen' pics.
Connect.
Learn.
SKY Event.
Q

EO is an abbreviation for a Presidential Executive Order, which Q asked anons to follow. Since they're signed with a pen, "follow the pen" is another instruction to track them. Q did not confirm the event in Singapore was the SKY Event, but his response provided some helpful information.

May 10 2018
Note the pictures we post are ALL originals.
Think about what that means.
Q

If you do a reverse image search on photos posted by Q in 2017 and 2018, you won't find these images posted elsewhere on the internet.

When Q doesn't post for several days, he refers to it as a "blackout" or "darkness." From May 22nd to June 3rd, 2018, Q was silent. This was his first post upon returning.

Jun 3 2018
BOOM.
 BOOM.
  BOOM.
  BOOM.
A WEEK TO REMEMBER.
DARK TO LIGHT.
BLACKOUT NECESSARY.
Q

In June of 2018, President Trump attended the G7 Summit in Quebec, Canada. On Saturday June 9th, he departed the summit earlier than expected and flew eastward from Quebec to Singapore, making a stop to refuel on the Mediterranean island of Crete, as noted by a local Greek news website *keeptalkinggreece.com*.

Air Force One landed on the island of Crete at 3:07 Sunday morning and took off 90 minutes later. On board US President Donald Trump, Secretary of State, Mike Pompeo, and several journalists. The plane landed for refueling on the Souda Naval base and took off [sic] for Singapore for the historic meeting between the US President and the North Korean leader Kim Jong Un.

According to Singapore news outlets, Air Force One touched down at Paya Lebar Air Force Base in Singapore at 8:20 pm (local time) on June 10th. Chairman Kim and the President were scheduled to meet on June 12th.

On June 10th, Q posted a photo of the Singapore skyline, which included the Gardens by the Bay Hotel. The post had no text, only an image. Q then posted the following message.

Jun 10 2018
Every single picture posted is ORIGINAL.
Pulled/Wiped or Taken.
Think about what that means.
Q

Q reposted a reply from an anon.

Anonymous • Jun 10 2018
Not necessarily from /ourguy/s...

I suspect that some of the photos posted by Q were taken by people scouting the locations that Kim Jong-un was about to visit. The NSA has access to electronic data stored on phones. If Q is with the NSA (or has access to the agency's files), it would be easy to retrieve an image from a bad actor's mobile device and post it on the board if he wanted to let them know they were being watched.

The following day, Q posted more photos from the Gardens by the Bay Hotel along with a message.

Jun 11 2018
No. 72
Where was Kim tonight?
How was this known?
You are watching a 'plan' being set in motion.
Enjoy the show.
Q

"No. 72" was a reference to post number 72 a month earlier. It was the first image Q posted of the Gardens by the Bay Hotel. As I mentioned, the filename of the image was NKSINGSEC.png. I assume this filename indicated the picture was taken from someone scouting security (SEC) for the meeting between North Korea's (NK) leader and President Trump in Singapore (SING).

In the above post, Q asked where Kim was that night. The filenames of the two images Q posted were MBS_KIM1.png and MBS_KIM2.png. MBS seems to be a reference to the Marina Bay Sands Hotel. This raises an interesting question: Did Q post images taken from Chairman Kim's phone?

An anon posted several photos along with an excerpt from an article describing Kim's sightseeing tour of Singapore that night. The images showed Kim and his entourage visiting several local attractions, including the Gardens by the Bay Hotel. A local news outlet reported that Kim and his security detail stayed at the St. Regis Hotel in the Tanglin area.

Q responded to the anon.

> Gardens by the Bay.
> See prev pic.
> Timestamp.
> Coincidence?
> Everything shown has meaning.
> You are watching a 'scripted' movie.
> Q

The post with a timestamp from May 10th that contained a photo of the Gardens by the Bay Hotel suggests that Q knew a month in advance that Kim would visit there. Q posted again.

> Jun 11 2018
> Does Kim look nervous prior to the 'BIG' meeting w/ POTUS?
> Did they already meet long ago?
> Is he preparing at his hotel w/ his advisors ahead of time?
> Or, is he out enjoying the 'FREEDOM' he never had in the past?
> Deal done?
> Safe?
> On guard?
> POTUS moves up departure - why?
> The World is Safer.
> IRAN developments...
> Q

News outlets reported that the meeting ended sooner than expected. Kim's relaxed demeanor and the fact that he and President Trump wrapped up talks early suggested their agreement had been worked out ahead of time.

Four Booms

We looked at this post previously. Now let's make some connections.

> Jun 3 2018
> BOOM.
> BOOM.

BOOM.
BOOM.
A WEEK TO REMEMBER.
DARK TO LIGHT.
BLACKOUT NECESSARY.
Q

On June 12th, an anon connected the four BOOMs from this post to four things accomplished at the meeting between President Trump and Chairman Kim. North Korea is formally known as the Democratic People's Republic of Korea, or DPRK.

Anonymous • Jun 12 2018
From the summit document... 4 BOOMS

BOOM 1: The United States and the DPRK commit to establish new U.S.-DPRK relations in accordance with the desire of the peoples of the two countries for peace and prosperity.

BOOM 2: The United States and the DPRK will join their efforts to build a lasting and stable peace regime on the Korean Peninsula.

BOOM 3: Reaffirming the April 27, 2018 Panmunjom Declaration, the DPRK commits to work toward complete denuclearization of the Korean Peninsula.

BOOM 4: The United States and the DPRK commit to recovering POW/MIA remains, including the immediate repatriation of those already identified.

Q replied.

Jun 12 2018 12:20 (EST)
What a coincidence.
4 points / 4 booms
Dark to Light 1:07
More to come.
Q

Q confirmed the anon's connections, and included the phrase "Dark to Light 1:07." Note that the June 3rd post also included the phrase "Dark to Light." An hour earlier, Q posted the message below and asked anons to view a video and note what was said at the 1:07 marker.

Jun 12 2018 11:08 (EST)
No. 100
Dark to Light.
1:07 [Marker]
https://www.youtube.com/watch?v=A838gS8nwas
Do you believe in coincidences?
Q

At the one minute, seven second mark of the linked video, the narrator says "Out of the darkness comes the light." According to news reports, President Trump showed Chairman Kim this video during their meeting. Did Q predict on the 3rd that the President would make a reference on the 12th to the phrase "Dark to Light?"

In the above post, No. 100 refers to a message by Q on June 10th which included three photos of tourist attractions in Singapore. "Blackwater on guard" is a hint that contractors from the security firm Blackwater were guarding attendees of the meeting.

Q !CbboFOtcZs No.100
Jun 10 2018
Start the Clock.
A Week to [Remember].
Think Logically.
First private [CLAS-5(6)]
Second public.
Blackwater on GUARD.
Evidence KILLS.
These people are STUPID.
Q

Misspellings Matter

Q has indicated that if we want to understand the full meaning of his messages, we must make note of the way his posts are worded.

Mar 3 2018
Where we go one, we go ALL.
Misspellings matter.
Sentence formation matters.
Learn.
Q

Typically, when Q makes a spelling error, it is noted either by anons or by Q. If it was not intentional, Q will follow up with a clarification. Below is an example.

May 30 2020
'War[e]fare' misspelling unintentional.
On the move.
Q

On June 11th, President Trump tweeted about North Korea and its missile launches. Just as Q had omitted the second letter "i" in the word "missile" on two previous occasions related to North Korea, so did the President in his tweet.

Donald J. Trump (from his Twitter account):
The fact that I am having a meeting is a major loss for the U.S., say the haters & losers. We have our hostages, testing, research and all missle launches have stoped, and these pundits, who have called me wrong from the beginning, have nothing else they can say! We will be fine!
3:04 PM - 11 Jun 2018

Q and the President both omitted the second letter "i" from the same word, which suggests coordination, especially given that Q drew his followers' attention to the spelling of this word six months earlier. This word was first misspelled (the same way) on November 2nd, 2017. Again, the context of the post was North Korea.

Nov 2 2017
Would it blow your mind if I told you BO has been to NK and perhaps there now?
Why did his administration do little to slow their nuclear and

missle capabilities?

◆◆◆

On June 12th, the day President Trump met with Kim, Q posted the following message along with a photo of a missile in flight over Whidbey Island, Washington.

Jun 12 2018
This is not a game.
Certain events were not suppose to take place.
Q

Note in the above post, the word "supposed" was misspelled. The same word was misspelled in a post from October 31st, 2017.

Oct 31 2017
◆◆◆
Was TRUMP asked to run for President?
Why?
By Who?
Was HRC next in line?
Was the election suppose to be rigged?
Did good people prevent the rigging?
◆◆◆

The letter "D" was missing from the word "supposed" and was pointed out by an anon, who also noticed that this post contained an image of George Washington crossing the Delaware River in a Durham boat.

Q responded.

Jan 28 2020
DurhamBoat.jpg
https://en.wikipedia.org/wiki/Durham_boat
Anons found the subtle hint dropped in the beginning.
Think Durham start.
Think 'Q' start.
You have more than you know.
Q

Jeff Sessions appointed John Durham U.S. Attorney for the District of Connecticut, on October 28, 2017, the same day Q began posting.

Whidbey Island Missile

After his June 12th post showing a missile in flight over Whidbey Island, anons began digging to find out what happened. News outlets reported that while looking through photos taken by a weather camera on the Kitsap Peninsula, Greg Johnson of Skunk Bay Weather spotted a photo with a mysterious object. The picture—taken at 3:56 am on June 10th—showed a bright orange vertical streak in the early morning sky over Whidbey Island. Close inspection of the photo revealed the unmistakable shape of a missile. A few news outlets attributed the image to lens flare or claimed it was a photo of a helicopter. There were many opinions circulating about this photo, but no authorities would identify the object that left a blazing trail through the sky. The most likely explanation of the photo would be the vertical launch of a missile from a submarine. Although the Navy denied any knowledge of a missile launch, Bangor Submarine base is nearby. It's the home port of submarines that carry vertically launched missiles.

Some people have mistakenly reported that the missile launch was an attempt to hit Air Force One while President Trump was in flight. One website that aggregates Q's posts had a title on several related posts to that effect. It's worth noting that Q doesn't write the titles on sites that aggregate his posts. A website administrator adds the titles, so they may not *always* accurately reflect Q's intended message. And they may be updated as more information comes to light. In this instance, we must remember the flight path Air Force One took en route to Singapore as previously outlined in this chapter:

CNN reported that the President left the G7 Summit in Quebec early in the afternoon on Saturday, June 9th.

Reluctant to participate at all in this year's G7, Trump chose ultimately to make a truncated visit, arriving behind schedule on Friday and departed before anyone else on Saturday. He made an early exit to fly directly to Singapore, where a high-stakes summit with Kim Jong Un awaits.

Source: https://www.cnn.com/2018/06/09/politics/g7-trump-climate-change/index.html

Some of the confusion lies in the fact that people assume Air Force One flew westward from Canada to Singapore when it did not. Air Force One flew eastward from Quebec on June 9th across the Atlantic Ocean to the Greek island of Crete for refueling before continuing to Singapore. Therefore, a missile launched from the Puget Sound near the Pacific Ocean on June 10th could not hit an airplane traveling eastward across the Atlantic Ocean when it had departed on June 9th.

On June 12th, the day the President met with Chairman Kim, Q posted the following message along with an image of a submarine.

Jun 12 2018
Reverse image search.
Think hack.
Comms dark.
Q

A reverse image search for the submarine photo returned a link to an article explaining how Chinese hackers stole highly sensitive weapons system information from Navy contractors. Was the missile launch the result of a foreign government or CIA hack of a weapons system?

Q provided another piece of the puzzle the next day.

Jun 13 2018
♦♦♦
Re: D OPs Hussein Hacking State Voting Sys
The TIP.
THEY MUST WIN.
AT ALL COSTS.
SR 187 DISCOVERY.
UK SIS.
C_A RUSSIA MASK HACK (SAME HAS CHINA SUB WASH - SET UP).
GOD SAVE US.
Q

I would draw your attention to the line: "C_A RUSSIA MASK HACK." Q is suggesting that the so-called "Russian hack" of the DNC files prior to the 2016 election was, in fact, a CIA operation designed to mask the identity of the person who actually gave the files to *WikiLeaks*.

The official story was that the Russian hacker Guccifer 2.0 stole the files and gave them to *WikiLeaks*. Former NSA Technical Director Bill Binney and former CIA employee Larry Johnson analyzed the metadata of the documents released by Guccifer 2.0. Binney also examined the metadata of the DNC files published by *WikiLeaks*. Their research concluded that the file transfers were consistent with data transfered to a thumb drive or a storage device rather than a Russian internet-based hack. This data alone does not prove that the emails were copied at the DNC headquarters. But it does show that the data posted by *WikiLeaks* passed through a storage device, like a thumbdrive, before *WikiLeaks* posted it on the internet.

Q has suggested that Seth Rich (SR), an IT employee with the DNC, retrieved the files and gave them to *WikiLeaks*. 187 is the California penal code for homicide and is commonly used by street gangs. SR 187 is how Q refers to the murder of Seth Rich—allegedly for leaking the files. The claim about Seth Rich being the source of the DNC leak is not meant to disparage his memory. It simply portays him as a whistleblower, who tried to expose corruption. The topic has become highly controversial and the parents of Seth Rich currently have a law suit pending against *Fox News* over their coverage of this tragedy.

The Vault 7 documents published by *WikiLeaks* exposed the CIA's UMBRAGE group and its related projects which allow the CIA to use bits of computer code collected from a known foreign source and plant the code on targeted hardware, leaving a digital fingerprint pointing to a foreign country. This tool could be used to implicate foreign nations in cyber attacks they didn't actually commit. Q implied that the CIA used this technique on the DNC server to blame Russia.

The phrase "SAME HAS CHINA SUB WASH - SET UP" implies that the same technique may have been used by the CIA to frame (SET UP) China for the unauthorized missile launch from a submarine (SUB) near Whidbey Island, which is in Washington state (WASH).

In a post that we looked at previously from February of 2018, Q foreshadowed the missile launch and explained its goal.

Feb 11 2018

◆◆◆

Ask yourself, would the PUBLIC understand the following statement: "Rogue actors (Clowns/US former heads of State) initiated a missile launch in order to 'force' the US into a WAR/

conflict against X?"

◆◆◆

The reason rogue actors could launch a missile and start a war is precisely because the public would not understand how such a thing could be possible. In August of 2018, Q explained that bad actors were desperate because President Trump would eventually release evidence of their corruption. They couldn't remove him from power, so they opted to launch a missile in an attempt to start a war.

Aug 11 2018
How do you prevent the public release of incriminating acts that would forever strip their power away?
How do you BIND the hands of POTUS?
Two-Pronged SITU.
>>Test strength of midterms through private analysis (win/loss ratio)
>>Analysis below key metric w/o chance for recovery - START A WAR.
Think missile(s) accidentally fired.
Against WHO?
Relationships are VERY IMPORTANT.
The SHARING of INFORMATION IS VERY IMPORTANT.
Q

Bad actors must try to prevent President Trump from releasing information about their crimes. One way to do that is by removing him from office. They evaluated their chances of removing him by election and calculated that this was unlikely to happen. Their other option was to launch a missile in the hope of starting a war and removing him under the 25th Amendment by accusing him of being mentally unfit.

President Trump's ability to neutralize the actions of rogue agents and stabilize international relations comes from his willingness to keep international channels of communications open. In 1962, during the Cuban missile crisis, John F. Kennedy averted war with the Soviet Union through the diplomatic use of backchannel negotiations. In a similar way, President Trump may one day sign a denuclearization agreement with North Korea (and perhaps other nations) because of his willingness to use backchannels.

Dec 19 2019

Backchannels are important.

Know your history and you will know why.

Q

ABOUT THIS SERIES

Q Chronicles is a series that explores the topics and signatures of Q as well as news relevant to the "Great Awakening."

ABOUT THE AUTHOR

Dave Hayes is a teacher, public speaker, and author. He has written more than a dozen books on faith and the spiritual life under the pen name Praying Medic.

GLOSSARY

Because Q's posts include terms you may not be familiar with, I've provided a glossary to help decode abbreviations, acronyms, symbols, names, and agencies. The decodes I've provided are not to be taken as the only possible correct ones. There are, no doubt, valid decodes I have not considered and have not included. Some abbreviations have been confirmed by Q to have multiple meanings. As Q's mission continues, some abbreviations that have been used in one way may later be used in a different way. In such cases, the context of a particular post should be used to determine the best interpretation. The terms in this glossary are not exclusive to posts found in this book. They pertain to the entirety of Q's operation to date.

Note: names and initials are alphabetized as they appear in Q posts which is usually the first name followed by the last name.

/calmbeforethestorm/ or **/CBTS/** — An 8chan board where Q has posted messages.

/greatawakening/ or **/GA/** — A read-only board on 8chan where Q has posted.

/patriotsfight/ or **/pf/** — An 8chan board where Q has posted messages.

/pb — Previous Bread. A term indicating that a current post refers to a message found in a previous thread (or in the vernacular of anons, a previous bread).

/pol/ — Boards on 4chan and 8chan where Q has posted messages.

/projectdcomms/ — A read-only board on 8kun where Q posts.

/qresearch/ — Boards on 8chan and 8kun where anons can interact with Q.

/thestorm/ — An 8chan board where Q has posted messages.

/_ — A three-sided shape used by Q to illustrate the power structure of the three wealthiest and most politically influential families in the world; the Saudi royal family (removed from power in 2017) the Rothschilds, and George Soros. Q's mission involves the gradual removal of all three sides of the triangle, representing the removal of these families from power.

@jack — Jack Dorsey, who is the CEO of Twitter, a social media platform, and the CEO of Square, a mobile payment processing company.

#2 — Andrew McCabe, Deputy Director of the FBI from February 2016 to January 2018. Later, McCabe became Acting Director of the FBI briefly—May 9th to August 2nd, 2017—after Director James Comey was fired, but McCabe then returned to his Deputy Director position until he was fired by Jeff Sessions in March of 2018.

#FLY# — Q uses the word FLY along with a name and pound sign (#) to indicate a person whose influence has been neutralized or a politician who has been removed from office.

#FlyCoatsFly# — Signified the removal of Dan Coats as President Trump's Director of National Intelligence.

#FLYJOHNNYFLY — Signified the resignation of John Conyers from the United States Congress.

##FLYMAYFLY## — Signified the announcement by Teresa May that she would step down as the Conservative party leader and Prime Minister of the UK.

#FLYROTHFLY# — Signified the reduction of political influence by the Rothschild family.

#FLYSIDFLY# — Two possibilities. This may have signified the end of Arizona Senator John Sidney McCain's time as a U.S. Senator, or it may signify the removal of the influence of Sidney Blumenthal, a trusted associate of Hillary Clinton.

#FLYALFLY# — Signified the resignation of Al Franken from the U.S. Senate.

#FLY[RR]FLY# — Signified the resignation of Rod Rosenstein as U.S. Deputy Attorney General.

[] — Brackets indicate different things depending on the context. Q answered an anon's inquiry by indicating that brackets signified a "kill box" but sometimes brackets are used to highlight letters that spell out a message hidden within a post, for example, [p], [r], [a], [y]. Brackets can also be used to disrupt computer programs used by opponents that search Q's posts for key words.

[30] — A time interval, typically 30 days or one month. In some cases, it will signify 31 or 28 days, depending on the number of days in the month.

[93 dk] — 93 dark seems to be a prediction of the 93 days between August 1st and November 2nd of 2019 that Q would not post after 8chan went offline and before its replacement, 8kun, went live.

[C] — Multiple meanings. Often used to indicate the CIA in the term AB[C]. Occasionally, it signifies former Director of National Intelligence Dan Coats or former FBI Director James Comey. It has also been used to signify COVID. In one instance, it refers to classified documents, and in another it appears to indicate the Ted Cruz's 2016 presidential campaign.

[D] — Two possible decodes. Often used to signify members of the Democratic party. Sometimes signifies declassification of documents.

[E] — Gate E at Terminal 2 in Shanghai Pudong International Airport (PVG).

[F] — Foreign

[R] — Several meanings. Used once to refer to the Republican party, and once to refer to the name Rothschild. Used multiple times to indicate Barack Obama, whose Secret Service code name was "Renegade." Obama was referred to by the single letter R in text messages between former FBI employees Lisa Page and Peter Strzok.

[T2] — Terminal 2 at Shanghai Pudong International Airport (PVG).

(6+) — George Soros, a hedge fund billionaire who is known for using his wealth to fund his own brand of political activism. Recipients of his philanthropy appreciate his money, but those who oppose his political views see him as a creator of chaos around the world, and a destabilizing force on economies and societies. Some countries have either banned Soros or restricted his organizations from operating within their borders. These countries include Pakistan, Poland, Turkey, Russia, Soros' home country of Hungary, and the Philippines. The Israeli government has said Soros is not welcome there.

(6++) — The Rothschilds, an influential banking family that exerted economic and political influence over Europe during the 18th and 19th centuries and over the world during the 20th and 21st centuries.

(6+++) — Saudi Arabia, a nation ruled by a hereditary monarchy—the House of Saud. The king serves as head of state and the head of the government.

(You) — When viewing posts on 4chan, 8chan, or 8kun, the word "you" is displayed in parenthesis to indicate that you are viewing your own post.

+ — George Soros, a hedge fund billionaire who is known for using his wealth to fund his own brand of political activism. Recipients of his philanthropy appreciate his money, but those who oppose his political views see him as a creator of chaos around the world—a destabilizing force on economies and societies. Some countries have either banned Soros or restricted his organizations. These countries include Pakistan, Poland, Turkey, Russia, Soros' home country of Hungary, and the Philippines. The Israeli government has said Soros is not welcome there.

++ — The Rothschilds, an influential banking family that exerted economic and political influence over Europe during the 18th and 19th centuries and over the world during the 20th and 21st centuries.

+++ — Saudi Arabia, a nation ruled by a hereditary monarchy—the House of Saud. The king serves as head of state and the head of the government.

*** — Three asterisks, or three stars, signifying retired Lieutenant General Michael Flynn. In the U.S. Army and some other branches of the military, a lieutenant general is a three-star general officer.

1+1 = 2 or 2 + 2 = 4 — When the facts of a story as reported don't add up or make sense, Q will use a math equation to suggest that the facts must be carefully evaluated or interpreted logically.

4-10-20 — Initials of Donald John Trump when the numbers are replaced with the corresponding letters of the alphabet.

4chan — An internet message board where users can post anonymously.

5:5 — "Five by five" is military jargon signifying loud and clear, or understood. Radio transmissions are rated for signal clarity and strength on a scale from 1-5 with 1 being the lowest and 5 being the highest. 5:5 indicates the signal is loud and clear.

5 Eyes or Five Eyes or FVEY   A multilateral intelligence-sharing alliance that includes Australia, Canada, New Zealand, the United Kingdom and the United States.

7 Dwarves — According to the Michael Kilian article Spy vs. Spy published in 2000 by *The Chicago Tribune*, the CIA has seven supercomputers named after the seven dwarves; Doc, Dopey, Bashful, Grumpy, Sneezy, Sleepy and Happy.

7th Floor — There are two possible decodes. According to an October 17th, 2016 article published by *The New York Post*, "The 7th Floor" was a group of U.S. State Department officials who met regularly on the 7th floor of the Harry S. Truman Building in Washington, D.C. The group's activities came to light in the fall of 2016 and appeared to have formed in support of Hillary Clinton during her email investigation. The FBI referred to them as the "shadow government" inside the State Department, which briefly attracted the attention of mainstream media. Most, if not all, members were terminated by Rex Tillerson in February of 2017. Depending on context, "7th Floor" can represent the upper echelon of the FBI.

8chan — An internet message board where users can post anonymously.

8kun — An internet message board where users can post anonymously. Created in 2019 after 8chan was deplatformed.

11.3 — The date of November 3rd. There is a second decode. The initials "KC" when the numbers are replaced with the corresponding letters of the alphabet. KC represents Kevin Clinesmith, the former FBI attorney who was the first person to be indicted and plead guilty in John Durham's investigation of the FISA applications submitted to surveil Carter Page.

11.4 — The date of November 4th.

15-10-5 or [5] [10] [15] — Q and the President occasionally post with predetermined time intervals (deltas) between their posts. In this case, Q had posted within five minutes of the President, and anons caught it. Q was directing them to find two past posts where the President tweeted a message 10 and 15 minutes from the time of his post.

44 — Barack Obama, the 44th President of the United States.

187 — California penal code for murder. Often found in criminal gang tattoos.

302 — An FD-302 form is used by FBI agents to summarize the interviews they conduct. A 302 contains information from the notes taken during the interview by the non-interviewing agent (there are supposed to be at least two agents present, one to interview and one to take notes).

470 Investigators — Department of Justice Inspector General Michael Horowitz is reported to have a staff of 470 investigators, attorneys and other personnel. Horowitz is coordinating with U.S. Attorney John Huber, giving Huber access to a staff considerably larger than that of a Special Counsel

702 — Section 702 of the Foreign Intelligence Surveillance Act. "This authority allows only the targeting, for foreign intelligence purposes, of communications of foreign persons who are located abroad."

2020_P election +1 — Q's way of indicating the day after the 2020 presidential election or November 4th, 2020.

A321 — The Airbus A321 is a member of the Airbus A320 family of short-to medium-range, narrow-body, commercial passenger twin-engine jet airliners manufactured by Airbus.

A or A's — Agency, agencies, intelligence agencies.

Adam Schiff — Democrat representative from California, and Chair of the House Select Committee on Intelligence.

Adm R — Admiral Michael Rogers, Director of the National Security Agency from 2014 to 2018. Rogers is a former U. S. Navy Admiral who served as the second commander of the U.S. Cyber Command.

ADV — Advantage

AF1 — Air Force 1, the call sign designator for the airplane in which the President of the United States travels, regardless of which particular airplane it happens to be.

AG — U.S. Attorney General

Agnes Nixon — TV soap opera pioneer who created the shows *One Life to Live* and *All My Children.*

AJ — Alex Jones, founder of InfoWars, a conservative media outlet operated by Free Speech Systems LLC.

AL — Senator Al Franken, who formerly represented the state of Minnesota, but resigned in 2017 after multiple women accused him of sexual impropriety and unwanted advances.

Alan — Alan Dershowitz, a lawyer, author, and Harvard law professor. Although he is a registered Democrat, Dershowitz has supported President Trump against those who have criticized him.

Alice — Hillary Clinton, as she was referred to in emails from Marty Torrey (published by *WikiLeaks*), who went by the moniker "Hatter."

Alice and Wonderland — A signature phrase that Q helped anons decode. Alice is Hillary Clinton. Wonderland is Saudi Arabia. Q says Saudi Arabia has been the source of funding for many U.S. politicians.

Alphabet — The parent company of Google, YouTube, and others subsidiaries.

AL-Q — Al-Qaeda, a militant Sunni Islamist organization founded in 1988 by Osama bin Laden.

AM — Andrew McCabe, Deputy Director of the FBI from February 2016 to January 2018. Later, McCabe became Acting Director of the FBI briefly—May 9th to August 2nd, 2017—after Director James Comey was fired, but McCabe then returned to his Deputy Director position until he was fired by Jeff Sessions in March of 2018.

Amanda Renteria — A political aide who has worked for U.S. Senators Dianne Feinstein and Debbie Stabenow. In 2018, she announced her candidacy for Governor of California but lost in the primary to Gavin Newsom.

Amb — Ambassador

AMB Matlock — Ambassador Jack F. Matlock Jr. was appointed by President Reagan to be the U.S. ambassador to USSR. Matlock has defended the Trump's transition team's contacts with Russian officials as normal diplomatic relations.

anarchy 99 — A reference to the fictional anarchist group and main antagonist of the 2002 film xXx.

Anderson Cooper — CNN News Anchor who previously served as chief international correspondent for Channel One News, where he reported and produced his own stories. Cooper graduated from Yale University in 1989 with a BA in political science. During college, he spent two summers as an intern at the Central Intelligence Agency.

Angela Dorothea Kasner — Angela Dorothea Merkel neé Kasner, Chancellor of the country of Germany.

Anne Wojcicki — The co-founder and CEO of 23andMe, a genetic testing company. She is married to Sergey Brin, the co-founder of Google. Her sister is Susan Wojcicki, the CEO of YouTube.

Anon or **Autist** — Anonymous people who monitor and post messages on 4chan, 8chan, or 8kun. Many are researchers. The autist label refers to the fact that "autists" can become hyper-focused on their research.

Antifa — An American militant movement that embraces a far-left political ideology. Members employ a variety of tactics, including online activism, damaging personal property, inflicting physical violence, and harassing those they deem to be fascists, racists, or politically far-right.

APACHE — A term that has multiple meanings. It may refer to the internet domain that hosts SecureDrop, a platform that journalists use to communicate anonymously with their sources. It could also refer to the open source software used on computer servers. Or it may refer to Apache Co. (NYSE:APA), an oil and exploration company. The Rothschild's Family Trust divested 30 percent of their interest in the company in late January of 2018.

ARM or ARM/MSM — The context of its use would seem to indicate ARM is a group connected to the mainstream media, who oppose the agenda of President Trump. (Q has not confirmed an exact decode.)

Article — Typically refers to the articles of impeachment brought against President Trump by members of Congress in January of 2020.

As the World Turns — A television soap opera that aired on CBS for 54 years. When President John F. Kennedy was assassinated in 1963, the news story about the assassination interrupted the show's broadcast.

AS — There are three possible decodes. It has been confirmed as the initials of Antonin Scalia, the Supreme Court Justice, who died mysteriously in 2016. Alternately, it may refer to Adam Schiff, the Democrat representative from California. In November of 2018, Abigail Spanberger was elected as the representative of Virginia's 7th congressional district. Spanberger is a former CIA agent. Context determines the best decode.

ATL — Hartsfield-Jackson Atlanta International Airport

ATL -> IAD — Atlanta Airport to Dulles International Airport

AUS — The country of Australia.

Autist or Anon — Anonymous people who monitor and post messages on 4chan, 8chan, or 8kun. Many are researchers. The autist label refers to the fact that "autists" can become hyper-focused on their research.

AW — Anthony Weiner, disgraced ex-congressman from New York who served time in prison, and former husband of Huma Abedin.

Awan — Family name of the Pakistani brothers Imran, Abid and Jamal, who operated an IT company that was hired by more than 40 Democratic members of Congress. Imran Awan pled guilty to bank fraud charges but a Department of Justice case regarding him is currently open.

AZ — Arizona, a state in the U.S.

B2 or **B(2)** — The B-2 Spirit, also known as the Stealth Bomber. An American military bomber featuring radar-evading aircraft shapes and built with radar-resistant materials. Q has used the term to refer to someone who seems unthreatening but is working covertly.

Bad actor — A person who has engaged in criminal acts or corrupt behavior.

Bakers — Slang term for anons who assemble 4chan, 8chan, or 8kun posts (crumbs) into threads (breads) for discussion.

BB — U.S. Attorney General William (Bill) Barr.

BC — Bill Clinton, 42nd President of the United States from 1993 to 2001.

BDT — Several possibilities: Blunt & Direct Time, Bangladeshi Taka (Bangladesh's currency). Bangladeshi Terrorist or a Bulk Data Transfer.

Betsy D or **Betsy DeVos** — Secretary of Education under President Trump, and sister of Erik Prince.

Biblefag — Slang term for a 4chan, 8chan, or 8kun user who posts scripture verses.

Biden — Joe Biden, 2020 Democratic candidate for U.S. President.

BIDEN/CHINA — Robert Biden (son of former Vice President Joe Biden) partnered with John Kerry's stepson, Chris Heinz, to form Rosemont Seneca Partners, LLC. The firm signed a billion-dollar deal with the government-owned Bank of China following a diplomatic trip to that country by then-Vice President Joe Biden.

Bilderberg Group — Variously referred to as the Bilderberg Group, Bilderberg conference, Bilderberg meetings or Bilderberg Club, it is a group of 120 to 150 elite members of society including individuals from governments, business, media, and academia from Europe and the United States, which meets annually to promote the concept of "Atlanticism," which is an agenda that supports the mutual interests of Europe and the U.S.

Bill Priestap — Director of FBI Counterintelligence from 2015 to 2018.

Black ops — Black budget operations. Government operations (typically military or intelligence) that are not publicly acknowledged and not under congressional oversight. Some of these operations are funded through the official federal budget. Some are funded by siphoning money from approved programs, some by money made through illegal activities, and some are funded privately.

Blackwater — Blackwater USA is an American private military company founded in 1997 by former Navy SEAL officer Erik Prince. It was renamed as Xe Services in 2009 and is now known as Academi after the company was acquired by a group of private investors.

Blizzard — Activision Blizzard, Inc. is an American video game holding company based in Santa Monica, California.

BLM — Black Lives Matter. (Not to be confused with the Bureau of Land Management.)

Blockade — Q indicated that Robert Mueller's investigation into 2016 election interference was designed by the enemies of Donald Trump to serve as a blockade to his success.

BO — There are three confirmed decodes: Bruce Ohr (former U.S. Associate Deputy Attorney General), former President Barack Obama, or Board Owner.

BOB — Robert Mueller, former FBI Director who served as Special Counsel in the 2016 Trump-Russia investigation.

BOD — Board of Directors

B_Ohr — Bruce Ohr, the former Associate Deputy Attorney General who was demoted for his role in the surveillance of the 2016 Trump campaign.

Bolton — An American attorney, political commentator, and Republican consultant. Bolton was President Trump's National Security Advisor from March 2018 until September 2019. He also served as the U.S. Ambassador to the UN from August 2005 to December 2006.

BOOM — As in "Lower the Boom." Chastisement, punishment, to deliver a knockout punch.

Boris — UK Prime Minister Boris Johnson.

Bots — Internet 'crawler' programs used to find and analyze data and run coded routines. May also be used as a derogatory term for people with a certain belief system, i.e., "Russian bots" or "Soros' bots."

Bottom to top — An order of operations that begins at the lowest level and proceeds toward the upper levels. These operations, because of their nature, take time to complete.

BP — There are two decodes: Border Patrol, or Bill Priestap (FBI former Chief of Counterintelligence).

Bridge — A term found in Q's posts that indicates someone who acts as a go-between for others. It has also been used in at least one post that discusses a "central" social media algorithm that helps track users. The word has other uses that are still not confirmed by Q.

Bring the thunder — Artillery/aircraft controller term for final authorization of a fire/bombing mission.

Bruce Ohr — Former U.S. Associate Deputy Attorney General, who was demoted for his role in the surveillance of President Trump. Husband of Nellie Ohr, an employee of Fusion GPS.

Bump — A comment that forces a conversation thread to rise to the top of a particular board.

Burner phone — A cheap, disposable phone used by those who do not wish to be tracked by intelligence agencies.

BUZZF — Buzzfeed, an American internet media company.

C19 — COVID-19.

C_A — Central Intelligence Agency, A civilian foreign intelligence service of the U.S. federal government.

CA — In most cases, it refers to California, but when used in a stringer with Uranium One (U1), it refers to Canada.

Call the ball — A phrase derived from U.S. Navy terminology for a naval aviator confirming he has the optical landing aids in sight prior to landing on an aircraft carrier. In Q's vernacular, it signifies committing to a course of action.

Carter Page — Briefly served as a staffer on candidate Donald Trump's 2016 Presidential campaign. Page became the target of an FBI investigation as a possible foreign agent, and then became the center of a controversy surrounding the surveillance of Trump's campaign.

Castle — Secret Service code name for the Executive Mansion or the White House.

CBTS — Calm before the storm.

CC — Chelsea Clinton, daughter of Bill and Hillary Clinton.

CCP — Usually stands for Chinese Communist Party, but has also been used as an acronym for Control and Command Positions.

CDC — U.S. Centers for Disease Control

CF — The William Jefferson Clinton Foundation

CF-i — The Department of Justice's investigation of the Clinton Foundation.

CFR — Council on Foreign Relations, a United States non-profit think tank specializing in U.S. foreign policy and international affairs.

CHAI — Clinton Health Access Initiative. In 2010, the Clinton Foundation's HIV/AIDS Initiative became a separate non-profit organization called the Clinton Health Access Initiative (CHAI).

Chair — Likely a reference to what the Catholic Church considers to be the throne of St. Peter on which the current Pope sits.

Chatter — Conversations between politicians, media and intelligence operatives that are detected by agencies like the NSA.

CIA — Central Intelligence Agency, a civilian foreign intelligence service of the U.S. federal government.

C-Info — Confidential or Classified Information.

Civ — Two possibilities: civilian, or civil.

Clapper — James Clapper, former Director of National Intelligence under Barack Obama.

CLAS or **[CLAS 1-99]** — Q has access to both classified and non-classified information. These terms refer to the names of people, agencies, and organizations that are currently classified.

Clock — Some believe the word clock is a reference to a clock diagram, "the Q clock" that pinpoints and predicts events in Q's mission. The clock image has been posted on Q's board many times, and anons have asked for confirmation, but Q has not confirmed the clock diagram yet.

My theory about references to a "clock" takes into consideration that Q and the President post close to each other in time—often less than ten minutes apart. A clock is necessary to track the time intervals (deltas), showing the relationships between their posts. Graphics can then be made showing the time intervals.

Clowns — The U.S. Central Intelligence Agency.

CLOWN DIR — Former CIA Director John Brennan

CM — Code Monkey, the administrator who provided technical support for Q's board on 8chan, and the current administrator of 8kun.

Coats — Dan Coats, former Director of National Intelligence under President Donald Trump.

CoC — Two confirmed decodes: Chain of Command, and Chain of Custody.

Cohen — Michael Cohen, former personal attorney for Donald Trump.

Cohn — Gary Cohn, President Trump's former Chief Economic Advisor.

Color Revolution — A technique of overthrowing governments by the use of insurgency tactics—generally both violent and non-violent.

COMM or **COMMS** — Different possibilities depending on context. An abbreviation for communications, committee, or community.

comp-to-comp — Computer-to-computer.

Con — Confidence game: a swindle in which the mark, or victim, is defrauded after his or her trust (confidence) has been won.

Corsi — Jerome Corsi is an author and political commentator. He was an avid Q supporter early in the mission but became the center of a controversy in the spring of 2018 when he claimed that Q had been compromised, and Q's posts could no longer be trusted.

CoS — Chief of Staff.

Crop or **[crop]** — A euphemism used by Q to taunt former FBI Director James Comey about his pending prosecution. (Comey has often posted photos of himself standing in a cornfield.)

Crossfire Hurricane — The codename for the FBI's counterintelligence investigation of Donald Trump's campaign prior to the appointment of Special Counsel Robert Mueller.

CrowdStrike — A tech company contracted by the Democratic National Committee to investigate their computer system for alleged hacking during the 2016 Presidential election.

Crumb — Slang term for a single post on 4chan, 8chan, or 8kun. Crumbs, when brought together, make a bread (thread).

Cruz or **[-Cruz]** — U.S. Senator Ted Cruz

CS — Several confirmed decodes: Senator Charles Schumer, former British spy Christopher Steele, or the tech firm CrowdStrike that was used by the Democratic National Committee. Context determines the best decode.

CV — COVID-19

C wave2 — A predicted second wave of the COVID virus.

C Wray — Christopher Wray, Director of the FBI who began serving in that capacity in 2017. From 2003 to 2005, he was the Assistant Attorney General in charge of the Criminal Division in the George W. Bush administration.

cycling 5s — Cycling every 5 seconds. Used in reference to Twitter and Facebook algorithms.

D5 — The metric used to rate the potential danger an avalanche poses on a scale from D1-D5, with D5 being most severe. Q uses it as a metaphor to convey the idea that a coming avalanche of justice will devastate corrupt people.

D or **D's** — Democrats

DA — District Attorney

Dafna Linzer — Since October of 2016, she has been the managing editor of NBC/MSNBC politics.

DAG — U.S. Deputy Attorney General

Dan — Usually a reference to Dan Scavino, the White House Deputy Chief of Staff for Communications and Director of Social Media.

DARPA — The U.S. Defense Department's Advanced Research Projects Agency. Q has suggested that DARPA developed much of the technology used by major social media platforms.

David Laufman — Former Chief of the U.S. Justice Department's Counterintelligence and Export Control Section.

DC — Washington, District of Columbia.

DC-CAP — Washington D.C., Capitol of the United States.

DDoS — Distributed Denial of Service, an attack used by hackers to take down a website or network by causing server overload. "Distributed" means the attack comes from multiple users and machines that overtax a website's resources.

Dead Cat Bounce — An investing term for a temporary recovery in a prolonged decline or bear market that is followed by the continuation of the downtrend. The name "dead cat bounce" illustrates the idea that even a dead cat will bounce if it falls far enough and fast enough.

Declas or **DECLASS** — The declassification of documents that will shed light on corruption.

Deep Dream — A reference to a Jason Bourne film in which a social media company named Deep Dream gathered personal information from subscribers and secretly funneled it to the Central Intelligence Agency.

Deep State — A term used for entrenched politicians, bureaucrats, and others who have their own policy agendas in government, and work to guard and maintain their positions of power and control. Therefore the status quo never seems to change no matter who is elected by the people.

DefCon — Defense Condition which is indicated by a number 1 through 5. DefCon 5 is a state of low alert. DefCon1 is a state of high alert. Q has used the term in some unorthodox ways. Look for context to determine the correct application.

Delta — Several possible uses: The U.S. Defense Department uses four conditions to indicate the relative level of a terrorist threat (Threatcon). Alpha is the lowest Threatcon level, bravo is higher and delta is the highest. In chemistry, delta (Δ) is used to indicate the change in a system during a reaction. For fighter pilots, it indicates a change to a later time, either minutes or hours depending on the context. ("Delta 10 on your recovery time" means the jet is now scheduled to land 10 minutes later.)

In most of Q's posts, the term "delta" indicates the time interval between one of Q's posts and a tweet by the President.

DE_POTUS — Democratically elected President of the United States.

D/ F — Domestic and Foreign.

DF — Dianne Feinstein, a Democrat U.S. Senator from California.

DHS — U.S. Department of Homeland Security, which is a cabinet department of the U.S. federal government with responsibilities in public security.

Digital Battleground — Q's term that describes a war of information being waged on the internet, and specifically—on social media.

DJT — Donald John Trump, the 45th President of the United States. Before entering politics, he was a businessman and television personality.

DL — Download

Dla Piper — The law firm that happened to employ Peter Comey, the brother of disgraced former FBI Director James Comey.

DNC — Democratic National Committee, the governing body for the United States Democratic Party.

DNC BREACH — In 2016, files from the Democratic National Committee were transferred to and made public. The incident was widely attributed to a Russian hacking operation, but Q has suggested the information was given to by a DNC staffer.

DNI — U.S. Director of National Intelligence.

DOD — U.S. Department of Defense, which is part of the Executive Branch of the federal government that handles functions of national security.

DOE — U.S. Department of Energy, a cabinet-level department of the federal government, concerned with energy and safe handling of nuclear material.

DOJ — U.S. Department of Justice (also known as the Justice Department), which is a federal executive department of the U.S. government responsible for the enforcement of the law and administration of justice in the U.S.

Donna — Donna Brazile, who served as the interim Chair of the Democratic National Committee in 2016 after the resignation of Debbie Wasserman Schultz.

Dopey — In a tweet, Donald Trump referred to Saudi Prince Alwaleed bin Talal as "Dopey Prince Alwaleed." Q has also referred to Alwaleed as Dopey.

DOSSIER — A collection of documents assembled by former British spy Christopher Steele, used to obtain a warrant to surveil Carter Page and the Trump campaign.

DrudgeR — The Drudge Report, a news aggregation service.

Durham — John Durham, U.S. Attorney from Connecticut. Tasked by former Attorney General Jeff Sessions to investigate government corruption.

DWS — Debbie Wasserman Schultz, a Representative from Florida who resigned as chair of the DNC after emails were published by that revealed DNC staff favoring Clinton over Sanders.

E — Two confirmed decodes: The rapper known as Eminem, or emergency.

Eagle — Secret Service code name for President Bill Clinton.

EAM LOYALISTS — In the U.S. military's strategic nuclear weapon command and control system, an Emergency Action Message (EAM) is a preformatted message directing nuclear-capable forces to execute specific Major Attack Options (MAOs) or Limited Attack Options (LAOs) in a nuclear war. "EAM Loyalsts" would be members of the military who would receive such a message and intend to keep their oath and serve their country faithfully.

EBS — Emergency Broadcast System

EC — This usually signifies Electronic Communication, as in email, instant messaging, or other communications. In more recent posts, it refers to Eric Ciaramella, a CIA analyst and former National Security Council staffer. Ciaramella is believed to have filed the whistleblower complaint used to impeach Donald Trump.

Ed O'Callaghan — The former Principal Associate Deputy Attorney General for Rod Rosenstein.

EG — Abbreviation for Evergreen, Hillary Clinton's Secret Service code name.

EH — Eric Holder, former U.S. Attorney General under Barrack Obama.

EM — Elon Musk, CEO of Tesla and SpaceX.

EMP — Electromagnetic Pulse

EMS — Emergency Messaging System

EO — Presidential Executive Order

Epstein — Jeffrey Epstein, an American financier and convicted child sex offender who died in his jail cell in 2019 while awaiting trial.

Epstein Island — Little Saint James Island, an approximately 75-acre island in the U.S. Virgin Islands, owned by American financier and convicted child sex offender Jeffrey Epstein from 1998 until his death in 2019.

Erik Prince — Former U.S. Navy SEAL officer best known for founding the government services and security company, Blackwater USA. He served as its CEO until 2009. Prince supported Donald Trump in his bid for President.

ES — Two confirmed decodes: Eric Schmidt (ex-CEO of Alphabet/Google) or Edward Snowden, a former CIA employee and NSA contractor. Snowden is usually indicated by @snowden but on rare occasions by ES. Context determines which is correct.

EU — European Union

Evergreen — Hillary Clinton's Secret Service code name.

Eyes in the SKY — Drone or satellite surveillance.

Eyes On — To watch or observe.

Ezra Cohen-Watnick — National security advisor to the U.S. Attorney General, and a former Senior Director for Intelligence Programs for the United States National Security Council (NSC).

F2F — Face-to-face meeting.

F9 — Two uses: SpaceX Falcon 9 is a two-stage medium-lift space launch vehicle. F9 is also a Facebook surveillance algorithm.

Facebook — A popular social network founded on February 4th, 2004—the same day the Pentagon's DARPA Lifelog Project was shut down. Lifelog was designed to track the same life events as Facebook.

Fag — Slang term for an anon. It is sometimes combined with areas of interest, i.e. biblefag, planefag, lawfag, etc.

Fakewood — Hollywood

Fantasy Land — A Q signature indicating a truth that is too wild for the average person to believe. Cognitive dissonance is caused by information that challenges a programmed way of thinking.

Farm — A nickname for the CIA's training facility, Camp Peary, near Williamsburg Virginia.

FB — Facebook

F + D — Foreign and Domestic

FED — Federal Reserve System, a private banking corporation that controls the U.S. money supply.

FED G — Federal Government

FF — False Flag. A secret operation that is intended to deceive. The deception creates the appearance that a particular party, group, or nation is responsible for some type of activity, while the actual source of the activity is concealed. The term originally referred to pirate ships that flew flags of countries as a disguise to prevent their victims from fleeing or preparing for battle. Sometimes the flag would remain, and the blame for the attack would be laid incorrectly on another country.

FIFTH COLUMN — A group within a country that are secretly sympathetic to or are working with its enemies.

FISA — The Foreign Intelligence Surveillance Act, which permits the surveillance of foreign citizens or U.S. citizens suspected of being foreign agents.

Five Eyes — Often abbreviated FVEY, it is an intelligence-sharing alliance that includes Australia, Canada, New Zealand, the United Kingdom, and the United States.

FOIA — The Freedom of Information Act. It allows individuals to request government documents on particular subjects and requires compliance within certain guidelines.

Follow the Pen — A pen photograph has appeared in a number of Q's posts. Sometimes the images precede a Presidential Executive Order or declassification of documents.

Fox & Friends — A weekday morning news show on *Fox News* television channel.

Fox Three — Military aviator jargon for firing an active radar-guided air-to-air missile.

Future Marker — A reference in a post by Q intended to mark a topic that will be discussed in greater detail at a future time.

Future proves past — A phrase suggesting that information contained in a current post will be proven true at a future time.

G — Google

Game Theory — The study of conflict and cooperation by opponents within a competitive game environment.

Gang of 8 — A term used to describe the eight leaders in the United States Congress who are briefed on classified intelligence matters. It includes the leaders of both parties from the Senate and House of Representatives, and the chairs and ranking minority members of both the Senate and House Intelligence Committees.

Gardens by the Bay — A nature park in central Singapore, adjacent to the Marina Reservoir. Kim Jong-un explored the park on his first night in Singapore preceding the Summit meeting with President Trump on June 11th, 2018.

GCHQ — An acronym for the Government Communications Headquarters, an intelligence and security organization responsible for providing signals intelligence (SIGINT) and information to the UK government and armed forces.

General K — President Trump's former Chief of Staff General John F. Kelly.

GEO or **geo-location** — A reference to geographic location.

GEO-T or **GEO-T/L** — Geological tracking, and location. Tracking a person's location by using global positioning satellites.

GEOTUS — Acronym for God-Emperor of the United States. A meme used to aggravate those who despise Donald Trump.

Gina Haspel — Director of the Central Intelligence Agency under President Trump.

GITMO — Guantanamo Bay Naval Base, a military prison and detention camp.

Giuliani — Former New York City Mayor Rudy Giuliani.

GJ — Grand Jury.

Gloria V — Gloria Vanderbilt, an American artist, author, actress, fashion designer, heiress, and socialite.

Godfather III — A Q signature that connects posts containing this phrase to a film from 1990 about the Corleone crime family's involvement with the Vatican.

GOOG — Google

GREEN_CASTLE — Q confirmed this was a reference to the U.S. Army Corps of Engineers who have an office in Green Castle, Indiana.

GS — George Soros, a hedge fund billionaire who is known for using his wealth to fund his own brand of political activism. Recipients of his philanthropy appreciate his money, but those who oppose his political views see him as a creator of chaos around the world—a destabilizing force on economies and societies. Some countries have either banned Soros or restricted his organizations. These countries include Pakistan, Poland, Turkey, Russia, Soros' home country of Hungary, and the Philippines. The Israeli government has said Soros is not welcome there.

GSA — General Services Administration. An independent agency of the U.S. government that helps manage and support federal agencies.

Guccifer 2.0 — An internet persona who claimed to be the hacker(s) who gained unauthorized access to the Democratic National Committee (DNC) computer network and then leaked its documents to *WikiLeaks*.

G v E/R v W — Good versus evil. Right versus wrong.

GWB — Former U.S. President George W. Bush.

GZ — Ground Zero

H — Multiple possibilities. Depending on the context, H could mean either Haiti, U.S. House of Representatives, or in rare cases, Hillary Clinton, who is known to sign letters and emails with the letter H.

Hannity intruder — Sean Hannity's wife found a man trespassing in their home on Long Island. The intruder claimed to be writing a book about the *Fox News* host and was arrested.

Hatter — Marty Torrey, as he was referred to in emails from Hillary Clinton (published by *WikiLeaks*), who went by the nickname "Alice."

H-BIDEN — Hunter Biden, the son of 2020 Presidential candidate Joe Biden.

Hillary Clinton — Former Secretary of State under Barack Obama. Democratic Presidential Candidate in 2016. Wife of President William Jefferson Clinton.

Hive-Mind — The ability of anons and researchers to coordinate their work, similar to how a bee hive operates.

HK — Hong Kong

Holder — Eric Holder, former U.S. Attorney General under Barrack Obama.

Honeypot — A scheme used to lure people into behaviors that are unethical, immoral, or illegal. Their participation can be recorded and used as leverage to control them.

Hops — FISA surveillance allows the collection of information on individuals in the targeted person's *immediate* circle of contacts. It also allows surveillance of other people who are *in communication with* the immediate circle of contacts. In this way, surveillance "hops" or acts as a "leapfrog" from a small circle of contacts to larger ones, extending a broader surveillance net.

HRC — Hillary Clinton, former Secretary of State under Barack Obama. Democratic Presidential Candidate in 2016. Wife of President William Jefferson Clinton.

H-relief — Haiti earthquake relief.

H Report — One of several reports released by the U.S. Department of Justice Inspector General Michael Horowitz.

HS — U.S. Department of Homeland Security

Huma — Huma Abedin, Hillary Clinton's Chief of Staff, and ex-wife of Anthony Weiner.

HUMA — Harvard University Muslim Alumni

Hunter — Q often uses this as a euphemism for those who are hunting criminals and bringing them to justice. It can also refer to Hunter Biden, the trouble-prone son of former U.S. Vice President Joe Biden.

Hunt for Red October — Multiple meanings including, but not limited to, the film by that title and a steel plant in Stalingrad, Russia, which appears on a CIA document, for which Q provided a link. Note: Q removed "the Hunt for," and in October of 2018, a new theme "Red October" appeared.

Hussein — Barack Hussein Obama, the 44th President of the United States.

Hussein's PL — Barack Obama's Presidential Library

HW — Hollywood

H-wood — Hollywood

I — The letter I has been used at least once to refer to criminal indictments.

IBOR — Internet Bill of Rights, a set of ideas proposed by California Representative Ro Khanna that would guarantee the rights of internet users.

IC — Intelligence Community

ICBM — Intercontinental Ballistic Missile

ICE — U.S. Immigration and Customs Enforcement.

ID/IDEN — Identification, or to identify an individual.

IG — Inspector General. Every U.S. government agency has an Inspector General. In most cases, the reference is to the Department of Justice Inspector General Michael Horowitz.

ILS — Instrument Landing System. Radio signals are transmitted from a runway and are intercepted by aircraft that use them as a guide for landing. Used by Q in discussions with anons to help build camaraderie.

In-Q-Tel — A venture capital firm that invests in tech companies for the sole purpose of keeping the Central Intelligence Agency and other intelligence agencies equipped with the latest in information technology. The name "In-Q-Tel" is an intentional reference to Q, the fictional inventor who supplied technology to James Bond.

Insurance Policy — According to publicly released text messages between FBI agent Peter Strzok and FBI attorney Lisa Page in 2016, a plan was developed to prevent Donald Trump from being elected. A backup plan (an insurance policy) was put in place to remove him from office if he were to be elected.

Intelligence A — Intelligence Agency

IP-Ghost — Using a device or software to conceal your IP address.

IRL — In real life, as opposed to online.

IRON EAGLE — A 1986 movie starring Lou Gossett Jr. about a retired Air Force Colonel and an 18-year-old whose father had been shot down in the Middle East and was sentenced to death. The two men obtained a pair of F-16 fighter jets and managed to fly to the Middle East for a rescue mission for the young man's father. Iron Eagle is a Q signature.

IRS — U.S. Internal Revenue Service, a government agency that is a bureau of the Department of the Treasury.

ISIS — Islamic State in Iraq and Syria. Listed as a terrorist group by the U.S. State Department.

Ism — A term Q uses to describe in generic terms, ideas such as racism, fascism, totalitarianism, etc.

JA — Julian Assange, founder of *WikiLeaks,* a watchdog organization that publishes leaked documents.

Jack — Jack Dorsey, CEO of the social media platform, Twitter. He is also the CEO of the mobile payment processing company Square.

James Alefantis — Named in GQ magazine as one of Washington D.C.'s 50 most influential people. He is a American chef and restaurateur.

James Baker — Former FBI Chief Counsel.

James Comey — Former Director of the Federal Bureau of Investigation (FBI) who was fired by President Trump in 2017.

James Dolan — From 1999 to 2006, Dolan served with the U.S. Marines in the Iraq war. He helped develop SecureDrop, an open source whistleblower submission system that eventually came under the control of the Freedom of the Press Foundation. Dolan's death at the age of 36 on December 27th, 2017, was thought to be a suicide and was followed by the death of John Perry Barlow in February of 2018.

Jared Cohen — A businessman who serves as the CEO of Jigsaw (previously Google Ideas) and an Adjunct Senior Fellow at the Council on Foreign Relations (CFR). Previously, he served as a member of the Secretary of State's Policy Planning Staff and as an advisor to Condoleezza Rice and later, Hillary Clinton.

Jason Bourne — A fictional agent and hero in a series of books and films. Bourne was the subject of a CIA mind-control experiment that made him into the perfect asset for the Agency.

JB — At least two confirmed decodes: former FBI Chief Counsel James Baker, or former CIA Director John Brennan. Context determines the correct one.

JC — At least two confirmed decodes: former FBI Director James Comey, or former Director of National Intelligence James Clapper. Context determines the correct one.

J C or J_C — John P. Carlin, former Director of the National Security Division of the U.S. Department of Justice.

JCS — The U.S. Military's Joint Chiefs of Staff.

JD — Jack Dorsey, the CEO of Twitter, a social media platform, and the CEO of Square, a mobile payment processing company.

JFK — Two confirmed decodes: John Fitzgerald Kennedy, 35th President of the United States, or President Trump's former Chief of Staff General John F. Kelly.

JFK JR — John Fitzgerald Kennedy, Jr. was the son of the 35th President John F. Kennedy Sr. He was a lawyer, journalist, magazine publisher, and actor. Kennedy died on July 16th, 1999 (along with his wife, Carolyn, and sister-in-law Lauren Bessette) when his small plane crashed into the Atlantic Ocean near Martha's Vineyard.

Jim Jordan — Representative from Ohio's 4th congressional district and member of the House Freedom Caucus. He has been the ranking member of the House Oversight Committee since 2019.

Jim Rybicki — Former FBI Chief of Staff.

JK — Two confirmed decodes: In Q's earlier posts, JK refers to Jared Kushner, senior advisor to his father-in-law, President Donald Trump. In later Q posts, JK refers to John Kerry, Secretary of State under Barack Obama.

JL — John Legend, singer, songwriter, musician, actor, and philanthropist. Legend participated in a telethon to benefit Haiti victims.

John Durham — U.S. Attorney from Connecticut. Tasked by former Attorney General Jeff Sessions to investigate government corruption.

John M — John McCain, U.S. Senator from Arizona. He served as a senator from January 1987 until his death in 2018.

John McCain — U.S. Senator from Arizona who served from January 1987 until his death in 2018.

Johnny — John Conyers, U.S. Representative from Michigan who resigned from Congress in 2017 after multiple allegations of sexual harassment. Now deceased, he was the longest-serving black member of Congress in history.

John P. Carlin — Former Director of the National Security Division of the U.S. Department of Justice.

John Perry Barlow — Poet and essayist, cattle rancher, and a cyber-libertarian, political activist, and lyricist for the Grateful Dead. Founding member of the Electronic Frontier Foundation and the Freedom of the Press Foundation. Barlow died in February, 2018.

Josh Campbell — Former FBI agent, appointed Special Assistant to former FBI Director James Comey. Contributor for CNN.

JP — John Podesta, White House Chief of Staff under President Bill Clinton, and Counselor to President Barack Obama. Chairman of Hillary Clinton's 2016 Presidential campaign. Currently serves as Chair of the Center for American Progress, a think tank based in Washington, D.C.

JPC — John P. Carlin, former Director of the National Security Division of the U.S. Department of Justice.

JS — John Solomon, investigative journalist, reporter, and Editor in Chief of *Just the News*.

KANSAS — Mike Pompeo, former CIA director and current Secretary of State. Pompeo also served as a U.S. Congressman from Kansas.

Kashyap Patel — Indian American lawyer Kashyap "Kash" Patel, who was the primary author of the House Intelligence Committee memo that was critical of the FBI and Justice Department handling of the investigation into alleged collusion between Donald Trump and Russia.

KC — Kevin Clinesmith, a former FBI attorney who was the first person to be indicted and plead guilty in John Durham's investigation related to "Crossfire Hurricane." Clinesmith admitted to altering an email used to obtain a warrant for broad surveillance of Carter Page, a U.S. citizen and member of the Trump campaign.

Kek — Laughter or amusement. Synonymous with "lol" (laughing out loud). Kek had its origins in World of Warcraft, where one faction's "lol" was translated as "kek" by the other.

Keith Raniere — Co-founder of NXIVM, a multi-level marketing company based near Albany, New York, that offered personal and professional development seminars through its "Executive Success Programs." NXIVM leaders were prosecuted for sexual abuse and sex trafficking of members.

Kerry — John Kerry, a former U.S. Senator and Secretary of State under President Barack Obama.

Kevin Clinesmith — Former FBI attorney who was the first person to be indicted and plead guilty in John Durham's investigation related to "Crossfire Hurricane." Clinesmith admitted to altering an email used to obtain a warrant for broad surveillance of Carter Page, a U.S. citizen and member of the Trump campaign.

Keystone — Several uses: decoded by Q to indicate the power given to average citizens when they're assisted by the President, the military, and its intelligence apparatus. Information is the *key*. The executive branch and military are the *stone*. Together, they form the *keystone*. Also refers to a trapezoidal-shaped building stone found at the apex of some arches and doorways.

Kim — Kim Jong-un is a North Korean politician who has been the Supreme Leader of North Korea since 2011 and chairman of the Workers' Party of Korea since 2012.

KKK — Ku Klux Klan, a group that became a vehicle for southern post-Civil War resistance against freedmen and the Republican Party leaders who sought to establish equality for blacks. As a secret, masked vigilante group, the Klan aimed to restore white supremacy by using threats and violence, including murder.

Klaus Eberwein — A former Haitian government official who was found shot to death just before he was scheduled to expose Clinton Foundation fraud before an anti-corruption committee.

Knowingly — Used by Q as a reminder that many actions taken by corrupt people were not done negligently, but knowingly. Negligence is generally not prosecuted. Certain acts, when done knowingly, are.

LARP — Live Action Role Play. On 4chan, 8chan and 8kun, it refers to a phony.

Lawfag — A slang term for an anon who has a background in law.

LdR or LDR — Two possible decodes. Lord de Rothschild or Lynn de Rothschild (aka Lady de Rothschild)—both members of the Rothschild banking family.

Leapfrog — FISA surveillance allows the collection of information on individuals in the targeted person's *immediate* circle of contacts. It also allows surveillance of other people who are *in communication with* the immediate circle of contacts. In this way, surveillance "hops" or acts as a "leapfrog" from a small circle of contacts to larger ones, extending a broader surveillance net.

LifeLog Project — A project of DARPA, the Defense Department's research arm. The goal of the LifeLog Project was to get citizens to voluntarily provide their private information to a military database. The program ended on February 4th, 2004—the same day Facebook was launched.

Lisa Barsoomian — Former Assistant U.S. Attorney who once represented Bill Clinton. She is the wife of former Deputy Attorney General Rod Rosenstein.

Lisa Page — Former FBI attorney, and legal advisor to then-FBI Deputy Director Andrew McCabe. Page became the focus of media attention for her role in the surveillance of Donald Trump's 2016 Presidential campaign.

Little St. James Island — Little Saint James Island, an approximately 75-acre island in the U.S. Virgin Islands, owned by American financier and convicted child sex offender Jeffrey Epstein from 1998 until his death in 2019.

LL — Loretta Lynch, served as U.S. Attorney General under Barack Obama. Lynch came under scrutiny when she met secretly with former President Bill Clinton on a tarmac at an airport in Arizona during an active investigation of Hillary Clinton.

Locked on target — Military aircraft use radar to track or "lock" onto the position of other aircraft. As Q uses the term, it refers to corrupt people who are being tracked.

Login Devices — Various secure computers, tablets, or mobile phones that Q uses to connect to the internet to post messages.

LOOP — In most cases, a reference to Loop Capital Markets, a Chicago-based investment firm. There may be other uses.

Lord d R — Lord Jacob de Rothschild of the Rothschild banking family.

LOSBR — Line-of-sight beam riding. A technique of directing a missile to its target by aid of radar or a laser beam.

Lurk — To read a 4chan, 8chan, or 8kun board without posting a comment. Lurking is not only acceptable, but recommended. If you make a bad or unoriginal post, someone will likely ask you to "lurk more" (sometimes written "lurk moar") before posting again.

LV — Las Vegas, a city in Nevada.

LZ — Landing Zone. Q's references are typically to locations where a military aircraft land.

M — Used at least once to refer to Moloch, the biblical name of a Canaanite god associated with child sacrifice.

Mack — Allison Mack, a Hollywood actress who played the part of Chloe Sullivan in the TV show *Smallville*. Mack pleaded guilty to racketeering and conspiracy as a member of the NXIVM sex cult that was founded by Keith Raniere. As part of her guilty plea, Mack admitted to extortion and forced labor.

Macron — Emmanuel Macron, elected President of France on May 7th, 2017.

MAGA — "Make America Great Again," Donald Trump's 2016 Presidential campaign slogan.

Maggie Haberman — White House correspondent for *The New York Times* and a former political analyst for CNN. Emails published by indicated that Haberman was particularly useful in releasing political talking points friendly to Hillary Clinton. She was also reported by to be one of many reporters who colluded with Hillary's campaign and the DNC during the 2016 election.

Maggie Nix — The daughter of Sarah Nixon and granddaughter of actress and TV soap opera writer and producer Agnes Nixon.

MagikBOT — A *Wikipedia* bot that makes automated or semi-automated edits to *Wikipedia* entries that would be difficult to do manually.

MAKE IT RAIN — Military jargon for the detonation of explosive ordnance (bomb), which sends a shower of debris on those who are nearby.

Manafort — Paul Manafort, a businessman, lobbyist, and member of Donald Trump's 2016 Presidential campaign. He was convicted of money laundering, tax evasion and failing to register as a foreign agent.

Mariah Sunshine Coogan — One of six people killed in a plane crash near Scottsdale, Arizona, on a flight to Las Vegas, Nevada, on April 9th, 2018.

Marina Abramovic — A Serbian performance artist mentioned in the John Podesta emails published by *WikiLeaks* drawing public attention to her "Spirit Cooking" art, as well as her relationships with political figures and celebrities.

Marine 1 — The President's helicopter operated by the U.S. Marines.

Marker — A reference in a post by Q intended to mark a topic that will be discussed in greater detail at a future time.

MAP — A graphic that displays Q's posts.

Master — The identity of the "Master" is uncertain. In a discussion about the Pope and the Rothschilds, Q wrote:
> The "Chair" serves the Master
> P = C.
> Who is the Master?

May — Theresa May, served as the Prime Minister of the United Kingdom and Leader of the Conservative Party from 2016 to 2019.

MB — Muslim Brotherhood, a political and military group based in Egypt. The government of Egypt banned the group and named it a terrorist organization.

MBS — Two decodes. Mohammad bin Salman, the Crown Prince of Saudi Arabia, Muslim reformer, and ally of Donald Trump. Depending on context, MBS can refer to Marina Bay Sands Hotel in Singapore.

McCabe — Andrew McCabe, Deputy Director of the FBI from February 2016 to January 2018. Later, McCabe became Acting Director of the FBI briefly—May 9th to August 2nd, 2017—after Director James Comey was fired, but McCabe then returned to his Deputy Director position until he was fired by Jeff Sessions in March of 2018.

Media Matters — Media Matters for America (MMfA) is a progressive tax-exempt, non-profit organization, with the stated mission of "comprehensively monitoring, analyzing, and correcting conservative misinformation in the U.S. media." MMfA was founded by political activist David Brock and is known for its aggressive criticism of conservative journalists and media outlets. Hillary Clinton and John Podesta were instrumental in helping form MMfA, which receives partial funding from George Soros.

Melissa Hodgman — Associate Director of Securities and Exchange Commission Enforcement Division. Wife of fired FBI Special Agent Peter Strzok.

MI — Military Intelligence

Memo — House Intelligence Committee 4-page memo on the FBI's FISA warrant against Trump campaign staffer Carter Page.

Merkel — Angela Merkel, a politician who has served as the Chancellor of Germany since 2005.

MF — Retired Lieutenant General Michael Flynn, served as the National Security Advisor briefly under President Trump in 2017. Flynn became a target during the SpyGate scandal and entered a guilty plea under pressure from Special Counsel prosecutors. Previously, Flynn served as Director of the Defense Intelligence Agency for two years under the Obama administration and was forced out due to his criticism of Obama's policy on the Islamic State.

Michael Atkinson — Former Inspector General for the U.S. Intelligence Community. He was fired after his involvement was exposed in facilitating the whistleblower complaint that led to the House impeachment of President Trump.

Michael Avenatti — The attorney who represented Stormy Daniels in her lawsuit against President Trump. Q has not mentioned him by name but has posted links to his tweets and his website. Avenatti is currently facing charges in New York and California.

Michael Gaeta — The FBI's legal attaché in Rome, Italy.

Midnight Riders — A term Q adopted for anons in the summer of 2020, that symbolizes the patriotism of Paul Revere, who rode a horse at midnight to warn of the British plan to arrest Samuel Adams and John Hancock.

Midyear — Midyear Exam, the FBI's name for its investigation of Hillary Clinton's use of a private server in her home for email correspondence while she was Secretary of State.

Mika Brzezinski — MSNBC reporter and co-host of the weekday show *Morning Joe*, and daughter of Zbigniew Brzezinski (President Jimmy Carter's National Security Advisor.)

Mike Kortan — Former FBI Assistant Director for Public Affairs, an influential position that controlled media access. He also served under Robert Mueller in the 2016 Trump-Russia probe.

MIL brass — Military leaders

MIL-CIV Alliance — An informal alliance between members of the military and civilians in an effort to inform the public about the realities of corruption.

MIL SATs — Military Satellites

Mitch McConnell — Mitch McConnell, U.S. Senator from Kentucky is also the Senate Majority Leader. Elected to that position unanimously by his Republican colleagues in 2014, 2016, and 2018, he is the longest-serving Senate Republican leader in the history of the United States.

MK_active — A suggestion from Q that the CIA's MK-Ultra mind control program is still active.

MKUltra — CIA mind-control project that involved the use of psychological experiments combined with the use of drugs.

ML — Marshal law, refers to a state where the military assumes control of civilian law enforcement duties.

MLK — The Reverend Martin Luther King, Jr. was the most influential black leader of the 1960s. He was a Baptist minister and an advocate of civil rights in America. He led the peaceful historical boycott of city buses in Montgomery, Alabama, in 1955. King was assassinated in 1968.

mm — Millions

MOAB — an acronym for Mother of All Bombs. The nickname for GBU-43/B Massive Ordnance Air Blast, which, weighing in at over 21,000 pounds, was the largest non-nuclear bomb ever used by the U.S. military. It was dropped on an ISIS-Khorasan camp in Afghanistan in April of 2017.

Moar — Slang term for "more" used on 4chan, 8chan, and 8kun.

Mockingbird — Operation Mockingbird was a CIA operation where the agency recruited news reporters and their managers to disseminate propaganda for the purpose of controlling the masses.

mod — Sometimes refers to a moderator, but can also refer to the act of modifying.

Moloch — The biblical name of a Canaanite god associated with child sacrifice.

MOS — Mossad, an Israeli intelligence agency.

Mr. Contractor — Edward Snowden, a former CIA employee and NSA contractor who illegally leaked information about NSA surveillance programs to the press in 2013.

Mr. Ryan — Jack Ryan, a character from *The Hunt for Red October.*

MS-13 — Mara Salvatrucha, also known as MS-13, is a criminal gang that originated in Los Angeles, California, in the 1970s and 1980s. It was primarily comprised of and helped protect Salvadoran immigrants. The gang's influence has spread throughout the Western hemisphere and Europe. In 2012, the U.S. Department of the Treasury labeled the group a "transnational criminal organization," the first such designation for a U.S. street gang.

MSDNC — An acronym coined by conservative political pundits (also used by President Trump) to mock MSNBC's cable television channel. It comes from the idea that MSNBC is the propaganda arm or mouthpiece of the Democratic National Committee (DNC).

MSM — Mainstream Media

Mueller — Robert Mueller, former FBI Director and Special Counsel.

MW — Maxine Waters, a U.S. Representative from California who has served in Congress since 1991. A member of the Democrat Party, she chaired the Congressional Black Caucus from 1997 to 1999.

MX — The country of Mexico.

MYE — Midyear Exam, the FBI's name for its investigation of Hillary Clinton's use of a private server in her home for email correspondence while she was Secretary of State.

MZ — Mark Zuckerberg, founder, CEO, and controlling shareholder of the social media platform Facebook.

Nancy Pelosi — U.S. Representative from California and Speaker of the House of Representatives.

Nancy Salzman — President and co-founder of NXIVM, a multi-level marketing company based near Albany, New York, that offered personal and professional development seminars through its "Executive Success Programs." NXIVM leaders were prosecuted for sexual abuse and sex trafficking members.

Natalia Veselnitskaya — A Russian attorney who gained notoriety for her meeting with Donald Trump Jr., Paul Manafort, and Jared Kushner prior to the 2016 Presidential election.

NATSEC or **NAT SEC** — National Security

N_C — National Security Council. Part of the Executive Office of the President of the United States. It is the principal forum used by the President for consideration of national security, military, and foreign policy matters with senior national security advisors and Cabinet officials.

NDA — Non-disclosure agreement. A commonly used legally-binding contract by which one or more parties agree not to disclose confidential information they have shared as a necessary part of doing business together.

Nellie Ohr — The wife of former Associate Deputy Attorney General Bruce Ohr. Both Ohrs have been implicated in the Obama administration's surveillance of the 2016 Trump Presidential campaign.

Newfag — Slang term for new user on 4chan, 8chan, or 8kun.

NG — National Guard

NK — North Korea, also known as the Democratic People's Republic of Korea (DPRK).

NOFORN — Regarding the classification of information by the U.S. government, this designation (meaning "no foreign nationals") is applied to any information that may not be released to any non-U.S. citizen.

N_Ohr — Nellie Ohr, an employee of Fusion GPS, the firm that conducted research used in Christopher Steele's anti-Trump dossier. Wife of former Associate Deputy Attorney General Bruce Ohr. Steele's dossier was the source cited by the FBI in its FISA applications against Carter Page. The surveillance of Page allowed the Obama administration to spy on the 2016 Trump campaign.

No name — John McCain, U.S. Senator from Arizona. He served as a senator from January 1987 until his death in 2018.

Non_Civ — Two possibilities: non-civilian, or non-civil.

non Page — As it relates to FISA surveillance, Q hints these are FISA targeted individuals *other than* Carter Page.

Normalfag or **normie** — Slang term for normal members of society who don't share the same interests as those who commonly use 4chan, 8chan, or 8kun boards.

No Such Agency — National Security Agency (NSA) is a signals intelligence agency within the U.S. Department of Defense. It collects and analyzes electronic signals intelligence of interest to the security of the U.S. and protects all classified and sensitive information stored on government information technology equipment. In addition, the NSA supports and contributes to the civilian use of cryptography and computer security measures.

NP — Usually refers to Nancy Pelosi, a U.S. Representative from California and Speaker of the House of Representatives. In a couple of cases (related to George Soros), it stands for nonprofit.

NPO — Non-Profit Organization

NR — Nuclear Reactor

NSA — National Security Agency is a signals intelligence agency within the U.S. Department of Defense. It collects and analyzes electronic signals intelligence of interest to the security of the U.S. and protects all classified and sensitive information stored on government information technology equipment. In addition, the NSA supports and contributes to the civilian use of cryptography and computer security measures.

NSC — National Security Council. Part of the Executive Office of the President of the United States. It is the principal forum used by the President for consideration of national security, military, and foreign policy matters with senior national security advisors and Cabinet officials.

Nunes — Devin Nunes, U.S. Representative from California and ranking member of the House Intelligence Committee.

NV — Natalia Veselnitskaya, a Russian attorney who gained notoriety for her meeting with Donald Trump Jr., Paul Manafort, and Jared Kushner prior to the 2016 Presidential election.

NWO — New World Order, sometimes referred to as a one-world government. A governmental concept where individual nations surrender their political sovereignty to the will of a centralized world governmental power.

NXIVM — A multi-level marketing company based near Albany, New York, that offered personal and professional development seminars through its "Executive Success Programs." NXIVM leaders were prosecuted for sexual abuse and sex trafficking of the group's members.

NYT — *The New York Times*, an American newspaper founded in 1851.

o7 — Used as an online salute. The letter o symbolizes a head. The number 7 is a hand in position to salute.

OCONUS lures — Oconus = Outside Contiguous United States. Lures = spies. The term was found in text messages between FBI agent Peter Strzok and attorney Lisa Page from conversations they had in December of 2015.

O-games — The Olympic Games are international sporting events held every four years.

Oldfag — Slang term for a longtime 4chan, 8chan, or 8kun user.

OO — The Oval Office, which is the working office space of the President of the United States, located in the West Wing of the White House.

OP — Usually stands for "original poster," the person who originally published the thread on 4chan, 8chan, or 8kun. Occasionally it stands for "operation" as in a military or intelligence operation.

OPS — An abbreviation for "Operations" such as military or intelligence operations.

OS — Congressional Oversight Committee

O-WH — The Obama White House

Owl — Occult symbol found throughout history.

over/under — An over–under or over/under bet is a wager in which a sportsbook will predict a number for a statistic in a given game, and bettors wager that the actual number in the game will be either higher or lower than that number.

P — Multiple uses: may refer to the Pope, but Q suggested it may also refer to the Payseurs—the descendants of the French Royal family who emigrated to the U.S. after the French Revolution. In more recent posts, it seems to indicate FBI agent Joe Pientka, who interviewed General Michael Flynn when he served as President Trump's National Security Advisor.

P_2020 — The 2020 Presidential election.

P_elec — Presidential election.

Pain or **[PAIN]** — A reference to the pending prosecution of corrupt individuals.

Painted — Some military weapon systems use lasers to guide missiles and bombs to their targets. When a target is illuminated by a laser , it is said to be "painted." As Q uses the term, it refers to corrupt people being identified for exposure or prosecution.

Paul Manafort — A businessman, lobbyist, and Member of Donald Trump's 2016 Presidential campaign. He was convicted of money laundering, tax evasion and failing to register as a foreign agent.

Paul Nakasone — The Lieutenant General who succeeded Admiral Michael Rogers as the Director of U.S. Cyber Command and NSA.

Pawn — An individual who is used by influential people to accomplish their objectives.

Pay-for-play — Bribery of a public official. Something of value is exchanged for an action taken by a public official. Sometimes expressed as "pay-to-play."

P_debates — Presidential debates

PEOC — Presidential Emergency Operations Center, an underground bunker-like structure beneath the East Wing of the White House.

Peter Strzok — FBI agent who was involved in the bureau's counterintelligence investigation of Presidential candidate Donald Trump. He was also a member of Special Counsel Robert Mueller's team until it was disclosed that he harbored an excessive bias against Trump. Strzok was one of the FBI agents who questioned Hillary Clinton regarding her emails, and he interviewed Lt. General Mike Flynn regarding his communications with Russian Ambassador Sergey Kislyak.

PG — Pizzagate/PedoGate, an internet controversy that surfaced in 2016, where restaurant owner James Alefantis and John Podesta were accused of pedophilia.

Phase [2] — The second phase of a covert operation that Q mentioned on February 21st, 2018.

Pickle — A euphemism that describes a difficult or messy situation with no obvious solution.

Pickle Factory — A term used for the CIA.

Placeholder — A current post that alludes to details which will be disclosed in a future post.

Planefag — Slang term for a 4chan, 8chan, or 8kun user who specializes in tracking airplanes by radar.

PM — Prime Minister

POTUS — President of the United States. As Q uses the term, it specifically refers to Donald J. Trump.

pp — People

PP — Planned Parenthood, the largest abortion provider in the United States, is a highly controversial organization with ardent supporters as well as staunch opponents.

P_PERS — A personal message from President Trump.

PR1 — Priority one, or top priority.

Prince Al-Waleed — Alwaleed bin Talal, a billionaire and philanthropist who was arrested November 4th, 2017, as part of the Saudi corruption crackdown.

PRO — Meaning "in favor of." Examples: O-PRO is supportive of Barack Obama, PRO-POTUS is supportive of President Trump.

PROJECT DEEPDREAM — A reference to a Jason Bourne film in which a social media company called Deep Dream, gathers personal data from subscribers and secretly funnels it to the Central Intelligence Agency.

PSYOP — Psychological Operations, which convey selected information and indicators to audiences in order to influence their emotions, motives, objective reasoning, and ultimately their behavior.

Punisher skull — Marvel Comics' superhero Frank Castle (The Punisher) typically wears a shirt with a skull emblazoned on the chest. The skull logo was unofficially adopted by some military special operations teams and has been posted by Q.

PVG — Pudong International Airport in Shanghai, China.

Q Clearance — Access to the highest level of classified information in the U.S. Department of Energy. Q suggested in his case, it refers to the highest level of access across all departments.

Q Clearance Patriot — The first appearance of the term "Q Clearance Patriot" was on November 1st, 2017, where Q introduced himself with this name and the initial Q.

Quid Pro Quo — A Latin phrase indicating something given or received for something else. In cases of public bribery, something of value is exchanged for an action taken by a public official.

R — In most contexts, a reference to Renegade, the Secret Service code name for President Barack Obama. Other uses are possible.

R's — Republicans

Rachel Brand — United States Associate Attorney General from May 22nd, 2017, until February 20th, 2018. She resigned to take a job as head of global corporate governance at Walmart.

Rapid Fire — A 1992 film starring Brandon Lee and Powers Booth, who battle a Chinese drug lord and corrupt FBI officials.

RBG — The late Ruth Bader Ginsburg was an Associate Justice of the U.S. Supreme Court. She was a liberal noted for her feminist views.

RC — Rachel "Ray" Chandler, photographer who co-founded Midland modeling Agency with Walter Pearce.

R+D — Republicans and Democrats

Rec — Usually stands for received, but occasionally stands for record.

RED1, RED2, RED3 — From a post on June 4th, 2020. These codes appear to indicate a predictable progression of events that may be taken by bad actors and the planned response by members of the military.

RED_CASTLE — A reference to the insignia of the U.S. Army Corps of Engineers.

Red Cross — The International or American Red Cross.

Red October — Multiple meanings including but not limited to the film by that title and a steel plant in Stalingrad, Russia, which appears on a CIA document that Q provided a link to. Note: Q removed "the Hunt for," and in October of 2018, a new theme "Red October" appeared.

Red pill — A reference from the film *The Matrix*. Taking the red pill causes one to awaken to a different reality.

Red Red — The International or American Red Cross.

Re_drop — A re-post of an older message, usually for the benefit of people who are new followers.

Renee J. James — A technology executive, who was formerly the president of Intel. She is currently Chairman and CEO of Ampere Computing and an Operating Executive with The Carlyle Group in its Media and Technology practice.

Renegade — The Secret Service code name for President Barack Obama.

Repost Lost — When a post has been deleted from the board, Q will sometimes repost it with this notice.

Rig for Red — A term used by submariners when the vessel is coming to periscope depth. Red lights are illuminated providing enough light to see while maintaining night vision. In most cases, Q does not post for several days following a Rig for Red message.

Rizvi Traverse Management — The secretive New York private equity firm founded by Indian-born Suhail Rizvi. Investments include ICM Talent

Agency, Summit Entertainment, Playboy Enterprises, SpaceX, Flipboard, and Square. Rizvi Traverse was the largest initial stakeholder of Twitter and was instrumental in bringing on board other investors like JP Morgan Chase and Alwaleed bin Talal. At Twitter's Initial Public Offering in 2013, Rizvi Traverse held a 15.6 percent stake in the company valued at $3.8 billion.

RM — Robert Mueller, Special Counsel who investigated President Donald Trump. Served as FBI Director from 2001-2013.

RNC — Republican National Committee, the governing body for the United States Republican Party.

Road block — Using the U.S. Military at the Mexico border to prevent the inflow of illegal aliens, drugs, cash, terrorists, trafficked children, and MS-13 gang members.

ROASTED — A reference to President Trump's participation in the Gridiron Roast Dinner on March 4th, 2018.

Robert Byrd — Former U.S. Democrat Senator from West Virginia. Byrd was the longest-serving U.S. Senator in history. According to *Wikipedia*, in the early 1940s, he recruited 150 of his friends and associates to create a new chapter of the Ku Klux Klan in Sophia, West Virginia. Byrd partook in a lengthy filibuster effort against the 1964 Civil Rights Act. Hillary Clinton said Byrd was her mentor in the Senate. Joe Biden spoke at Byrd's funeral.

rogue1_McMaster — Former National Security Advisor H.R McMaster, who Q says was secretly sympathetic to the deep state.

rogue2_Coats_DNI — Former Director of National Intelligence Dan Coats, who Q says was secretly sympathetic to the deep state.

Rogue3-6 — Unidentified deep state sympathizers who were installed early on that made referrals to President Trump to hire H.R. McMaster, Dan Coats, Christopher Wray, and John Bolton.

rogue7_Bolton — Former National Security Advisor John Bolton, who Q says was secretly sympathetic to the deep state.

Rosatom — A Russian state-owned energy company that purchased the North American company, Uranium One, during Barack Obama's presidency.

ROT — Rotation. A different view provided by the rotation of a camera.

ROTH — Rothschild

Rothschild — An influential banking family that exerted economic and political influence over Europe during the 18th and 19th centuries and over the world during the 20th and 21st centuries.

RR — Former U.S. Deputy Attorney General Rod Rosenstein. He conducted oversight of Robert Mueller's investigation of President Donald Trump.

RT — Multiple possible meanings including retweet, real-time, the news outlet *Russia Today*, and former Secretary of State Rex Tillerson. The context will dictate the best decode.

Running RED — A phrase first used on September 19, 2020 in reference to the upcoming battle to confirm President Trump's selection for the Supreme Court, Amy Coney Barrett. The suggestion was that Barrett would be confirmed, despite the battle that would be waged. The phrase was used again the following day as the last line of a post, suggesting that it could be considered a Q signature.

Ryan — Paul Ryan, former Wisconsin Representative and former Speaker of the U.S. House of Representatives.

SA — The Kingdom of Saudi Arabia

SA --> US --> Asia --> EU — A flow chart showing an order of operations. According to Q, the removal of corruption began in Saudi Arabia and will then happen in the United States, followed by Asia, then the European Union, and other nations.

Sage — By entering the word "sage" in the email field on a 4chan, 8chan, or 8kun thread, you can comment on a thread without bumping it to the top of the board. (Typically used to comment on bad threads to avoid giving them more visibility.)

Sally Yates — Served as Deputy Attorney General under Barack Obama, and briefly as Attorney General under Donald Trump but was fired for insubordination.

Sam Clovis — A policy advisor to the Trump campaign in 2016.

SAP — Special Access Program, a security protocol used by the U.S. federal government that provides highly classified information with safeguards and access restrictions that exceed those used for regular classified information.

Sara — Sara A. Carter, a national and international award-winning investigative reporter who is currently a Fox News contributor.

Sauce — Slang term derived from the word "source." When information is provided on 4chan, 8chan, or 8kun that is not common knowledge, the one posting the information will frequently be asked to provide a source (sauce).

SB — Super Bowl, the annual championship game of the National Football League.

SC — Two confirmed decodes: Special Counsel, or the Supreme Court. The context will dictate the correct one.

SCARAMUCCI MODEL — Anthony Scaramucci served as President Trump's White House Director of Communications from July 21st to July 31st, 2017. During those ten days, Sean Spicer and Reince Priebus resigned. The point Q wants us to understand is that a temporary hire can accomplish unpleasant tasks easier that someone in a permanent position.

Schneiderman — Eric Schneiderman, former New York state Attorney General who resigned May 7th, 2018, due to allegations of past sexual assault by four women.

SCI — Sensitive Compartmented Information. A protocol for securing highly sensitive information using control systems approved by the Director of National Intelligence.

SCI(f) or SCIF — Sensitive Compartmentalized Information Facility. An enclosed area that is used to process sensitive and classified information and restrict access to people who do not have the proper security clearance and need to know.

Scot-Free — A phrase used in a post by Q to indicate someone who goes unpunished, while also alluding to the motion picture studio Scott Free Productions that produced the film *White Squall*.

SD — State Department (formally called the U.S. Department of State). The department of the U.S. executive branch responsible for carrying out foreign policy and international relations.

SDNY — Southern District of New York, a powerful U.S. Attorney's office that controls the fate of many of the nation's important legal cases.

SEALS — Special forces teams of the U.S. Navy tasked with conducting small-unit special operation missions. The acronym comes from "Sea, Air, and Land."

SEC — In most cases, it refers to "secure" or "security," i.e., NAT SEC (National Security). In some cases, it refers to the Securities and Exchange Commission. The context will provide the correct decode.

SecureDrop — A program that allows intelligence community employees to communicate with journalists securely.

Sergey Brin — Sergey Mikhaylovich Brin, the Russian-born former president of Alphabet (the parent company of Google and YouTube). Brin co-founded the search engine firm Google with Larry Page in 1998.

Sessions — Jeff Sessions, former U.S. Senator from Alabama. Served as Attorney General under President Trump from 2017-2019.

SFO — San Francisco International Airport

SH — Steve Huffman is the founder and CEO of Reddit, an online discussion site. He is also known by his Reddit nickname "Spez."

SHADOW ARM — The term "arm" is used by Q in various ways to allude to the idea that the corporate media covertly act as the propaganda wing of the Democratic Party.

Shall we play a game? — A line spoken by a computer (WOPR, or War Operation Plan Response) to Matthew Broderick's character David in the 1983 film *War Games*. David thought he'd hacked a software developer and gained access to new games, but he unwittingly hacked into a Department of Defense system and nearly started a global thermonuclear war. Q uses the phrase in some cases to challenge anons and, in other instances, to taunt his enemies.

Shell1/Shell2 — A reference to "shell" companies. A shell company is a business created to hold the funds and manage the financial transactions of another entity. They don't have employees, don't make money, and don't provide customers with products or services. They only manage the assets they hold.

Shill — Someone who spends time and resources promoting (or attacking) a product or idea in public forums with the pretense of sincerity.

Shooter — A reference to the perpetrator of a mass shooting.

SID — Likely a reference to Arizona Senator John Sidney McCain III. A second possibility is Sid Blumenthal, a longtime confidant to Hillary Clinton.

Sidley Austin — Chicago-based law firm Sidley Austin LLP is the sixth-largest U.S.-based corporate law firm with approximately 2,000 lawyers and annual revenues of more than two billion dollars.

SIG — Special Interest Group, a group of individuals, brought together by a shared belief or interest, often aiming to influence politics or policies.

SIGINT — Signals Intelligence. The interception and decoding of electronic signals, whether used in communication between people or other applications (i.e., radar and weapon systems). Analysts evaluate raw electronic data and transform it into actionable intelligence.

Silent War — A phrase used once by Q in November of 2017, to indicate an ongoing, covert war against the principles of freedom and democracy in the U.S. In 2020, the phrase was used more regularly and became a Q signature that will be explored in depth in a future volume in this series.

SIS — Secret Intelligence Service, another name for the UK's MI6. This agency is the UK counterpart to the CIA. SIS was also the acronym used for the Signal Intelligence Service, the United States Army's codebreaking division, before World War II. It was renamed the Signal Security Agency in 1943, and in 1945, it became the Army Security Agency. During World War II, its resources were reassigned to the newly established National Security Agency (NSA).

SIT ROOM — Situation Room. Officially known as the John F. Kennedy Conference Room, the "Situation Room" is a conference room and intelligence management center in the basement of the White House run by the National Security Council staff for the use of the President and his advisors to monitor and deal with crises at home and abroad and to conduct secure communications with outside persons.

SKY EVENT or **SKY Event** — Q posted a reference to this twice, but has not confirmed a decode yet.

Sleeper — a term for someone who joins a community pretending to share their values, while secretly opposing them. At a strategic time—when the "sleeper" is signaled to "awaken" or become active—they carry out their covert mission of disruption or sabotage.

Smollett — Jussie Smollett, an American actor and singer, who was indicted on February 20th, 2019, for allegedly paying two Nigerian-Americans to stage a fake hate crime assault on him.

Sniffer or **Sniffers** — Generally, a bot designed to search the internet for specific data on websites. Q has alluded to highly sophisticated artificial intelligence programs that aggregate data and interpret it. Valerie Jarret has also been identified by Q as a "sniffer."

Snopes — A fact-checking organization that produces reports on rumors, urban legends, and odd news stories. Snopes has been criticized for its liberal-progressive bias.

Snowden — Edward Snowden, the former CIA employee and NSA contractor who stole and made public two classified NSA surveillance programs—PRISM and XKeyscore.

Snow White — A signature by Q referring to the CIA, so named because of the Agency's seven supercomputers that are named after the seven dwarves.

SOCIALM — Social media.

Soros — George Soros, a hedge fund billionaire who is known for using his wealth to fund his own brand of political activism. Recipients of his philanthropy appreciate his money, but those who oppose his political views see him as a creator of chaos around the world—a destabilizing force on economies and societies. Some countries have either banned Soros or restricted his organizations. These countries include Pakistan, Poland, Turkey, Russia, Soros' home country of Hungary, and the Philippines. The Israeli government has said Soros is not welcome there.

SOTU — The annual State of the Union speech given by the President of the United States.

SP — Samantha Power, U.S. Ambassador to the United Nations from 2013 to 2017.

Spade — Katherine Noel Brosnahan, known professionally as Kate Spade and Kate Valentine. She was a fashion designer and businesswoman, who founded the designer brand "Kate Spade New York." Spade's death in June of 2017 was ruled a suicide. She was reported to have hung herself from a doorknob using a red silk scarf.

Spartans in Darkness — "Spartans in Darkness: American SIGINT and the Indochina War, 1945-1975" is a report written by Robert J. Hanyok, of the Center for Cryptologic History, National Security Agency. A link to the document was posted by Q as reference material.

Speed — A film starring Keanu Reeves and Sandra Bullock about a bus that had a bomb connected to the speedometer by a villain. If the bus speed dropped below 50 miles per hour, the bomb would detonate. The conundrum for the hero was how to defuse the bomb without stopping the bus. "Speed" is used as a signature by Q to indicate a delicate situation involving corrupt people that is being dealt with by patriots in a way that will avoid unnecessary harm to the public and keep government services open.

Spirit Cooking — (from *Wikipedia*) Marina Abramovic worked with Jacob Samuel to produce a cookbook of "aphrodisiac recipes" called Spirit Cooking in 1996. These "recipes" were meant to be "evocative instructions for actions or for thoughts." For example, one of the recipes calls for "13,000 grams of jealousy," while another says to "mix fresh breast milk with fresh sperm milk." The work was inspired by the popular belief that ghosts feed off intangible things like light, sound, and emotions.

In 1997, Abramovic created a multimedia Spirit Cooking installation. This was originally installed in the Zerynthia Associazione per l'Arte Contemporanea in Rome, Italy and included white gallery walls with "enigmatically violent recipe instructions" painted in pig's blood. According to Alexxa Gotthardt, the work is "a comment on humanity's reliance on ritual to organize and legitimize our lives and contain our bodies."

Abramovic also published a Spirit Cooking cookbook, containing comico-mystical, self-help instructions that are meant to be just poetry. Spirit Cooking later evolved into a form of dinner party entertainment that Abramovic occasionally lays on for collectors, donors, and friends.

Splash — A Naval aviator term for shooting down an enemy aircraft. An airplane shot down over the ocean will "splash" into the sea.

spy_T — The government spying operation against President Donald Trump.

SR — There are two confirmed decodes: Barack Obama's National Security Advisor Susan Rice, or Seth Rich, the Democratic National Committee staffer who was murdered on July 10th, 2016.

SS — U.S. Secret Service, a federal law enforcement agency under the Department of Homeland Security charged with conducting criminal investigations and protecting the nation's leaders and their families.

Standard Hotel — The Standard Hotels are a group of five boutique hotels in Los Angeles (Hollywood and Downtown LA), New York City, and Miami Beach. Q's references pertain to the Hollywood location.

Stanislav Lunev — A former Soviet military officer who defected to the United States in 1992. He is the highest-ranking GRU (Russian intelligence) officer ever to defect to the United States. He has worked with the CIA and FBI and is currently in the federal witness protection program.

Stormy Daniels — A pornographic actress, stripper, screenwriter, and director. In 2018, Daniels became involved in a legal dispute with President Trump and his attorney Michael Cohen. Daniels claimed that Trump and his surrogates paid $130,000 in hush money to silence her about an affair she says she had with Trump in 2006. Trump's spokespeople have denied the affair and have accused Daniels of lying.

Strike Package — As used by the military, a strike package is a group of aircraft having different weaponry and capabilities that are launched as a unit to perform a single attack mission.

Sum of All Fears — A Q signature and a reference to the Tom Clancy novel and film by that name. The plot: a sociopath develops a plan to get Russia and the U.S. to destroy each other in a nuclear war, paving the way for him to set up a fascist superstate.

super T — Super Tuesday. The first Tuesday in March, when a large number of states hold their presidential primary elections.

SURV — Surveillance

Susan Rice — Served as U.S. National Security Advisor for Barack Obama from 2013 to 2017. She also served as U.S. Ambassador to the United Nations from 2009 to 2013.

Swamp — Washington D.C., which is rumored to have been built on a swamp. Research more at Histories of the National Mall: http://mallhistory.org/ explorations/show/was-the-national-mall-built-on

T2 — Terminal 2 at Shanghai Pudong International Airport (PVG).

Taken — A 2008 film about a retired CIA agent who traveled across Europe relying on his knowledge of tradecraft to save his estranged daughter, who, along with her girlfriend, was kidnapped by Albanian sex traffickers.

target C — This appears to be Q's way of indicating that Ted Cruz's presidential campaign was targeted for surveillance by the Obama administration.

target POTUS — Q's way of indicating that Donald Trump's presidential campaign was targeted for surveillance by the Obama administration.

TG — Trey Gowdy, former South Carolina Representative and former federal prosecutor who served as Chair of the House Oversight and Government Reform Committee.

The Analysis Corporation (TAC) — A corporation founded in 1991 in McClean, Virginia, by Cecilia Hayes. TAC works on projects in the counterterrorism and national security industries. John Brennan was appointed TAC president and CEO in 2005.

The Bloody Wonderland — Q's reference to Saudi Arabia, which was notorious in the past for its frequent use of public execution.

TheMagikBOT — A *Wikipedia* bot that makes automated or semi-automated edits to *Wikipedia* entries that would be difficult to do manually.

TOR — An internet browsing service that allows users to view web pages anonymously by routing traffic through an overlay network made up of thousands of relays.

TP — Tony Podesta, an influential Washington D.C. lobbyist who stepped down from his firm, The Podesta Group, as a result of Special Counsel Mueller's investigation and the firm's unregistered lobbying for the European Centre for Modern Ukraine. Podesta Group failed to file as an agent of a foreign power under the Foreign Agents Registration Act (FARA). Tony is the brother of John Podesta, the chairman of the 2016 Hillary Clinton presidential campaign.

Trip, Tripcode or **Trip code** — A hashed password used on internet boards like 4chan, 8chan, or 8kun that provides a unique user identity while maintaining anonymity.

Trump Swift Boat Project — An operation by Hillary Clinton's campaign in 2016 designed to smear her political opponent Donald Trump. It was mentioned in an email exchange published by *WikiLeaks*.

TSA — Transportation Security Administration, an agency of the U.S. Department of Homeland Security created as a response to the September 11th attacks. TSA has authority over the security of the traveling public in the United States.

TT — Two confirmed decodes. The context will determine the correct one. It can refer to Trump Tower in New York. It can also be an abbreviation for Tarmac Tapes. According to Q, the NSA has a recording (tape) of the conversation that Bill Clinton had with then-Attorney General Loretta Lynch on the tarmac at Sky Harbor Airport in Phoenix, Arizona, on June 27th, 2016.

TTM — Trailing twelve months, or the twelve months that follow.

T-Tower — Trump Tower. A skyscraper on Fifth Avenue, between 56th and 57th Streets, in Midtown Manhattan, New York City. Trump Tower serves as the headquarters for the Trump Organization.

U1 — A abbreviation for the North American company, Uranium One, which was sold to the Russian energy company, Rosatom.

U1 -> CA -> EU -> ASIA -> IRAN/NK — According to Q, this is the route of travel for uranium transferred when the company, Uranium One, was sold to the Russian company, Rosatom: from Canada, to the European Union, to Asia, to Iran/North Korea.

UBL — Usama bin Laden (AKA Osama bin Laden) was a founder of the pan-Islamic militant organization al-Qaeda.

Uhuru Kenyatta — Kenyan politician and the fourth President of the Republic of Kenya.

UID — User ID for internet connection or specific internet-connected device.

UK/AUS assist/set up — According to Q, the UK and Australia, through the Five Eyes agreement, assisted the Obama administration in surveilling Donald Trump's presidential campaign.

Unmask — Exposing the concealed name of a U.S. person in surveillance data.

UN — United Nations, an intergovernmental organization responsible for facilitating cooperation in international law, international security, economic development, diplomacy and human rights. It was founded in 1945 to replace the League of Nations.

Upstream collection — A term used by the National Security Agency for intercepting email, telephone, and text message data from the major internet cables and switches, both domestic and foreign.

US — The United States of America

US ATT — U.S. Attorney

USA V. [1-2-3-6] — A reference to future legal cases where currently unidentified people will be named as defendants in cases against the United States.

US Cyber Task Force — In February of 2018, Attorney General Jeff Sessions ordered the creation of the Justice Department's Cyber-Digital Task Force, which "will canvass the many ways that the Department is combatting the global cyber threat, and will also identify how federal law enforcement can more effectively accomplish its mission in this vital and evolving area."

USD(I) — The Under Secretary of Defense for Intelligence

US-G — United States Government

USMC — United States Marine Corps, a branch of the U.S. Armed Forces responsible for conducting expeditionary and amphibious operations with the Navy, the Army, and the Air Force.

USSS — United States Secret Service, a federal law enforcement agency under the Department of Homeland Security charged with conducting criminal investigations and protecting the nation's leaders and their families.

v2 — Version 2: a reference to the second term of Donald Trump's presidency. The implication is that it will be run differently than his first term.

Vault 7 — A series of documents published by *WikiLeaks* in 2017 that detail the capabilities of the CIA to perform electronic surveillance and cyber warfare. The files, dated from 2013–2016, include details on the agency's software capabilities, such as the ability to compromise cars, smart TVs, web browsers, and the operating systems of most smartphones, as well as operating systems like Microsoft Windows, MacOS, and Linux.

Vindman — Retired Lieutenant Colonel Alexander Vindman, a member of the National Security Council who testified against President Trump during the House impeachment hearings.

VIP — Very Important Person. Usually a reference to people who wear Q related shirts at President Trump's rallies. On a few occasions, the President has pointed to these patriots in the crowd. Many VIPs have posted rally photos on Twitter. Q has reposted links to them on the board.

VJ — Valerie Jarrett, a businesswoman and former government official who served as the senior advisor to U.S. President Barack Obama. Jarrett was born in Iran to African-American parents; her family moved to London for a year, and then to Chicago in 1963.

VP — Vice President

We don't say his name — John McCain, U.S. Senator from Arizona. He served as a Senator from January 1987 until his death in 2018.

Wendy — Nickname for Maggie Nixon. The daughter of Sarah Nixon and granddaughter of actress and TV soap opera writer and producer Agnes Nixon.

Wet Works — Slang for assassination. The term was used in the John Podesta emails published by *WikiLeaks*.

Wexner — Les Wexner, the billionaire founder and former CEO of Victoria's Secret parent company L Brands. Wexner was a confidant of Jeffrey Epstein.

WH — White House, the official residence and workplace of the President of the United States. White House is also used as a metonym for the President and his advisors.

Wheels up — An aviation term indicating an aircraft is taking off, and its landing gear are being retracted. Q used this term as a signal that an individual he referred to as the "stealth bomber" was commencing operations.

Where we go one, we go all — A line from the film *White Squall* which was based on the sinking of a school Brigantine sailing ship in 1961. The phrase "Where we go one, we go all" is a signature found in many of Q's posts.

Whistleblower — Q is usually referring to the whistleblower who filed a complaint to the Intelligence Community Inspector General about President Trump's phone call to the President of Ukraine.

White Squall — A 1996 coming of age film in which a group of high school and college-aged misfits sign up for training aboard a sailing ship under the instruction of a hard but courageous skipper. Scenes from the film have been highlighted by Q as themes that illustrate different aspects of his mission.

WHO — World Health Organization

Who performs in a circus? — Clowns, which is a reference to the CIA, an agency Q also refers to as "Clowns In America."

WikiLeaks — A watchdog organization founded by Julian Assange that publishes documents leaked from various government and corporate sources.

Wizards & Warlocks — An internal name used by NSA employees and contractors—guardians of all electronic information.

WL — *WikiLeaks,* a watchdog organization founded by Julian Assange that publishes documents leaked from various government and corporate sources.

Woodshed — Nickname for the White House Situation Room, a 5,000 square foot complex of rooms in the ground floor of the West Wing.

Wray — Christopher Wray, Director of the FBI.

WRWY — We are with you.

WW — World Wide

WWG1WGA — The abbreviation for "Where we go one, we go all," a line from the film *White Squall* which was based on the sinking of a school Brigantine sailing ship in 1961. The phrase "Where we go one, we go all" is a signature found in many of Q's posts.

Y — Generally, refers to the goat head and owl symbolism, images, and icons used by the occult. It has also been used in references to former FBI Director James Come[Y] and with reference to his book, A Higher Loyalty [Y].

YT — YouTube, an American video-sharing platform headquartered in California that now operates as one of Google's subsidiaries.

Zero Bubble — Used in submarine operations when a vessel's stern (rear) and bow (front) are at the same depth, with no incline. In Q's vernacular, it goes along with Rig for Red, coming to periscope depth. Both seem to be related to his frequency of posting.

Other Books from Dave Hayes / Praying Medic

Find all titles on PrayingMedic.com

Series: Q Chronicles

- Book 1 - The Calm Before The Storm
- Book 2 - The Great Awakening

Series: The Kingdom of God Made Simple

- Divine Healing Made Simple
- Seeing in the Spirit Made Simple
- Hearing God's Voice Made Simple
- Traveling in the Spirit Made Simple

Series: The Courts of Heaven

- Defeating Your Adversary in the Court of Heaven
- Operating in the Court of Angels

Series: My Craziest Adventures with God

- My Craziest Adventures with God - Volume 1
- My Craziest Adventures with God - Volume 2

And more...

- Emotional Healing in 3 Easy Steps
- The Gates of Shiloh (novel)
- God Speaks: Perspectives on Hearing God's Voice
- A Kingdom View of Economic Collapse (ebook)
- American Sniper: Lessons in Spiritual Warfare (ebook)

Made in the USA
Monee, IL
30 October 2020